To Jane Lydia
with love
6x
Christmas 2002.

TALKING SWING

TALKING SWING

The British Big Bands

Sheila Tracy

MAINSTREAM
PUBLISHING

EDINBURGH AND LONDON

First published in Great Britain in 1997 by
MAINSTREAM PUBLISHING COMPANY (EDINBURGH) LTD
7 Albany Street
Edinburgh EH1 3UG

ISBN 1 85158 963 5

A catalogue record for this book is available from the British Library

Typeset in 11on 13½ pt Janson Text
Printed and bound in Great Britain by Butler and Tanner Ltd, Frome

CONTENTS

ACKNOWLEDGEMENTS

I would like to thank all the people who made this book possible by giving me their valuable time and entrusting me with their treasured photographs. Also my grateful thanks to Tony Harrison of the Coda Club and Roy Oakshott of BBC Radio 2 for providing me with many valuable contacts.

PRELUDE

GEORGE SHEARING

In *Talking Swing*, Sheila Tracy takes us on a journey down memory lane. Through these pages I was able to relive some of the most enjoyable times of that period. 'Enjoyable?' you question. Yes, enjoyable – even though there was a war in progress. Somehow we lived for the moment with a good old British sense of humour and the requisite tenacity to make the best of what would otherwise have seemed like a raw deal.

You will read about the practical jokes we played on each other. 'Lumbering' we called it. Like the time when I played a solo on a composition called 'Midnight in Mayfair' with Ambrose. During the slow section, the whole band sang just loud enough for me to hear, 'George Shearing plays like Charlie Kunz'. I must say that they were quite successful in preventing me from continuing for several seconds. The audience realised that something was going on onstage. That something was contagious enough for them to join in.

I could go on, but in so doing I would rob you of the enjoyment and fun you'll have here with every turn of a page. I know that the memories dealt with in these pages will live on in my mind for the rest of my life. So just sit back and let *Talking Swing* talk to you. You'll enjoy it, believe me!

INTRODUCTION

Bands, Booze and Broads, published in 1995, was never planned as a book. It was a series of interviews I'd carried out in the process of making various documentaries on the American bands of the swing era for BBC Radio 2. Immediately it appeared I was asked if I was planning to do a similar book on British bands and for some time I resisted, but eventually, with several of our prominent musicians well into their eighties and nineties, I thought it better to delay no longer! I have followed the same format as before, talking to whoever was available and there is absolutely no reason why any particular sideman has been omitted apart from lack of opportunity and lack of space.

I had no idea what I was letting myself in for until I began listing the British bands people would expect to see in this book, and there was no way I could include them all. You will not find any of the specialist bands such as Victor Sylvester and Edmundo Ros, nor the smaller line-ups such as Sid Phillips and Tito Burns, and as I couldn't include all the notable BBC dance orchestras over the years, I decided to include none. I omitted that famous wartime line-up the Squadronaires for the simple reason that it was virtually the Ambrose Orchestra. That still left me with seventeen bands to be allocated a chapter each. Ambrose, Geraldo and Ted Heath are by far the longest as those are arguably the three best bands this country has ever produced, and everybody who was anybody played in them. The last chapter I've reserved for reminiscences of some of the other famous and not so famous bands that were around before, during and after the Second World War.

The Prelude and the Coda are kindly provided by two of Britain's all-time jazz greats: George Shearing, born in Battersea in 1919, and George Chisholm, born in Glasgow in 1915. Both are in a class of their own and both played a very large part in London's West End music scene in the '30s and '40s. George Shearing became an international star when he emigrated to America in 1947. George Chisholm became not only our most eminent jazz trombonist but also one of our top entertainers before falling ill in 1993. Sad to say he is unable to contribute personally, but I have included an excerpt from an interview he gave me in 1987 which I think provides a fitting postscript to the story of an unforgettable era.

Sheila Tracy
Kingswood, Surrey

AMBROSE

1897–1971

Theme 'When Day Is Done'

A Londoner whose family emigrated to America when he was a schoolboy, Bert Ambrose started his musical career in the States where in his teens he was playing sixth violin in an orchestra in a famous New York restaurant. Six months later he was conducting it. He then took his own band into the Club de Vingt, haunt of the very cream of New York's high society. So successful was he, they even named a drink after him, the Ambrose Cocktail.

He returned to London in 1920 to become musical director of the Embassy Club fronting a quintet, but was soon back in the States, ostensibly to recruit a band of American musicians to play in London. However, New York's newest club, the Clover Gardens, persuaded him to accept a residency with his new band and at that time he became the highest paid bandleader in America. On his second return to London he brought a few of his best musicians with him who, joining forces with Britain's finest players, produced not only the best band in the country but arguably one of the best in the world. Ambrose paid top salaries and it was every player's ambition to be in his band, not just for the money but as a guarantee of a future job with any other bandleader.

A seven-year residency at the Mayfair Hotel with the Saturday Night Dance Dates from ten-thirty to midnight on the BBC made Ambrose a household name. From the Mayfair he returned to the

Embassy Club and from there to Ciro's followed by the Café de Paris. No society event was complete without Ambrose and His Orchestra and he was a great favourite of the royal family, often playing at Buckingham Palace and Windsor Castle. The summer would find the band playing the smart continental resorts such as Monte Carlo, Cannes and Biarritz, where its leader was able to indulge his love of gambling, often flirting with disaster.

He returned to the Mayfair in 1939 but the outbreak of war signalled the end of an era and Ambrose would never recapture those halcyon days of the '20s and '30s, although he continued to lead bands of varying sizes up until 1960 when he moved into management.

GEORGE ELRICK *Drums/Percussion/Vocals 1930–32*

I was at the Chez Henri Club playing in a five-piece outfit where the Prince of Wales used to come and play on my drums and suddenly it closed so I was without a job. I'd just got married so I told my wife I wanted to take her up to Scotland. Before we left London, Clive Erard, one of the three Rhythm Brothers, said to me if you're going to Scotland go through Glasgow because Ambrose is there. Go and ask him for an audition.

Ambrose was at the Empire Theatre, which I later played several times, and round the corner past the stage door there's a little lane and I drove in there. I sent in a message saying I wanted an audition with Ambrose, so Joe Brannelly came out. He was his banjo player but also his road manager and he said, 'We've got a drummer.'

'Yes, but I'm a percussionist as well as a drummer.'

'Percussionist?'

'Yes, and if you want to see what I play come around the corner and look.'

When he saw all my instruments, he said, 'Good God, do you play all this? Hold on.' He went inside and came out again, 'Ambrose will see you at three o'clock.'

We put all my instruments up on the stage and I was the first in the country to have pedal tympani as I'd got the Premier drum company to write to America and get them for me. Ambrose said, 'Gee whiz!' and Sid Phillips said, 'Where did you get those? Can you do glissandos?'

'I can do anything on them.'

'Give me a glissando from A flat to D flat.' So I did. 'That's marvellous, I'll put them in my orchestrations.' And they're in both the Ambrose recordings of 'Coronation Scot' and 'Midnight Travel' I think it's called. They're both fast and halfway through it goes boo-oo-oo-oom.

Ambrose talked to me about touring and how much did I want and I said I was free to tour and 'you tell me how much you pay'. When he told me I was quite happy but the Musicians Union had laid down that I get paid for every instrument I double on, so all that went on top. He made me work for it because I became one of the three Rhythm Brothers and when Maxie Bacon was off I'd do his comedy numbers too so I became the handyman of the band!

Evelyn Dall, the singer with the band, was a lovely girl and I was the only one allowed to go horse riding with her. Ambrose trusted me, I don't think he trusted the others. I remember when we were in Newcastle and had a matinée, it was a sweltering hot day and he said we could take our coats off. It came to Evelyn Dall's number and he introduced her and she walked on in a flimsy dress with nothing on underneath. When the lights hit her she was in her birthday suit and of course the band all started to giggle and Ambrose was looking around to see what the hell was going on. When he turned and saw her, he conducted the band facing us but with his back to her and following her so that we couldn't see her!

Ambrose fancied himself as a golfer; in fact he fancied himself as anything. I was a very good snooker player at that time and I'd been taking a lot of money off the boys, so when we were in a hotel in Leeds where there was a billiard room, they planned for me to play Ambrose.

I didn't know it but they all had bets on me and of course I won the game. He looked at me in a different manner after that. I was always the kid, you see, but it was different after I beat him, and they were all pleased. Ammy was a difficult man you know and he was a terrible fiddle player, but he very rarely played it!

BILLY AMSTELL *Clarinet/saxophone 1931–40, 1946*

I joined and played second alto to Joe Crossman. You've no idea how unworldly I was at that time and when I walked into the Mayfair it was like going into heaven! To begin with I was like a fish out of water. Bert Read was the piano player and because they'd sort of discovered me, Bert gave me a couple of solos on a recording session. I had a solo on 'Smile Darn You Smile' and one on the other side and Joe Crossman didn't talk to me for a couple of months! I played second alto to Joe for about a year and it was a wonderful experience watching him. He was a very emotional player, maybe because he was Jewish, and he used to schmaltz around like mad. There's little me from the East End, I schmaltz around with him and he got to like me for it.

In a week or two my salary was up to twenty pounds a week. That was in 1931. I couldn't believe it. I was the youngest of seven children and we were a very close-knit family. We went to Monte Carlo in the summer. Monte Carlo! My parents were so proud of me.

After about a year Danny Polo joined Ambrose, taking Joe Crossman's place and Joe went over to Lew Stone at the Monseigneur. The first evening Danny Polo was in the band, Ambrose came on to the stand, looked at Danny Polo and me, looked at Joe Jeannette the tenor player, and said, 'Why don't you two change over?' So I took Joe Jeannette's tenor, he took my alto, and from then on I became a tenor player and I've been a tenor player ever since.

In 1927 at the Mayfair Ambrose had some Americans in the band, Sylvester Ahola on trumpet, Joe Brannelly on guitar. When you hear the records from 1927 and then the mid-'30s, you can hear how the band got better and better. When Lew Davis joined in 1933 and the band had three trombones it was the talk of the profession.

You know, as a musician, to keep up a standard of playing you have to practise but Ambrose had no time to practise and he would get a little bit rusty. Some notable character would call out 'Ambrose play the violin', and unaccompanied he would play 'Body and Soul'. We sat there and listened and you couldn't help admiring him because you need a bit of pluck to play on your own, out of practice with all the corner men listening to you. But he did very well.

When we did a broadcast from the Mayfair there would be a notice on the piano 'The band is playing a little louder than usual as we're on the radio'. We didn't play special arrangements for the dancers but we did for the radio. It was like a football match for the Saturday night broadcasts, but the notable people didn't come in on a Saturday, only the ordinary people and they enjoyed it and we enjoyed it. Ambrose never made the announcements, he was too shy, he left it to Sam

Browne. We'd start about nine and play the more commercial numbers and then at ten we'd have a break, check the programme and go on the air for an hour and a half. That's a long time.

We had people who came from America and the first thing they wanted was to hear Ambrose. Hoagy Carmichael was one of them because Ambrose had recorded 'Stardust'; Edward G. Robinson was another. He kept trying to push a pound note into Ambrose's hand as a tip and Ambrose pushed it back and it was going to and fro and in the end Ambrose, to avoid a scene, took it and threw it on the piano. The band was very much admired in America as it had a 30-minute record show on the American Network every week, the only British band to do so. Another interesting thing is, Ambrose was the only British band to record 'Rhapsody in Blue', a Bert Barnes arrangement. Bert Barnes never got the recognition he deserved. He was a grand piano player and a grand arranger. When they think about arrangers, all people talk about is Sid Phillips. Sid was very good but so was Bert and he played piano on that recording of 'Rhapsody in Blue' and Danny Polo played the clarinet cadenza. Lovely player.

We went from the Mayfair to the Embassy Club, back to the Mayfair, to Ciro's, back to the Mayfair, to the Café de Paris. Ambrose only worked four places and they were the best. When he played at the Embassy Club, which was an intimate place, he only had three saxes and two brass but for broadcasts the band was bigger and we didn't broadcast from the club but from the studio. We could never have got everyone on the stand.

There were always notable people at the Embassy Club. Edward, Prince of Wales came to dance around with Mrs Simpson and you could see they were very much in love. He was a likeable guy, he always had a wink for the band but he was a bit of a naughty boy and as they were dancing around he used to look down her dress. He did, honestly, and we could watch because we knew the music backwards! Prince George would also come in to dance but he never danced with Princess Marina. I think the reason might have been one of her legs was a little bit shorter than the other and it was to save the embarrassment. You could tell she was in love with him; I don't know about him because he was a bit of a lad too, like Edward.

They always went abroad together and came to Monte Carlo to see Ambrose. They wore tropical shirts, flannel trousers, sandals; nobody knew who they were but we did and Edward used to play golf with

Ambrose at Mont Agel just outside Monte Carlo. Ambrose was a good golfer because it was part of the social scene.

Once he took the whole band down to Stoke Poges, the most exclusive golf course in England, and we each had a caddie. I could hit the ball but I wasn't a player, not in any shape or form, but there were some good golfers in the band. Ted Heath was a good player, Max Goldberg, Danny Polo. I remember as Max Bacon went to hit the ball I jumped on his back! The caddies roared with laughter as they'd never seen anything like that before because only serious golfers went there. We had lunch at the clubhouse afterwards and that was the kind of thing Ambrose would do.

He made a fabulous amount of money. In the early '30s he changed recording companies and they gave him £10,000 just to change. He always knew when a tune was going to be a hit. When we went abroad we always stayed at class hotels. He insisted we stay at the Metropole in Monte Carlo.

Ambrose was a gambler and when we were in Biarritz he lost £28,000 in one go. He hadn't any money to pay the band. He was very intimate with certain guys in the band, Sam Browne, Max Bacon, Joe Brannelly, and do you know why they were so intimate? They were all gamblers. Sam Browne flew back to London, got the money, flew back to Biarritz, gave it to Ambrose so he could pay the band.

In 1937 we made three films and we got paid a pound an hour for being at the film studio and we could be there for eight, nine or ten hours in a day. Then in the evening we would go back to the Café de Paris and there was the Saturday night broadcast – that was another four pounds. Somehow or other we'd fit in a recording session maybe before or after the film. I think I earned about £200 in three weeks and that was a lot of money.

Sam Browne was a master of singing. Nothing was too difficult for him. I think in his early days he'd played drums; he had good pitch and a good ear for music. Elsie Carlisle had a voice with a tear in it and they were a good team. Later there was Anne Shelton and Vera Lynn, but the one that knocked them out was Evelyn Dall. We had the three Rhythm Sisters with the band and nobody looked at them, nobody. When there were girls with the band it would be 'Hello kid', and that would be it, no conversation. But when Evelyn arrived, oh oi gevult what a smasher! When she ran on at the Tower Ballroom, her first appearance in England, and there were 6,000 people there, her boobs bounced up and down as she ran to the microphone and the boys took their eyes off the music and Ambrose is going mad! No funny business, and at the first rehearsal Ambrose said, 'Hey fellas lay off, she's engaged.' That was to put us off you see. But what a great personality. I think Evelyn had been over to England some years before in cabaret at the Dorchester and Ambrose spotted her because when Sam Browne and Elsie Carlisle left the orchestra, he remembered Evelyn and sent to America for her. Let's face it, she was never a really top-class singer but she looked like a million dollars. When Ambrose went to America on business and we were on the halls, Evelyn fronted the band for a short time.

When he went back to the Mayfair the bombing was on and all the people would go down into the shelter in their dressing gowns. That was early in 1940. Most of the boys joined the Squadronaires. I would have loved to have gone in the Squadronaires but, number one, they didn't ask me and, number two, I wasn't ready. I joined the air force in August 1940 and when I came out in 1944 I joined Geraldo; 22 months later I went back to Ambrose and we opened at Ciro's. He had a very good band but times had changed and it was never the same again. I stayed with him a couple of years and in 1946 we went to Monte Carlo again.

It was a happy band and I always maintain a band is a reflection of the guy in front. Ambrose wasn't an outgoing man but he had charm. It was always a pleasant experience to talk to him. Everybody got on well in that band. The only slight abnormality, if you can call it that, was that my friend Danny Polo liked a marijuana once in a while and thought I should have a marijuana too! He took me down to the boiler room at the Mayfair one Christmas and I felt like I was six feet tall! I did that two or three times but it scared me 'cause it was too good to be true. Oh it's nice, it makes you feel great; you'd look at a lamp-post and laugh!

WOOLF PHILLIPS *Trombone 1935, 1946*

I would sit with my brother Sid at Campbell Connelly's doing arrangements and this particular one was of 'Isn't This A Lovely Day', beautiful song, Irving Berlin. He was working it out and then he said for me to do it, so I started working on it and when I'd finished he looked at it and said, 'We'll just change this little bit here. That's okay, score it.' 'Score it?' So I did. I scored it, the copyist copied it, and Ambrose recorded it. I was 15 years old. Sid said, 'Don't tell anybody, it's our secret!'

At 16 I left the music publishers to tour with the Teddy Joyce Juvenile Band and we were working in Plymouth when King George V died and I left and joined Ambrose. I remember thinking I must get a haircut, and Ambrose went mad. He said, 'You look like a boy of 12 on the stage!'

The band was being conducted by Evelyn Dall, a blonde bombshell, on that particular tour of Moss Empires. She could sing, she had much more personality than Bert, and we knew what we were doing so there wasn't any problem there. Ambrose would stand on the side of the stage or out front and didn't actually appear on stage at all. It was called the Ambrose Orchestra conducted by Evelyn Dall.

I only did that tour with Ambrose although I played with him at the Café de Paris just before the war and worked for him again near the end of the war and afterwards before I formed my own band in 1947.

IVOR MAIRANTS *Guitar 1938–39*

I loved him, he was a marvellous fellow but he would never explain what he wanted from the band. He would put his bow hand in front of his mouth and whisper to me, sitting in the front, 'Listen to those foghorns, it sounds like a ship coming in.' He was talking about the saxophones who were marvellous, but to him they weren't playing as they should have done. And he would say about Max Bacon, 'Listen to him, all he does all night is chew sweets instead of keeping tempo.' Max was a marvellous drummer although someone else used to complain about him, and I won't say who, saying, 'Listen to him, why doesn't he play sideways instead of thumping?'

Ambrose's tempos were perfect. Whatever I learnt about tempos of popular numbers, I learnt from Ambrose. He used to go chip, chip, chip with the heel of the bow. If you didn't play exactly the tempo he wanted he would do this and make you come to heel. He was wonderful. You would play the best for Ambrose.

Tommy McQuater once got the better of him. We were going on a Dutch tour and he wanted more money than anybody else as he was the lead trumpet and was very, very good. Ammy loved good playing; he would pay anything for good playing, and he said, 'What am I supposed to say? I could dig a knife into his heart!' Tommy got the better of him and got more money.

To give you another side of Ambrose, there were two fiddle players at the Café de Paris and the management said they couldn't afford fiddle players any more because business wasn't good and so on. They told Ammy to sack them but he didn't have the heart to give them two weeks' notice so they stayed on right to the end and got paid. That was Ammy.

When the announcement came on Sunday, 3 September that we were now at war with Germany we didn't know what to do; nobody knew what to do. All the places closed down but we didn't know whether we were going to be bombed or not and we had to put pieces of paper across the windows.

One day I got a call from Ambrose. He was reopening at the Mayfair and I must come and join him. We played in the restaurant and I remember one day a little girl – well, not so little – came in for an audition with her mother. Ambrose was very shy and didn't like to hurt anybody but he had to audition her, so he hid himself behind a pillar while she sang. She wanted to sing 'Begin the Beguine' but didn't know what key so we just played it in the normal key, which was F. Well she could sing anything in any key and she was lovely and that was how Anne Shelton joined the band. She sang the same hours as the band; nobody cared about teenagers in those days, very little mattered and there was very little government interference and her mother would come with her wherever she went. That band at the Mayfair was virtually the Squadronaires before the Squadronaires were formed. There was Stanley Black, Billy Amstell, Joe Crossman, Andy McDevitt, Tommy McQuater, Les Carew and George Chisholm.

The blitz started while we were there and I used to take Billy Amstell home. He lived in Kilburn and I lived in Cricklewood so it was on the way and very often the bombs just missed us or the fire missed us or whatever, but we used to go backwards and forwards at night in the middle of an air-raid; it was just normal. One night when I got out of the Mayfair at two a.m. to collect my car which was parked in Berkeley Square, a bomb had fallen and blown the roof off. We drove it home all right but when I went to put the car in the garage, there was no garage! My garage, which was just around the corner from my house, had been flattened. The main London to Edinburgh railway line was just behind us and that was what they were aiming for.

It was very late by that time, what with the bombs and things, and I was really tired. My wife and the two kids came out of the Anderson shelter and she said, 'We must leave here, it's not safe to allow the children to stay here.'

'I'm so tired,' I replied, 'I just can't stand up any more, I have to go to bed, and if the bombs continue to fall they'll have to because I have to go to bed.'

I got up the following morning thinking the immediate necessity was to live somewhere where it was safe. So I phoned up the Mayfair Hotel and booked a suite for us. We had peace and comfort the time we were there and then Lew Stone and Ben Frankel, whose children were in Devon, recommended a place where I could send my children. So we went down to Devon to deposit the children in Thurlestone and came back again.

Very shortly after we came back Ambrose gave in his notice to the Mayfair. He wasn't given the sack, he gave in his notice because he wanted to go to Torquay to get out of the way of the bombs so he asked me to take over for the final two weeks. At the same time, the whole contingent joined the air force and became the Squadronaires, so there I was in charge with no band! I found musicians just for the two weeks and Lew Stone, who was working at the Dorchester, said, 'Why don't you come with me, we've got an air raid shelter here.' That was okay with me.

TOMMY McQUATER *Trumpet 1936–40*

I joined Ambrose in 1936 and then in 1938 they closed the restaurant because of a war scare and I went with another band called the Heralds of Swing in one of the clubs in Regent Street. When that folded, I went back with Ambrose and we opened at the Mayfair and we were there until we went into the RAF and formed the Squadronaires. George Chisholm and I lived next door to each other and he joined Ambrose in 1937 just as Lew Davis was leaving, so the trombone section was Eric Breeze, Les Carew and George.

Those were very good times, all that society stuff when we were either at the Café de Paris or the Mayfair or Ciro's. I didn't drink a lot in them days although I enjoy my drink now, but I never get drunk. I think your body has a certain metabolism. I remember the Prince of Wales coming in drunk and playing the drums. It's this thing they have that they can do anything they like, but it was rubbish really. Max Bacon couldn't have cared less, he just got off the stand. We played from nine o'clock until about two in the morning and then we'd go along to the Nest in Kingly Street and have a blow. A lot of the American musicians would come into the Nest and I don't know whether I should say this or not, but as you walked in the door you could smell the marijuana. I never touched it, I didn't need it, but it was all over the place. George Chisholm took a job there so he could play with the lads and they would blow until about six o'clock in the morning. Sometimes we'd go home to bed for just a little while and then go to Decca for a ten o'clock call. Then you'd sleep in the afternoon ready to go to work at night.

I can remember one great evening in 1937 when the Woolworth heiress Barbara Hutton hired the Café de Paris for a party for the golfer Henry Cotton. We were playing when this great big gentleman wearing tails that were borrowed, because they were too short, walked towards Ambrose but went on past him to Bert Barnes at the piano and said, 'Mr Ambrose may we have a waltz?' So Bert stood up and said, 'Certainly,' and swung him around the floor! We were hysterical. Ambrose ran up the stairs because he thought there was going to be a fight and we couldn't play for laughing.

In the summer we went down to Cannes for six weeks. Ambrose was a terrible gambler and the week we were waiting to get paid there was no money, so Sam Browne, the singer, got the money from London put into the bank in Cannes so we could pay the hotel and were allowed to leave! Ambrose had gambled the lot. I knew him well enough to wonder each week whether we were going to get paid because he paid the best money, always.

I got on well with Ambrose although we used to fight with each other, but if you're a trumpet player you're going to fight with somebody sometime, but I got on well with him in the end.

STANLEY BLACK *Piano 1938–40*

As a bandleader he was magnificent. There would be a morning call for a band rehearsal and there would be a bevy of arrangers all with things tucked under their arm, and all I can tell you is that when the arranger had done his bit and taken the band through his arrangement Bert would come on and tap him on the shoulder and say, 'Good, my boy, you sit down and let me take it through.' And when Ammy took it through it was different. He wasn't a great musician in the sense of being able to read at sight but he had an aura about him. Maybe it was an aura of money, because he paid the best rates anywhere in the West End, but this aura would walk into the room before he did and there was a sudden hush.

The Ambrose band was looked upon as a kind of university, how to play in a dance band, in a very good dance band. He brooked no nonsense at all. If a musician started in the band there were 14 pairs of ears and Ambrose would have six of his own and if anything wasn't quite the way he wanted it he would have his fiddle under his arm and he'd look around at the drums, then he'd look at the guitar, not a word, but they would know by his expression he wasn't amused.

I joined him at the Mayfair which was a carbon copy of most other places only a bit bigger. We used to start about eight thirty playing very quietly because in those days you gave the diners indigestion. Everything had to be quiet. He was a maniac for the internal precision of the band, even early in the evening with maybe just a couple of tables occupied.

He had an outfit called the Ambrose Octet which he would send out on a nearby tour, somewhere like New Cross or the Holborn Empire. The Octet comprised some of the regular band; George Chisholm was in the Octet, I was in the Octet, so while we were out earning a crust tearing from the New Cross Empire to the Holborn Empire our understudies would be on at the Mayfair, and when we got there they would go home and we would take our places in the regular band later in the evening.

We had a guitarist, Albert Harris, from America and Albert's mother came to the Regal Ballroom, Marble Arch, to see our stage show. The film ended, then they had the newsreel and then there would be a 'live' show three times daily. Albert's mother came to see the early evening show and then came backstage and we asked her what it was like: 'It was rather strange – quite suddenly we saw Ambrose's pianist leave the keyboard, go offstage and then he came back being led by another young man who then sat at the piano.' Of course, that was

George Shearing leading me! His ears used to pop if he passed a lamp post. He had an uncanny sense of hearing. I would walk offstage and then George led me back on!

ERIC DELANEY *Drums 1939*

I was with the Ambrose Octet with Anne Shelton and George Shearing and when the war started George used to take me home at night because of the smog and blackout and everything! We were on the road doing the theatres and Teddy Foster was in charge of it while Ambrose was with his big band in town. Dougie Robinson was with us as well. George, Dougie and I used to hang around together.

KENNY BAKER *Trumpet 1941*

My first introduction to Ambrose was when he had this lovely band at the Mayfair. Luckily I'd got my foot in the West End by getting an audition with Lew Stone and got the job while he was in the pit at the Palace Theatre, Cambridge Circus, where he was conducting the show *Under Your Hat* with Jack Hulbert and Cicely Courtneidge, and of course I was delighted.

There were occasions when Chick Smith, one of the other trumpet players, would go and work with Ambrose at the Mayfair when we finished at the theatre. One night, when he'd got to know me, he said, 'Would you like to do a dep for me with Ambrose? It's just down the road at the Mayfair.' He'd fixed it with Ammy to have the night off, so I went in and played the book that Chick should have played. About three days later Chick said, 'Did Ammy pay you?'

'No, he never mentioned it.'

'Well the best thing is to go round and see him.'

'I can't go and ask him for money.'

'Yeah, he's all right, he's fine,' said Chick.

So at the end of one of the evening performances I went back to the Mayfair and asked to see Mr Ambrose. He came out and said, 'Oh it's you, what do you want?'

'Chick Smith said you've got to pay me.'

And in this lovely voice, I can't imitate him but he was a lovely man was Ambrose, 'How much do you want, son?'

'I don't know.'

'Will three quid be all right?'

'I suppose so,' and he brought out the biggest load of money I'd ever seen and just peeled off a few notes and gave them to me. That was my first introduction to Ambrose.

From then on I worked for him on and off at various stages. Money was no object; he was earning quite a lot and he was well in with royalty, the palace and Windsor Castle and things like that. I remember talking to him about his gambling and he told me he had a beautiful Rolls-Royce and when he had a couple of free weeks he decided to go down to Biarritz. He got through all the money he'd taken, everything he'd got in the bank, and gambled the Rolls as well and had to ring home, or write home, whatever you did then, to get transport back! That was Ambrose, he'd gambled the lot.

When it came to playing the violin he was about as good as Jack Harris. He had a funny way of never telling you what you were going to play. He'd stand on the bandstand in front of the band and he'd get his violin under his chin and he'd go eech, eech, eeeeech and the boys would say, 'Lady is a Tramp'. The next one he'd go eech, eecheeeee, all squeaky and horrible – 'Night and Day'. We all knew what was coming up! Lovely guy to work for.

I remember doing some recordings with him and he had some funny ideas. He left the band to sort things out; he was very clever because he wasn't a good musician but he knew what the public wanted. We'd be rehearsing something and he'd come up and say 'Aaaah, that sounds terrible'. He'd go over to the sax players and say, 'Sounds like a wart'.

'What do you mean?'

'It sounds terrible.' So they'd fix it and eventually he'd say: 'That's good, that's it, leave it.' Before the war, Joe Brannelly, the guitar player who went into music publishing, said that the guys used to run the band really. Ambrose ran it but left the music side for them to sort out. Sid Phillips did a lot of the arrangements and the band was marvellous before the war, a really polished band.

Tommy McQuater, who worked with him before the war, was earning quite a fortune as in those days sixty or seventy quid a week was an awful lot of money, and I think he paid, without argument, the best money in town.

I did Buckingham Palace and Windsor Castle with him quite a few times and we did evening society gigs, very enjoyable. Ambrose had a charming personality and he was lovely in front of the band. When he died, I went to his funeral with dear old Tommy McQuater and I always felt it was very sad that there were only two or three people there.

HARRY GOLD *Saxophone 1945*

When Ambrose was at the Mayfair Hotel in 1945 he had a saxophone player, Mossy Kaye, who had come out of the army where he'd been taking drugs to keep him awake, and eventually his nerve went because of lack of sleep and he was discharged. So he joined Ambrose. Now the bandleader in all the West End bands never came on for the first hour. The band would begin by playing printed arrangements, just choruses, and then when the bandleader came on the special arrangements came out so people would think he made a difference!

On this occasion Mossy Kaye wasn't feeling too well and he went off the stand before Ammy came on. He'd gone to the side and was sitting on a skip with his head in his hands. Ammy came on and said, 'Where's Mossy?' He went over and said, 'What's the matter Mossy?'

'I can't stand it, I can't stand it,' said Mossy.

'Move over,' said Ammy, 'neither can I!' Lovely sense of humour he had.

Ammy had another habit. If he wanted to tell somebody something was wrong he wouldn't say anything to the person but say to the guy next to him, 'Why's he doing that?' He was a strange man, very funny. I did some gigs for him and I also did some arrangements for him for recording sessions, and as I was also working for the People's Entertainment Society I would use a lot of the guys from his band on those gigs.

One night when we were playing a gig at Buckingham Palace with Ammy some of the guys were ribbing me saying, 'This is a bit different from the Co-op dances,' and Ammy heard them. He whipped round and said, 'Stop that talk. You're like dustbins with the lid off.' He was really angry. The King and Queen couldn't have heard it but he heard it.

The Queen would come over sometimes and talk to Ammy. We had several breaks where we had food and drinks laid out in a lovely room. That side of the business was quite different from the hoi polloi side. In those days playing for the King and Queen was quite something. We never went in the front of the palace, we always went in the tradesmen's entrance, but it was all very lavish, awe-inspiring you might say. Very exciting for a young lad.

HARRY HAYES *Alto saxophone 1948*

I was with Ambrose at the Nightingale Club on first alto with Johnny Dankworth on second alto, Ronnie Scott, Bob Burns and Harry Klein. The trumpets were Kenny Baker, Tommy McQuater and Freddy Clayton. Wonderful band but nobody came in! It was a disaster – the old Ambrose magic had gone.

IVY BENSON

1913–1993

Theme 'Lady Be Good'

Ivy Benson formed her first band in 1939 and got her big break when war was declared and 'call up' papers started to arrive for the musicians with the popular bands of the day. The arrival of the GIs set the seal on her success. 'We felt like a million dollars just looking at them' was the comment of one out of the thousands who flocked to dance to Ivy Benson and Her Orchestra at Covent Garden, turned into a temporary ballroom for the duration.

When a journalist from the *Melody Maker* suggested writing a book about her and calling it *Lady Be Goodman*, she adopted 'Lady Be Good' as her signature tune. The band starred in the 1943 film *The Dummy Talks* with Jack Warner and Claude Hulbert and were soon to become the most popular attraction on ENSA tours overseas.

When the British Bandleaders Association was formed, Billy Ternent stood up at the very first meeting and announced, 'We don't want any damn girl bandleaders in this association.' Ivy walked out never to return, but she received a lot of support from Joe Loss and against all the odds fronted a highly successful band for over 40 years before trading it in for an electronic organ and 'retiring' to Clacton-on-Sea where she continued to entertain the customers at the resort hotels until her death in 1993.

IVY BENSON

At the beginning it wasn't easy but it got better because people came to see me out of curiosity. Girls on trombones, girls on trumpets. This must be seen to be believed! They came and they were really surprised at the high standard. I wouldn't have it any other way. I knew I could have gone out with a band that looked pretty and did a few sexy movements but that was second in my mind. They had to play and play well, and because of that the girls accepted the fact they had to be good musicians and they worked to that end.

I was working 52 weeks a year in 1942 and we would have to talk about which weeks we would take out just for a holiday. It was Jack Hylton who got me a year's contract with the BBC. The men musicians were getting called up and Jack had suggested me, saying he was sure I'd be able to handle it. So along with Henry Hall and Billy Cotton I became the BBC's resident band. There were a lot of objections over that as the men didn't like me getting that plum job. They didn't mind me getting the little ones but they thought that was too big for a girl's band. It was really tough and the times I wanted to pack it in because it worried me, it really did. I didn't have any backers or managers, I was doing everything myself.

We were based in Bristol for a year where we broadcast to the troops every hour of the day and night. Sometimes we had to be in the studio at two or three in the morning and you should have seen some of the girls. They were in their night attire with curlers in their hair. If it had been television it would have been hilarious! The husband of my pianist was in the 7th Army and she cried all the time she was playing, saying, 'He'll never come back,' and I used to try to cheer her up. The studios were underground and we had to learn how to do fire fighting, wear tin helmets and get up on the roof. The girls thought it was great fun; it made a change from playing dominant sevenths and C sevenths!

After Bristol, Jack Hylton put me into the London Palladium for 22 weeks. Max Miller was on the bill with us and Anne Ziegler and Webster Booth.

They'd turned Covent Garden into a ballroom and I was booked as one of the resident bands. Billy Sproud and His Band were there with me and we alternated, an hour at a time, and the atmosphere was unbelievable. You would never think they were waiting to be shipped abroad and things like that. It was packed to suffocation with GIs, all dancing, all happy, full of fun. We never worried about the bombs, the attitude used to be if it happens it happens. They came in for a good time and they were going to have a good time. They didn't care about the bombs.

Little did I know what problems those GIs were going to pose for me later on! When I went abroad after VE Day that's when I started to lose half my band to the GIs, playing all the American bases here and on the Continent. My girls were mostly north country girls, Lancashire, Yorkshire, and up until then they'd been more interested in having a job than looking for a husband. They loved playing and they loved being in the band and some of them stayed with me for years, but the GIs changed all that. They had a different approach, there were no half measures about them. 'Com' on honey let's go out,' and I was thinking 'Oh Gawd' and one by one they left me. They were so generous and they didn't care what they spent on them. They talked about the States and asked them how they'd like to live there, and there was I thinking, 'How would you like to live in England?' There was the girl I had from Manchester, my pianist. 'Oh there's Skip, can I go and talk to him?' 'Yes, Marjorie, don't be long.' I never saw her again to this day! I found her costume in the dressing-room and I finished up on piano for the rest of the month. It was amazing.

Then there was the problem of dressing the girls during the war years. There was a time when the GIs helped me out. They got hold of some parachute silk for me and I was able to have sixteen dresses made out of it. It was all such a long time ago I don't think I'm getting anyone into trouble talking about that!

I remember when we were in the middle of an air-raid in Manchester. I had two of the youngest members of the band by the hand and we were racing through the streets. Then Mecca decided to send me up to Glasgow with an 18-piece band and I wasn't there two weeks when they bombed Glasgow. I think they were following us around!

Parents asked me to look after their daughters and what a task it was. If I went abroad, which I did often, I had to take the young ones, under 18, the London ones to Scotland Yard and the northern ones to Bow Street Magistrates Court, and I had to sign papers saying I would look after them and bring them back safe and sound. Their accommodation was vetted before they got there and if I moved from one town to another I had to report to the consulate each time, so it was very hard work. I would get letters from parents thanking me for bringing up their daughters. They never queried anything, they just took it for granted I was looking after them.

I had the offer of a booking in Las Vegas for the band after the war and I was over the moon, but the Federation of American Musicians stopped me going and that was only because our union wouldn't let their bands into Britain and it was a retaliation. I had an offer to go to the Lido in Paris and I couldn't go there either because of the French Musicians Union. I loved going around with the band and they loved it and were happy and gave me 100 per cent musicianship, as much as they possibly could, and it was very sad when I had to say goodbye to them later on.

My love of Jimmy Dorsey's alto playing made me go to see him at the Statler Hotel in New York. They treated me wonderfully and I had dinner with both Jimmy and Tommy. We discussed music and I told him all my problems of running a girl's band and he laughed at me! We had a lovely picture taken and he gave me his saxophone sling and he wrote on the back of it: 'From one saxophone player to another.' I don't have it any more because Johnny Dankworth said, 'Oh I'd love that,' and, silly me, I gave it to him!

I went to a Benny Goodman concert while I was there and I went to hear the Lombardos at the Hotel Roosevelt and I had dinner with the three brothers and then Guy Lombardo gave me his baton and told me to conduct the band! So I've got a lovely picture of me conducting Guy Lombardo's band in New York.

ELSIE FORD *Bass 1939–46*

My father was very against it when I said I was going to join a dance band. He was a classical musician and didn't want any daughter of his going on the stage – he hadn't had me trained to play music of that kind!

I remember when the band went to Berlin just after the war ended and there wasn't a pane of glass in the windows of the place where we stayed. We couldn't drink any water, we couldn't even clean our teeth in it, it all had to be out of a bottle because there were 30,000 dead bodies under Berlin. The troops loved us, pretty girls and music, they broke down the doors to get in! The band went to Osnabruck for three weeks and we were asked to parties every night after the show so we weren't getting to bed until morning, and the amount of drinking that went on! I had a room-mate who could drink like a fish and it made not the slightest difference to her. We lost count of how many gin and limes she had on her 19th birthday. I said, 'I don't know why you bother, you might as well drink water!'

GRACIE COLE *Trumpet 1945–50*

We did an ENSA tour for the British Army of the Rhine in December, eight weeks touring Germany and Belgium, and it was very memorable because on Christmas Day 1945 we broadcast 'live' from Hamburg and we followed the King's Speech. Immediately that was over they announced, 'Now we take you to the Garrison Theatre in Hamburg to join the Ivy Benson All Girls Orchestra'. It was so thrilling to be following the King's Speech because the whole nation was listening!

When we were working the Palace Theatre, Grimsby, and joined up with the George Evans Orchestra, that was really exciting because it was boy, girl, boy, girl. Later on when Bill [Geldard] came and asked if I'd like to join the band I was well knocked out as it was love at first sight! I left Ivy on 18 guineas a week and I got ten pounds a week with George which was good for him because that band was known as Evans on Sevens and I was actually asked to join on ten!

Ivy was none too pleased when I told her I was leaving. We were at Butlin's at the time and she was a bit taken aback because she was settled with the band and the trumpet section and it was all working well. But it was just one of those things; I had met Bill and I was impressed with the Evans band. George was a wonderful musician and I thought it could be good for me but also I was being persuaded by my future husband!

PAULA PYKE *Drums 1946–61*

I was 17 when I joined Ivy and when we went abroad I had to go to the British Consul and he would ask questions like was I getting enough food and was everything all right. There were six of us in the band who were under age and we had to do that in every town we played in. I remember we played in Berlin and we had to travel from West Germany into the eastern sector and when we got to the border all these Russian guards were just young boys, they looked about 18 or 19, and they couldn't read our passports. Ivy handed hers over upside down and he looked at it like that and handed it back! The snow that day was about four feet deep and Robey Buckley, who came from Australia, had never seen snow before and she just rolled in it! We started playing snowballs and in the end the guards joined in!

Ivy mothered me when I first joined and I grew up with the band. She would confide in me and I was the first to know when she was going to get married. 'I want you to be my witness Paula,' she said. She was a good boss and a good friend.

GLORIA RUSSELL *Vocalist 1947–57*

When I joined Ivy we went straight over to Germany, Austria and Italy and she was very strict with the under-age girls. I had to be in at night and I wasn't allowed out with the others. Any of us under age had to stay in the hotel and she would be there. The girls that were older, of course, she never queried; 'It's your life, you go out and do what you want to, but be careful and watch what you're doing.' She was like a mother to us really!

I shall never forget my first night with the band. I'd never even been out of Exeter before and here I was on stage with the Ivy Benson Band at the Hamburg Opera House! I had to sing 'Open The Door Richard' and I had to wait for this beat at the end. I stood there waiting for this beat and missed it so I turned my back on the audience and ran back to my seat. Meanwhile Ivy's conducting the band and smiling at the audience over her shoulder, and as she turned back she glared at me, 'Don't you dare do that again.' And then the smile was back on!

When we went to Egypt we were on our way from one army base to another and we had to stop as everyone wanted to spend pennies. We got to some old army building in the desert and it had toilets that were just holes in the ground in these little cubicles. Suddenly there's a terrific scream from Ivy and we all rush in and she's saying, 'There's an animal down there,' pointing down the hole, and there was this desert rat absolutely drenched looking up at us!

It was on our way home from Egypt that I was sitting in the plane with Ivy and I was looking out of the window and thought, that's strange, there seem to be flames coming out of that engine. 'Ivy, look, do you think those are flames?'

'Yes luv, I think they are.' So she calls the stewardess and the seat belt signs go on and we had to go back to Marseilles where we stayed for four days while they sent to Prestwick for a new engine!

I remember the time when we smuggled some Hungarian acrobats across the border. We met them when we were touring for ENSA in Austria and we were on our way to Trieste. They wanted to get back to Hungary but could only get back through Italy because they didn't have the right papers or something. So we decided to smuggle them over the border into Italy in the back of our lorry with all the stands and dresses. Ivy told me to go and sit with the lorry driver and when we got to the border I was to distract the guards so they wouldn't look in the back of the lorry. Of course the first thing they ask at the border is, 'What have you got in the lorry? Open up.' So while they're doing this I'm chatting away and telling them I'm the singer with the band and before they get past the first rack of dresses in the back they've lost interest and off we go. We got to Trieste and let them off the lorry and never heard from them again, so I suppose they got back to Hungary!

SYLVIA ENGLAND *Trumpet 1947–51*

In 1950 we were returning from entertaining the troops in the Canal Zone and I was sitting next to Ivy on the plane, cleaning her diamond rings with gin!

'Did you say your sister played trombone?' Ivy asked.

'Yes, but she's only just started with a brass band.'

'That doesn't matter, I can soon teach her all she'll need to know.'

So I took Dorothy back with me and Ivy spent hours teaching her bass clef, the dance band idiom, section playing and so on. Dot stayed with Ivy for six years and became her lead trombone. She had a beautiful tone and style and after hearing some records of Ivy's, Tommy Dorsey signed a photograph: 'To Dorothy, from one good trombonist to another'!

Ivy was a great teacher. Her determination, persistence, dedication and knowledge were legendary. When I had to take over lead trumpet it was the most terrifying experience of my musical career, but if Ivy made up her mind that one of us had to do something for her, we most certainly had to get on with it and do it. By sheer determination and will power she would work with us until we were as good as she wanted us to be.

JUNE PRESSLEY *Tenor saxophone 1956–58*

When I auditioned for Ivy my father took me to the Isle of Man and it just happened that the Sunday we were there I was all over the *News of the World* in a two-piece bathing suit! There was a photographer who watched me walking backwards and forwards to my job in Fraserburgh where I was a beautician. He asked if he could take my photograph and he sent it off to the Sunday papers.

Two things I remember about Ivy. First was going into the dressing-room and she didn't have any clothes on. I'd never seen a woman without clothes, I'd never seen a man, I'd never seen anyone without clothes! She was stark naked! That was a shock to me coming from a one-horse fishing town. Secondly, she ran up to Johnny Dankworth and Cleo Laine, who were also appearing at the Villa Marina, and said, 'Look at my new sax player' and showed them the newspaper and I was on the front page with this big picture. I think that's how I got the job, because of the publicity.

I'd spent most of my time playing piano so the sax was relatively new and I'd only played it for about two years. I played alto in my dad's band but Ivy had a good alto player already and she told me she wanted a tenor player so I went home and bought a tenor saxophone from my cousin for fourteen pounds and Ivy taught me how to play it.

The first star we played for after I joined the band was Frankie Vaughan. He was very handsome and all the girls were always hanging around his dressing-room. I remember it was when string vests came into fashion and Frankie Vaughan opened the door and was standing there in his string vest. I wrote to my father saying I'd seen Frankie Vaughan in his string vest! He wrote back and said, 'You'll never play like Coleman Hawkins if you're going to look at Frankie Vaughan in his string vest!'

My first pay packet was twelve pounds and as I'd been earning two pounds at the beauty salon, it seemed a lot of money. But of course you had to pay your own digs and everything.

We were all so pure in those days and all Ivy's girls were very moral as far as I can remember. Ivy wasn't pleased when I got engaged to Duncan because it was another one leaving the band. She was going to have to find another saxophone player and train her again and I could understand that. She said, 'You can't marry Duncan Campbell, they're all queer those trumpet players!' I believed what she said but I didn't know what it meant!

Ivy never favoured the saxes, she favoured the trumpets. She used to give Sylvia Monks, the lead alto, 'Zambesi' to play and Sylvia hated it. I remember arriving at one venue and there were only photographs of the brass section, no saxes at all, I'll never forget that.

I was always scared of Ivy, but I was scared of every adult. It was a respect thing. I remember when we had the Christmas parties at Ted Heath's house. I don't drink, don't smoke, but I'm a junk food eater, chips and all that, and Ted Heath was the same. They were all on the wine and Moira Heath said I could go through to the kitchen and sit with Ted and eat some chips. It was like sitting next to God; I was so scared because that's the way I was brought up, to respect your elders, your teachers and people in charge. I looked up to Ivy Benson because she was a household name but Ivy never gave me any need to be scared of her. I was just scared because she was a famous lady and I never felt good enough.

SHEILA TRACY *Trombone 1956–57*

My first sight of the Ivy Benson Band was at Lyons Corner House, Marble Arch, and they were wearing orange strapless dresses with green ivy leaves appliquéd down the front. I thought they looked really glamorous!

I had one more term to go at the Royal Academy of Music and was wondering what on earth I was going to do to earn my living when someone suggested I should write to Ivy Benson. I had a letter by return asking me to go along and meet Ivy and the girls. Ivy was charming and obviously desperate because I hadn't a clue how to play the theme from *Rififi* which she put in front of me. For a start it was manuscript and I was accustomed to printed dots, but she offered me a job there and then and I joined them at the Ideal Home Exhibition in Edinburgh's Waverley Market at the end of the spring term. Dad was delighted as I'd saved him a term's fees!

GILLIAN DENNIS *Alto saxophone 1958–66*

Ivy would always check to make sure we were safely back in our hotel at night, especially the young ones. And this particular night we'd met up with some of the boys from the Eric Delaney Band and they said to come out to a night club with them.

'Oh no, Ivy would be absolutely furious if we did that,' we said.

'Well try and sneak out.'

We couldn't get out by the door without being seen so we got the sheets off the bed and knotted them together and threw them out of the window. One of the girls stayed behind to pull the chain in the toilet so Ivy wouldn't know we'd gone, and that's how we went out for the night!

JOHN DANKWORTH

1927–

John Dankworth first came to notice playing traditional style clarinet with The Garbage Men led by drummer Freddy Mirfield. Following two years at the Royal Academy of Music, when he took up the alto, he became interested in bebop and together with Ronnie Scott was a founder member of Club 11 in Great Windmill Street which became known for its experimental bebop music.

He was a member of the Tito Burns Sextet, again alongside Ronnie Scott, and in 1949 was named Musician of the Year in the *Melody Maker* Jazz Poll. The following year saw the start of the celebrated John Dankworth Seven. His talent as a composer equals his ability as a performer and his compositions have brought him increasing acclaim over the years. They include *Improvisations* for Jazz Band and Symphony Orchestra, the ballet *Lystrata* and *The Diamond and the Goose* for Choir and Symphony Orchestra. Film scores include *Saturday Night and Sunday Morning, The Servant, Modesty Blaise*. He has also written two musicals, *Boots With Strawberry Jam* in collaboration with Benny Green and *Colette* which he wrote for his wife Cleo Laine.

In 1970 John Dankworth and Cleo Laine founded the Wavendon Allmusic Plan to which young musicians come from all over the world to attend jazz courses and master classes and where 'The Stables' has become one of the country's most popular venues for jazz musicians.

This husband and wife team, with an international reputation second to none, believe in backing the future of music as well as enjoying their well deserved reputation, and Britain should be justly proud of them.

JOHN DANKWORTH

After three and a bit years of the Seven, my agent Harold Davidson suggested I have a big band. It seemed a good idea because it was still the heyday of the big bands and everybody was trying to vie with Ted Heath at the time and bands like Joe Loss, Teddy Foster, Ken Mackintosh and the Squadronaires were still touring.

I left all the financing and every other aspect of it to Harold to organise and started writing for it. I had written for Ted Heath on occasions before so it seemed like heaven to have my own band and not be limited to a five-minute rehearsal for a three-minute piece before we went on the air!

In October 1953 we went to the Royal Forest Hotel, Walthamstow, and did something that I don't think has often been done in this country: we had the band rehearsing there for a couple of weeks before the first engagement. The band was hand-picked and I asked the members of the Seven whether they would like to be in it and some of them did and some of them didn't. I needed a lead trumpet and the one I'd admired as a lead for so long was Derek Abbott who had been with Geraldo for years. Then there was Maurice Pratt, a fine trombone player, Bill Le Sage, who stayed on from the Seven, and Allan Ganley, was the original drummer.

Our first booking was at the Astoria Ballroom in Nottingham in October 1953 and we devised this scheme of having different colour jackets for each section. I think it was green for the trombones, fawn for the saxophones, red for the trumpets and goodness knows what for the rhythm section. It looked a bit kaleidoscopic but it attracted attention as nobody seemed to have done that before. We had seventeen players including me. Six saxophones, eight brass, three rhythm and three singers as well. I guess as Ted Heath had three everybody thought they'd better have three in order to beat Ted Heath! I had two from the Seven: Frank Holder, who not only sang but also played the Latin American instruments, and Cleo Laine. Then there was Tony Mansell who later went on to sing with the Polka Dots.

Life on the road with a big band is full of hairy moments ranging from perhaps a bass player not turning up or falling ill on the morning of a big concert to a player being taken suddenly drunk, so to speak! All these things have happened and worse. Come to think of it one of the hairiest moments was when we were booked to play in Jersey and were due to fly in two small planes.

It was mid-summer but I was told that sometimes Jersey got fog which played havoc with the aeroplanes so I insisted that the 20 of us went in two lots of ten, both of which were plausible bands. I went in the first plane which had Frank Holder, two trumpets, two trombones, a pianist and a drummer, and two saxes. We went over there and lo and behold the second plane was delayed by fog and never got there!

We put all 17 stands out so it looked as if the platform would be bulging with musicians and we played with half the seats empty. It must have sounded awful! Thank goodness we were there for two nights so by the second night the others had arrived and we did the full thing.

We did the rounds and we did pretty well I suppose. I think I tried to make it a bit too different at the beginning and it didn't gel for about a year or so. We'd been making records but they didn't really sell very well and both of the big hits I had came out of the blue. George Martin was my record producer, long before he'd heard of the Beatles, and he happened to catch one of our BBC late-night slots on Wednesday evenings. Those were the days when you had a 'live' big band broadcast for an hour and a half at a time.

I always thought I had a different sense of humour and I felt something needed to be done for a bit of a laugh. So I had the idea of doing variations on 'Three Blind Mice' in the way that various bands might do them – Benny Goodman, Gerry Mulligan, Eric Delaney and so forth – and every week we did one of these impersonations of the way a band would play 'Three Blind Mice'. George happened to hear them and asked if I couldn't think of a way of putting them on record.

I went home and thought about it and I just thought up this story of three blind mice who lived in a recording studio: one used to live in a mill and played a bit of Glenn Miller so I called him Miller; and then there was a very righteous little fellow so they called him Benny Goodmouse; one was Irish so they called him Mulligan and on it went.

We were considered the jazziest band on tour but the non-jazz disc jockeys picked it up and it had quite a success. It was also successful in

41

the States and Cannonball Adderley phoned me to ask if he could do a cover record of it. I agreed and it never occurred to me that it would be in opposition to my record, but it was and it actually did better than my own record out there! But I was the composer so I got the royalties.

I took the band to the States for about three weeks in 1959. We played at the Newport Jazz Festival and got terrific write-ups. I think a lot of the jazz critics were getting a bit fed up with the round of the bands they'd been reviewing for years and they were quite interested in what we did. The *New York Times* said it had a freshness about it and a swing that had been missing in American bands for years. We then went on to play two other dates in New York including Birdland, and that's where Cleo met Ella Fitzgerald even though Cleo wasn't singing as the band was booked as a band, no singers invited. She came with me because she was my newly wedded bride and I got her to come up and sing two or three numbers and Ella was in the audience.

We then went on and played a week in New Jersey where they had a Music Circus. It was just a way of putting on different sorts of music in an enormous tent. We opened the first half and Duke Ellington the second half. We knew a lot about the Ellington band and Duke because he'd been touring England and we'd always met him backstage but this was the first time we'd shared the bill with him. I could spend an hour talking about that one alone! He was very keen on the band and had heard it in England when he came to one of our gigs and we played 'Mood Indigo'. I can't think how we had the effrontery to do that but we did, and to my surprise he said he would very much like me to send him that chart. I couldn't believe that he was serious but I realised much later, working with Mercer Ellington's band which is essentially the same as his father's, they play 'Mood Indigo' so many times they get fed up with their own arrangements of it, and when they hear a new one, they think let's give that a go for a few months. So I realised he was serious and I never sent it to him so that was my loss.

During the week we played in New Jersey with Duke, his drummer, who was not the permanent drummer, didn't know there was a matinée so Duke came to me and asked if I could lend him Kenny Clare.

'I'm sure Kenny will do it if you could give us the drum book and he can have a look through it.'

'Sorry there is no drum book!'

I told Kenny there was no drum book and he said, 'Oh that doesn't matter, I know most of those charts anyway.'

Of course he went on and played brilliantly and afterwards I said 'How did he do Duke?'

'I'd trade him for my guy any time.'

If he hadn't known me and felt it was a bit cheeky I think he would have offered Kenny the job right then. He was too much of a gentleman to do it because he knew he'd be stealing from me. The guys in the Ellington band told me that's the nearest Duke ever gets to offering anybody a job and Kenny should have taken it. To his great credit Kenny felt loyal to me and didn't take it.

I made a slight change in the band when I replaced the sax section with a small band. There were still three saxophones, myself, a tenor and baritone, but instead of the other saxes I had a trumpet and a trombone making a small band within a band. A lot of people said it made the band brass heavy but it was an interesting departure and a lot of people still comment on that particular band as being the one they felt was most distinctive.

In 1960 I changed again and went back to a slightly more conventional band and that was the time that Dudley Moore was the pianist. I've had so many big bands that I never know which one to revive! Not many of the things from the original '55 band get played these days but a few of them do. I think we've played 'Perdido' quite a lot over the years, that's about the only one that has survived 40 years of changes of style.

Then I started a publishing company and my partner in that venture, David Dearlove, was invaded in the office by a young composer who wanted him to listen to some of his demos. He left them and later David came to me and said that one could be of interest because it had 'something'. He played me this one piece and, frankly, I didn't see anything to go mad about except that it was in three-quarter time which made it that little bit different to the material being used. He persuaded me to record it and so we tucked it in as title number four in a three-hour session. You know what a rush that is sometimes, and we recorded it in about 25 minutes! I heard it back later and I thought it wasn't quite right, the tune wasn't quite forward enough and there wasn't quite enough percussion on it. So we did what must have been one of the first overdubs in history. We went back into the studio with George Martin and we somehow contrived to re-record it and mix in a piccolo and another Latin American instrument to make the rhythm stronger and the tune a bit more recognisable.

The company was EMI and they were going to put it out as a jazz record, but when I heard it back I felt very strongly that it had a much wider appeal than that. I went to Manchester Square and sort of blathered my way through department after department saying, 'You know that record of mine that's going out on the jazz label? Well, I think it should be on the other label.'

'Oh no, no we can't do that, it's too late to change.'

Somehow I managed to talk them into it and they put it out as a commercial record and within a week or two it was being played a heck of a lot and very quickly went into the charts. It never got to number one but I think it got to about number five and it was in the charts for nearly six months which is a long while by any standards. So what it lacked in number one status it had in sustaining status. It kept on selling.

That was 'The African Waltz' which a lot of people think was written by me but it wasn't. David Lindup and I sorted it out together and did what we thought was a good arrangement and that was the last hit record I had. The second and last!

CLEO LAINE *Vocalist 1951–58*

I auditioned for the Dankworth Seven in 1951 at the 51 Club and that was my breakthrough into the professional world. Before that I'd been auditioning most of the time and singing in pubs, doing talent competitions and trying to break into the business. I can't quite remember how it came about but there was a bass player in my life at the time who also wanted to manage me and he got an interview with Harold Davidson who said the only person he had on his books who needed a singer at the time was this group who were auditioning in the 51 Club and I could go down there and try my luck. I don't think he held out much hope for me.

I actually passed the audition, they offered me six quid a week and I got seven out of them. So that was the start. The beginning was quite traumatic really because they weren't very fond of singers, but luckily I passed the test and they seemed to respect my singing abilities for some reason or other and I made it. My leg wasn't pulled too much because I heard some terrible stories about how bands in general treated singers. I was on my guard most of the time but they were pretty respectful.

When John formed the big band there were three of us; I was the only girl with Frank Holder and Tony Mansell and we had a lecture from J.D. at the outset. He said, 'This band will never become a singers' band.' I suppose he was thinking in terms of Lita Roza, Dennis Lotis and Dickie Valentine who were very, very big with Ted Heath, although you couldn't call that a singers' band, but they were very big compared to what John wanted us to be. He just wanted us as an addendum, we had to be suffered rather than wanted! We sat on the stand, except for concerts, and did our smiling and whatever! We did about six numbers each a night because dancers liked to hear the singers but John really wanted it to be a band that was listened to for the band music, not the singers. That's why I left in fact, because I didn't want to be a band singer all my life and I knew it wasn't going to help me much.

The Seven helped me a great deal. They were my tutors in many respects. I learnt a great deal from listening to their talk and I really became one of the boys in the Seven. I went everywhere to late-night parties and their 'talk-ins' and whatever and that is where I learnt most of what I know today about jazz and musicians and the music that was going on in those days. My learning experience was with that band and it was tremendously good. I don't think that I could have done what I have done so far without the Seven and also the big band.

In the very early days I didn't have much say at all. I was just handed the arrangement and that was it. Get on with this girl! Then I put in my own interpretation in some sort of way and it developed from there. As I became more confident I ad-libbed more and started to put my spoke in. Certainly as the big band developed the arrangements were honed around me rather than just the odd chorus. Dave Lindup used to do quite a lot in the band. He was John's kind of amanuensis.

I always got on very well with the musicians and I don't think they were interested one way or another when I became involved with John. All they were interested in was their music, not the love life of anybody else! If I'd wanted to I could have stirred up a lot of trouble talking about the love life of musicians on the road so I was sure they weren't going to stir up any trouble for me! But, quite honestly, there was no trouble to stir up.

It was pretty tough for the singer because you got on the coach and quite often arrived half an hour, sometimes an hour, before you were due on. Often there was nowhere to clean up and make yourself presentable and people expected you to be presentable. My dress at the beginning was not really very sensible as it was white and it was the only one so it got gradually greyer and greyer, and in those days there was never a one-day cleaning service on the road.

You go into these town halls and so on and where do you plug in an iron? Often I ironed in the lift; I just took the light bulb out of the top of the lift and ironed there. I think I have a picture somewhere of me ironing in the bloody lift, this dreadful dress that an Oxford Street lady had talked me into buying saying it was the greatest. It didn't stand the test of time by any stretch of the imagination and it got limper and limper and greyer and greyer, and I got scruffier and scruffier! You were the one girl with 20-odd men on the road and they didn't really help you very much. If you had a heavy case it was definitely feminist time – they'd be treating you like you were a feminist! There wasn't much gallantry.

In 1958 I decided to leave the band. I felt that I'd come to a full stop as far as work was concerned, also I wanted to do something different. When I told John I was leaving he said, 'Marry me!' He thought I'd stay on if we got married but I left anyway so he didn't benefit from the marriage. He thought he was going to get a cheap band singer but he got an expensive wife!

When the band went to Birdland I wasn't hired, I was just a wife on the road. I don't know why it was decided I should sing a couple of songs but it was an opportunity and a pretty scary opportunity. There must have been a lot of interesting people in the audience and the one person I did meet that night was Ella. I met her in the toilet afterwards. She didn't comment on my singing at all, she just said, 'You've got nice legs'!

I met her several times after that and the last time was in San Francisco when she was making a first appearance after her heart bypass and at that time she was very concerned about her legs as she needed another operation on the big vein in the leg that contributes to heart problems. She was having some sort of operation on that which she hoped would ease the agony. Obviously it didn't as she lost both her legs eventually. She just loved singing, that was her whole life, and I can imagine that when it all had to stop she must have been completely and utterly distraught, mentally.

FRANK HOLDER *Vocalist 1950–57*

I was fortunate in that I used to bum around the jazz clubs and people had told me John Dankworth wanted me to join the Seven. Anyway, I was walking up Shaftesbury Avenue one day and John hailed me, pulled me into a café and said he'd like me to join the band. 'The only thing is we can't pay you very much money, not what you're worth nor what you're earning now.' I thought, 'Come off it' and said, 'Yes please, I'd like to.'

A year later Cleo joined and we auditioned where the Ronnie Scott Club is now, downstairs in a club called the Cosmopolitan. After we'd heard her John said, 'You're the singer, she's in your charge,' so I ended up showing Cleo the ropes and helping her to develop.

John would write all these lovely arrangements and he would have to teach Cleo these on the coach with the clarinet because she didn't know much about phrasing and things. He would be playing things for her all the way on the journey and through that they ended up with this formula of the alto and the voice, which of course became a world hit for them.

When I went with the band I suggested we wear different jackets and things and at first the guys looked at me as though I was mad. Anyway we ended up with the saxes in one colour, the rhythm section in another, and John of course wore his own suits, and so did I.

I was always a sort of a show type person and having suggested the coloured jackets, now I said we ought to do something to entertain the people. Tony Kinsey and Jimmy Deuchar said, 'Look this is a jazz outfit, you can't come in here and change it.'

'I don't want to change it,' I replied, 'but let's make some money.' I said nothing more.

Then we played a Sunday concert in Buxton and we had a packed house but people started to walk out, and by the time the interval arrived the place was more or less half full. The guys were down in the dressing-room saying, 'What are we going to do? This is not good.'

'I tried to tell you before so don't ask me. Look, I've never done an impression in my life but I'll go on and do an impression of the Ink Spots and you guys do whatever comes into your mind that you think will be funny.'

So we go on and I'm singing 'Don't talk to them trees' etc: This is the scene: John, Eddie Harvey, Don Rendell and Jimmy Deuchar were

47

playing cards on the stand and Eric Dawson, who had a natural sort of Afro hairdo, started bowing the bass, and Bill Le Sage put his feet up on the piano and started to read a newspaper upside down and then started tearing it up and throwing bits all over the place. The audience was falling about; a simple thing like that and at the end of it we got rapturous applause. Immediately after that we did 'I Hear Music' at one ridiculous tempo and, again, great applause.

That became the formula of the band; we did a comedy thing in either half of each concert and at a dance. Also John began to sing a bit more and created the Jay Birds, a singing group consisting of himself, Don Rendell and Eddie Harvey. When the big band started we took the same formula as in the Seven; we always kept the bit of comedy, and even to this day John will do something like that. My joining them and playing Latin American instruments was all part of the show and John had a way of throwing his clarinet up in the air when he got exuberant in the Latin stuff and sometimes he catches it and sometimes he doesn't! One day he forgot his clarinet and Don Rendell's is right beside him and as he got excited he reached for Don's clarinet and Don said, 'No, please John!' But he started to play, slung it up and it came crashing down on the floor. From then on Don used to guard his instrument very, very carefully.

John was a very playful character, he tended to be full of life, and when we finished dances late at night and had to be up early in the morning to travel to the next gig, we'd go to sleep on the coach. Now John was always playing practical jokes and the guys would say, 'John please go away.' I told Cleo that when he came larking around to punch him, so one day she did this and she had fairly large arms and John was so mad. He also did it to Eddie Blair and Eddie grabbed his hand and, accidentally or not, caught his thumb and pushed it back and it must have hurt a lot. Those were the days when we were all young and playful and it was a marvellous time.

During that time there was nothing between John and Cleo. She was like one of the fellas and John was the leader and he was very strong-minded. We did a tour in Germany and the lads would all run off on their own somewhere and leave John behind because otherwise we all ended up doing what John wanted to do even when we were relaxing. Being a girl, Cleo was left with the comedian on the show and the driver and the story goes that John got jealous of this huge German driver who was big and broad. Now nobody knew he cared for Cleo at all, because John never showed any emotion – he's not the type. Anyway one night he got mad and shouted at this driver, 'You leave my singer alone, get away from my singer.' That's when it started to develop slowly, but we didn't have any inkling and it was never such that one could say John and Cleo were an item, never. Then suddenly they're together, they're in love and it all started to happen, which was tremendous.

A thing that happened to me personally was the time we played Nottingham and all the others were ahead of me booking into the hotel. As I came up to the desk this person said, 'I'm sorry we can't have you here.' Silence. John said, 'What do you mean by that? He's booked in here, he's part of our band.' She's now stuttering, 'I'm sorry we can't help you.' So Don Rendell says, 'Look he is part of us and if you can't have him you don't have any of us.' She was dithering, so everybody left and we didn't stay there. That was in 1952.

It happened again when I was with the big band and we were playing at the Samson and Hercules Ballroom in Norwich. I was booked into these digs but didn't get a chance to go there before the gig and at one o'clock or so I knocked on the door and said, 'My name is Frank Holder and I'm booked in here with the Dankworth Orchestra.' This person looked at me and said, 'I'm sorry you must be mistaken, you're not booked here.' 'Look it was booked, check the name.'

'I'm sorry we can't have you, we have to think of our guests.'

I had always been a ballad singer, but because of my bongos and such I'd become an entertainer. Then I discovered that a lot of my ballads were being cut out and Cleo was getting them. At the Isle of Man, John did 'The Nearness of You' for her at a funeral tempo, very slow, and then shortly after that he'd play 'You Go To My Head' for me, and as I got up to sing the tempo was like a dance tempo. I could sing it but it wasn't fair, it should have been done as it was arranged. So I did something that no artist or musician should ever do, and I've often regretted it: I just walked off the stage.

John came off and funnily enough he wasn't angry. 'What happened to you?'

'John if you don't know, you never will, but before you say anything will you please take a month's notice, I'm off.'

And so I finished at the end of that summer season in the Isle of Man. But we had some wonderful times and John was phenomenal. As everybody knows, the band could be playing and if there's a mistake, he not only hears it because he has perfect pitch, but he can go round looking upside down at the music on the stand and correct the note. Oh yes, they were really wonderful, wonderful days.

BILL GELDARD *Trombone 1954–57*

I was under contract to Oscar Rabin but he let me go early without paying him anything! John's band was different to what we thought it might be but it was a good band, and though it was more jazzy than most, it wasn't quite the big jazz band it became later. With me in the trombone section were Maurice Pratt, Keith Christie and Eddie Harvey. John was a nice man to work for. He's a good musician so he has that going for him for a start; he's a good arranger, good composer and we never had any problems with John. He was relatively considerate as a bandleader.

Every year the bands played at the Jazz Jamboree. Tommy Trinder was the compère and it was a mixture of big bands and small groups at the Gaumont State in Kilburn, which would be packed. It started at lunchtime and the bands would be allowed ten minutes each apart from Ted Heath who would close the show around mid-afternoon with 15 minutes. Jazz Jamborees were always on a Sunday and as bands had to get away for Sunday concerts, that decided which spot you had on the bill. If you had a concert the other end of the country then you had to go on first.

Ted Heath always had something special done for the Jazz Jamboree, but in 1954 John put one over on him because it was so unexpected. He always had lots of good commercial ideas, John, and he worked out this arrangement so that as we sat there in regular band formation it would go along the line starting with the saxophone on the end who would stop playing for a moment and flick a letter over on the front of his stand, and this went the whole way around the band until the letters spelt out 'Welcome to the Jazz Jamboree'!

This was all timed to fit in with the music, really slick, and of course it brought the place down. I don't know what Ted thought about that but we stole one over him that year! That was the year Gracie's [Gracie Cole] girls' band were the first on and they tore the place up as nobody was expecting anything like that!

GARRY BROWN *Trombone 1954–59*

When I joined, the band was struggling a little bit – I think it was struggling financially – and then we had some Saturday broadcasts. Every Saturday we would travel down from some place like Barrow-in-Furness overnight and sit in Lyons Corner House and have a coffee and go straight into the studios, do the broadcast twelve-thirty 'til one, get back on the coach and go off somewhere else.

I remember arriving in Whitehaven, way up in Cumbria, one night at something like seven o'clock and we were on the stand about nine. I don't think there were any hotels in Whitehaven at that time so Kenny Clare, Dave Lee, Danny Ellwood and myself went to get some digs.

It was a miserable rainy night and we got to this house, knocked on the door, and the landlady said she had a room so we asked to have a look at it. We went upstairs into this loft where there were eight beds! Dave Lee asks why eight beds as there are only four of us, and she said, 'Oh you have to share, I've got another four people in.'

'Might I ask who?' says Dave.

'They're lorry drivers.' Well, we had nothing against lorry drivers but Dave said, 'Lorry drivers?' and she said 'Pickfords, you know'. The look on her face as if to say 'This isn't any rubbish!' We had no option and we came in at one and they left at five in the morning!

When John came up with the idea of 'Three Blind Mice', the letters started to flow in. When we recorded it and the record placings came out we were in the Top Ten! Suddenly the band was very famous, so much so that we were in the middle of this Scottish tour and at the end of it they decided we'd have to do it all over again! We finished the tour on the Saturday night in Kirkcaldy and then they flew Tubby Hayes up as a special guest and we did that tour twice in two weeks! After that we went to the Isle of Man and the Villa Marina, which had been the Joe Loss stronghold for the strict tempo dancers, and we weren't at all a strict tempo band. The band was so far ahead of its time, the technique, the quality, the precision and the professionalism of John. He stood no nonsense, which was good. When we got this booking I can remember saying, 'John, you know we're going to need things like the Gay Gordons!' Anyway, he did arrangements of those things and the band was very successful.

We did a series of Wednesday broadcasts called 'Johnny Come Lately' from Aeolian Hall and John and Dave Lindup would bring their manuscripts in still wet and they were copying while we were doing the rehearsal. John would have eight or nine new numbers in and they were never very easy numbers. He would have a guest artist like Spike Milligan playing trumpet or Gerard Hoffnung playing tuba. The band was meant to play so many numbers from the Plug List and we didn't have many of those! The BBC insisted on this so John did some arrangements of these songs, taking a chorus of each which he would play when the news came on and we were off the air!

When John and Cleo got married they announced it at one of our broadcasts and afterwards they took the whole band down to Gerrard Street for a Chinese meal. They have such an affinity with music and each other. All that stuff they do is so brilliant and there's no one else who does it like that, there never has been and there never will. They look at each other when John's playing alto with Cleo singing and you can see them signalling. I guarantee if he changes, she changes with him, just like that, even when they're not playing with their own band. I saw them at Carnegie Hall and it was magic.

PETE WARNER *Tenor saxophone 1955–57*

I was touring Ireland with Ken Mackintosh and I had this phone call from the Dankworth office and I thought it was somebody joking! I couldn't believe that I was being asked to join the great John Dankworth, and of course I said yes.

It was a very different band, clinically brilliant, and the arrangements were wonderful but, and I don't mean this in a derogatory way, it seemed like a gentleman's jazz band to me. If it ever started to swing a little bit evilly, John would back off. But I've heard recordings of it since and now I really can't believe how good it was. I must really have not been in my right mind to have taken it so lightly because it was a great band.

When we were in the Isle of Man, one hot day I ran down to the sea and leapt in and it was as if someone had hit me on the back of the head with a sledgehammer. Fortunately the water wasn't very deep and I was on all fours and managed to crawl out but I got this terrible pounding headache which went on for ten weeks. I eventually had to leave and go home.

Basil Kirchin heard that I'd left Dankworth and sent me to his doctor who gave me some pills and the headache went just like that! He asked me to join his band and it was the best thing I'd ever done in my life because that band really did swing, African evil – get down to it!

VIC ASH *Tenor saxophone/clarinet 1963–66*

Bobby Breen was the singer when I joined the band and one of his features was 'Laura'. The end of the lyric is 'Laura and she's only a dream', and for some reason Bobby would always end it with 'Laura and she's only a fool'. This kept going on and on and in the end John got quite angry about it. One day in the coach, I think we were going up to Manchester and we were winding Bobby up as he was singing to himself these words 'Laura and she's only a dream'. He had an incredible lisp, dear Bobby. 'Yeah, great, Bobby, that's right.' Anyway come the concert that night, he's concentrating in the wings and he came on, got to the last eight bars and sang, 'Laura and she's only a drool'. True story!

We did dances but I guess mostly concerts because it was a jazz band. As a bandleader John was great and I have great respect for him as a musician – wonderful. Of course at that time 'African Waltz' written by Galt McDermot was still a big hit for him.

ERIC DELANEY

1923–

Theme 'Oranges and Lemons'

Eric Delaney led his very first band at the age of ten when he appeared in a cine/variety show at the Troquette, Elephant and Castle, billed as Britain's Youngest Swing Drummer. His mother had given him his first drum, costing sixpence in Woolworth's, when he was 18 months old. When he formed his own line-up on leaving Geraldo, his theme 'Oranges and Lemons', and his own 'Delaney's Delight' featuring his tuned tympani, put his band firmly on the musical map where it has remained, in one form or another, ever since. In 1996 he joined forces with the Wigan Youth Jazz Orchestra, a magnificent mixture of youth and experience!

ERIC DELANEY

I left Geraldo in May 1954 to form my own band and take it on the road in the October. I'd made a record, 'Oranges and Lemons', so I was a big name by then. People like Jack Payne were playing it and it was top of the hit parade and it had so much publicity, I had to go on the road.

I was stuck for a lead trumpet player and Albert Hall, who was with Gerry, said 'What about me?' and so he left and came with me. For a few years we'd seen Geraldo driving about in his Rolls-Royce with this young lad sitting there next to him. He never spoke to us and we used to wonder who he was. Well that was Derek Boulton who was in the Geraldo office. So I'm leaving the band and he comes up and asks if I need someone to look after my band because he said, 'You've got to go on the road'. So that's Derek Boulton gone from the Geraldo Orchestra and we opened up our own office in Bond Street.

When the personnel of the band came out in the *Melody Maker*, straight away people in the business were saying, 'That won't last, no way', because I had so many jazzers, especially Jimmy Skidmore because Jimmy wasn't a reader. Anyway we had a fortnight's rehearsal in a ballroom in Kingsbury in north London, all day and half the evening in order to get a reasonable library off.

We then go on the road and at one particular time in the concert the audience are laughing, tittering, and we can't understand what's going on. It was Albert Hall who sussed it out standing at the back and looking down. He said, 'It's bloody Skidmore.' What happened was when the saxes had a passage to play on clarinet, unbeknown to us Jimmy didn't want to play clarinet. He would be the last to put down his tenor and the last to pick the clarinet up. Then he'd look at it, look at the reed, put it to his mouth to lick it. By now the phrase has gone, so he doesn't get to play it! The audience got to notice this and everywhere we went the audience warmed to Skidmore so much.

When we went on the road with my band show I had a different setting for every number we did, like the battleship for 'Hornpipe Boogie'. We did Sunderland Empire on the Monday night and the 'gods' hadn't been opened for ages and it was so dusty the whole of the audience were covered in plaster and everything with the vibrations of these cannons going off!

I got Alan Roper to do as much of the pad as he could, especially the big things, and I invited him to stay with me at my home in Edgware for two weeks. I paid him a fortnight's salary and we were able to talk day and night and it was at that time we did 'Roamin' in the Gloamin' and 'Truckin' two-beat style, and that's why the band was so popular, it had a style. Think of John Dankworth's 'Three Blind Mice', we're the only British band mentioned in that. The only reason he couldn't mention my name was because of contractual reasons. I wanted a two-beat feel in the quick steps because the two-beat foxtrot had caught on. I liked Mickey Ashman's playing, bass player with Chris Barber, and as

Jack Seymour, who did the arrangement of 'Oranges and Lemons', was leaving I thought I'd get Mickey Ashman. Also one of the trumpets was leaving and I liked this Kenny Ball, so I got Kenny in the band and I had two trad players in the band. It wasn't long before I was called to a meeting by the band and they said, 'Either they go or we go,' so I had to get rid of them. Kenny will tell you to this day that was the finest thing that happened to him, Delaney giving him the sack!

I'm still Tom Tom the Piper's son who sent them stone deaf with a tuneable drum! That's me. I had five trumpets and four saxes, three tenors and a baritone, that's how it started because I wanted the punctuation and the brilliance and the excitement of the Kenton Band, hence the five trumpets. I liked the Woody Herman thing, three tenors and a baritone, so I just did that and it worked very well.

It was great leading my own band although I had to be on my own more because one had meetings and I was seldom on the coach. It was so hectic, all the different appearances at music shops and that sort of thing. Selco Toy Company put out the Eric Delaney Drum Set which after a few years became the Ringo Starr Set! I had the lights in the drums which I hadn't used with the Geraldo Orchestra. I remember my dad putting them in, sawing the flap out in the bass drum so I could put two hinges on it to change the bulb. It was a great gimmick, a wonderful effect. Although it can be annoying at times when you get people coming up to my road manager at concerts and saying, 'We're looking forward to the concert tonight. Does he still put the lights in the drums and does he still go round?' Not, 'Can he still play but do the bloody drums light up?' Sometimes that bugs me a bit.

We were playing Glasgow Empire for a week when Bill Haley came over and did a one-night stand. They were sleeping on the pavements outside a couple of days beforehand to get tickets, and the radio and the papers were full of it and it was obvious then that things were changing. That was when I decided to form a small band and Tony Fisher was the man who came to light there. I wanted a tenor player and as we'd had this young whippersnapper running around the band during rehearsals in the '50s, Jimmy Skidmore's son Alan, we got young Alan in the band, so the front line was Alan Skidmore, Tony Fisher, Ron Asprey.

Then I wanted something different and I thought about having a vibraphone player so I rang up Ronnie Scott and asked him if he knew of anyone and he said 'I've got a young lad coming out of the air force who's working at the club, Jim Lawless.' So Jim joined my band. Steve Gray was the piano player and we used an organ to make it sound like a big band, and Steve couldn't quite get the hang of playing this organ with the volume pedal, and as we wanted a block sound we had to tie his foot to the pedal!

When I recorded the *Repercussion* album with Louie Bellson in London in 1960, Steve Gray did the arrangements; 633 Squadron was a big thing for us and I do it now with the Wigan Youth Jazz Orchestra.

DON INNES *Piano 1954–56*

Eric Delaney was forming a band and I'd been working at Chappell's doing arrangements and you get fed up with that after a while because you find yourself doing about 12 arrangements of the same tune for different bands and very often not a very good tune! I rang Eric and asked if the job on piano was still going and it was and I got it.

Eric was a great showman. The band was very facile and the trumpet section was really very good. It was built around Eric's drum features and he had tymps as well so he would play a lot of stuff on the tymps and then get on the drums. The first trumpet player, Albert Hall, a well known jazz guy at the time, had a switch which he pressed and Eric's drum kit would revolve. One night at the end of the evening the plug got pulled out of the wall without the hand switch being switched off and no one noticed, so the next night at the beginning of the evening, during a waltz, the 'roadie' put the plug into the wall while the band was playing and Eric began to revolve!

I remember we had the deck of a ship rigged up on stage with a naval gun and at the end of the piece it would go off with a bang, with a cloud of dust coming out of it. That was worked by a switch and once again that went wrong one night and went off in the middle of a slow ballad. Marion Williams was singing, very nicely, and halfway through this gun went off!

Eric is a good sport, a good-natured guy. A friendly man, a laughing man. He reminds me of Norman Wisdom. It was a happy band but you're living in each other's pockets, working together, living together, eating together. A couple of the guys, Bert Courtley and Jack Seymour, left to form the Courtley-Seymour Band in 1956. After a few months their piano player was leaving so they asked me to join them, and as they were working in London at the Wimbledon Palais, I left Eric and joined them.

When I gave in my notice Eric said, 'It's those two so-and-sos,' and he began to laugh. He knew it was Bert and Jack but he was all right. I was with the band a couple of years but we were travelling hundreds of miles and you eventually get a bit fed up with it.

DEREK HEALEY *Trumpet 1958–59*

Eric loved travelling around and he had a big furniture van with all his drum kit and scenery. He spent a fortune on scenery did Eric. We used to do weeks at places like Finsbury Park Empire and we did this 'Hornpipe Boogie' where the duck would fall out of the ceiling down to the floor. I had to pick it up, and as you picked it up you unzipped it and the eggs fell out. This was a big joke!

He had big guns on a ship and we'd be swabbing the decks with this 'Hornpipe Boogie' and cannons used to go off. One night one of the stage hands had put too much gunpowder up in the flies and when these guns went off we'd never heard a bang like it in our lives! The duck falls down but so did all the rust and dust from up in the flies, and of course when I picked up the duck our jackets were all black with the muck that had fallen down.

Eric would spin round on a rostrum so that people could see his feet 'cause he had two bass drums. The switch was near me and I was in charge of switching him on when he started playing and he'd start slowly spinning around. We're packing up at Bentwaters, the American base, and the trumpets are Ronnie Horler, George Bradley, Dougie Roberts, Ian Hamer and me. Jack Seymour was the bass player and he'd just told us a joke and we were all laughing away while Eric was packing up. It took him ages to pack everything up with all his gear and somebody inadvertently caught the switch and he started spinning round while he's packing up. Of course he flipped; having heard us laughing, he thought we'd done it on purpose. He picked every one of his drums and cymbals up and threw them right down the middle of the ballroom floor and this American Master Sergeant comes over and says, 'What's the matter, somebody steal his bottle of whisky?'

TONY FISHER *Trumpet 1959–65*

I joined him when he changed from a big band to a small band; it was only a six-piece and I was a founder member. We had about two weeks' rehearsal in England and the first gig was at an American base in Germany, Ramstein Air Base, and we spent the whole of August there and the band got itself blown in. Then we came back and started doing one nighters.

That band in Germany was a good band and we had some good players. It was a very high standard and people still say that small band of Eric's was a real musical band. He had all the best guys writing specifically for him, people like Neil Richardson and Dave Lindup. Kenny Salmon was on organ. This was pre-synthesizer days, and Eric's idea was to have the organ with me as the one trumpet over it making it sound like a brass section. In a way I was on a hiding to nothing because I had to play the first trumpet parts from the old five-trumpet pad, and when you play on your own it's a nightmare! We would sometimes start with 'Si Si' which starts on a high G and in a one trumpet band that's not too thrilling, there's nowhere to hide! Other musicians would listen to our broadcasts and say, 'Who the hell is that playing that roasting trumpet part?' I was only a young kid and you do what you have to do, and it did me good of course.

Nevertheless I enjoyed that band enormously as it was very much left to me what I wanted to do. Eric is a great bandleader because he never dictated it should be this, that or the other. I had a valve trombone and I suggested we use this in the band and I got to use it a lot so he let me do things I wanted to do. And a lot of what I do now developed from Eric's band, being 'exposed' like that, particularly when the writing was so difficult.

When Kenny Salmon left, I recommended a fellow called Malcolm Saul to Eric because he and I were together as kids in a Carroll Levis show in the 1940s. Malcolm was a very fine piano player, jazz, everything, and he fitted in beautifully. But he was a real dream boat, he'd forget his own name! We'd arrived at this gig having driven overnight from somewhere and we were very tired so Malcolm looked for somewhere to have a kip for an hour and found this big empty wardrobe. He got himself in there, fell fast asleep, and someone closed the wardrobe door not realising he was there. When he woke up he burst out of this wardrobe and found himself in the middle of the girls' dressing-room, who were there to do a show with the band. So that didn't go down too well with the girls, this man falling out of the wardrobe! That was Malcolm's life to a tee.

We were playing an air base in Germany and there was a big panic when Eric didn't arrive because he was in jail! We all fell about laughing when we heard this. It was a beautiful summer's day and Eric was in his convertible Sunbeam Alpine, top down, with his shorts on, driving along, and these two elderly German ladies thought they saw a naked man driving around in a car in this little village. They immediately phoned the police who came and grabbed Eric and he was rushed off to the jail. They bailed him out in time for the gig!

SHEILA SOUTHERN *Vocalist 1959*

Eric was the most magnificent showman. He had a double drum kit on a revolving pedestal with three tuneable pedal tymps surrounded by wooden painted flames, and each one was lit up inside with a different colour. He'd have the lights taken right down and he'd lean over the tymps and boing . . . and as he moved over each tympani his face was a different colour – green, red, blue! There was a character in a cartoon called Gerald McBoing Boing and that's what the fellas would call him!

He did this huge tympani solo with the band giving the great big build-up and he would leap over his tympani, which were up on a high rostrum, down into the middle of this drum kit and would go into a drum solo that would last about ten minutes. The lights would be flashing in the drums and then when he gave the word, someone would throw the switch and he would start to revolve and as he played quicker the thing revolved more quickly. You can imagine the audience went crazy, especially the American forces – they loved it. When he'd finished he'd lean back and shout to me in the wings. 'Flo, do a waltz.' After all that crazy stuff I had to go on and sing a waltz! Did I get mad at him! But I love him for it; he's great.

JIM LAWLESS *Vibraphone 1960–63*

Eric Delaney wanted to change his line-up and decided on a

vibraphone. He looked around and saw that I was playing at Ronnie Scott's club so he phoned Ronnie up and said, 'What's this Jim Lawless like?' and Ronnie's very words were, 'He's bloody good enough to play in your band!' So with that he phoned me that week and asked if I'd like to join his band. 'I'd love to but you haven't heard me play yet,' and he said, 'If Ronnie Scott says you're good enough, it's good enough for me.' I joined that Friday and we were working in Battle near Hastings, and the following day the band was going to Germany for a month working at an American base. That meant I would have a chance to look at the pad and at the end of that time he'd tell me whether he wanted me to stay or not. After two weeks he told me he'd like me to stay and I stayed for three years.

Eric was absolutely mad, he didn't know whether he was coming or going! But he was a very hard taskmaster in the nicest possible way. I joined him as a vibraphone player and left him as a percussionist because he had me doing everything you could think of, which obviously did me a lot of good. He showed me how to play tymps, encouraged my interest in Latin American stuff, brought a xylophone and a glock into the band, and so I was playing everything by the time I left him.

Musically the band was tremendous, and Eric made me work very hard. I had lots of features and he would say, 'Let's try and get some comedy into this,' and we would lark about. That's where I started my larking about days, you see! We'd try to get a laugh out of any situation because he was just the same as me and he could be quite outrageous at times. People say I'm outrageous but I must have got it from Eric! I used to think if it's all right for a bandleader to lark about like that, it's all right for me! Yes, he was a terrific bloke to work for – smashing bloke.

TEDDY FOSTER

1907–84

Theme 'You Made Me Love You'

Almost every sideman you meet seems to have played at one time or another in Teddy Foster's band. Teddy Foster himself played trumpet and sang in his husky voice with Billy Cotton, having fronted his first band, the Collegians, in 1929 at Tony's Ballroom in Birmingham when his signature tune was 'Collegiate'. After touring with the Billy Cotton Band he led a small line-up, The Kings of Swing, using 'St Louis Blues' as his opening theme. In 1943 he was resident at the Casino in Birmingham and was broadcasting weekly in *Saturday Night at the Palais*. In fact he became one of the most popular touring Palais bands of the '40s and '50s. He gave up bandleading in 1960 to form a theatrical agency and subsequently 'discovered' Julie Rogers, whom he married.

SYD LAWRENCE *Trumpet 1946–47*

The day after I was demobbed from the RAF I was playing with Teddy Foster in Nottingham and then we shot up to Green's Playhouse for three weeks. I had an enjoyable time with Ted's band although I didn't earn a lot of money! It was a fine band to play in, eight brass, five saxes, four rhythm. All good players as he'd got all the young fellows coming out of the forces, and everybody liked Teddy.

I was with him for the worst winter anyone could remember and we toured in one of Teddy's cheap coaches. There was no heater but we didn't care because we were all young. One night on the outskirts of Birmingham the coach driver took a wrong turning down a suburban road with a lot of semi-detached houses. It was piled high with snow and of course he had to turn around in this little street and everybody was digging the coach out. It was awful and we were aiming for an army camp in Oswestry!

We got there, but only just in time to get changed and go on. When we left the camp that night, this old–fashioned oil stove had appeared in the coach and the smell was terrible but we were desperate to keep warm!

JOHNNY ROADHOUSE *Alto saxophone 1946–48*

Teddy Foster was on his way to Scarborough and they were short of a saxophone, and Ronnie and Derek Price, who were in the band and used to come and practise in my house, said they knew of a saxophone player in Manchester who might be able to help. So Ronnie telephoned me and asked if I could join them at Scarborough. In fear and trepidation I packed my bag, because to me Teddy Foster was a big-time band, I never thought I could aspire to such greatness! They put me on second alto and I got through the night all right so they offered me the job on trial to see if I fitted in.

I'd arrived in my Manchester suit and the first thing Teddy said when he saw me was, 'You're not coming in my band with those clothes.' So he took me down to Praed Street in London where his brother or cousin had a tailor's shop and he fixed me up with a nice bird's eye suit with drapes. He didn't charge me then but took it out of my money every week. He wouldn't have me in his band dressed in my Manchester clothes! It made sense because he wanted a certain image.

I stayed with them for two years and that time was the most remarkable musical experience of my life. Teddy Foster had a reputation for making a few changes in the band but he always had really good musicians and damn good arrangements, and I believe it was the first eight-brass, five-sax band in this country and Teddy was quite a fair trumpet player in his day. He had people like Duncan

Campbell, Ronnie Hughes, Geoff Love, Basil Kirchin, Derek Humble, Syd Lawrence. I had the privilege of playing with some of the greatest musicians in the world although I didn't realise it at the time. Some of it must have rubbed off on me because I've survived in the music business all these years. I may be a bit short of technique compared with some of the people I work with but I've got by on sound and interpretation, a bit of luck and using my loaf!

I graduated to lead alto when David Ede left the band to join Oscar Rabin. So we had to hold auditions for a second alto player, and travelling around the various dance halls up north in Geordie land we'd heard this young 16-year-old saxophone player. We got him down to Manchester for an audition and got out the library. I thought we'd put him on first alto to test him and he played the parts better than I could and he was sight reading them! His name was Derek Humble and so I had to sit and play first alto with Derek on second alto and, young as he was, he was a fantastic musician. I learnt a lot from him but I think he learnt from me as well as I had more experience.

Teddy Foster was quite a disciplinarian in his way but the band would take the mickey out of him something shocking. We used to travel around by coach and we had a song we used to sing which he didn't like a bit. We sang it to the tune of 'California Here I Come' and it went, 'Teddy Foster is the name, puts you on the road to fame, he'll make you or break you on BBC, his trumpet's so umpetee it isn't true, believe me. On percentage is the rule and if you take it you're a bloody fool, so sing up boys with all your might, Teddy Foster is the name.' He'd be sitting at the front of the coach and we used to sing that to him at the back and he would be squirming! This percentage business meant he could cut our wages saying, 'You know how it is lads . . .'

We were always instructed not to drink before we went on the stand because once you get on there for a concert you can't get off for a pee, the usual thing with musicians drinking before the show. This particular night at St Helens, the rake on the stage was such that you almost fell over when you stood up. This poor trumpet player had had a few drinks and he just had to let it go. Teddy was down front doing an announcement at the time and the piano player started to giggle. Teddy turned around and there were these rivulets running down the rake of the stage to the footlights. I believe after that night the trumpet player had to find other work! If ever anyone got drunk on the stand they had to leave, Teddy wouldn't allow anything like that.

We wore grey band jackets with T.F. on the pockets, and when we were on the stand the lads would eye the girls as they were dancing past, trying to make dates, the married ones as well! When we came off in the interval we used to walk around in our band jackets because if you had a band jacket on the girls made for you. There was a bit of a row one night when we were at Wimbledon Palais and Teddy was getting all uptight and he said, 'If you don't behave yourselves I'm going to take the band jackets off you in the interval and then you'll be stuck.' So we all behaved ourselves because those band jackets were a magnet for the girls!

Everything was new to me because this was my first taste of what you might call the big time. The money wasn't that good; I think we got 10s 6d for an overnight allowance and my wages would average out at something like £12 10s a week. It wasn't that bad. Everybody used to criticise Teddy Foster for his meanness but I managed all right.

BOB EFFORD *Tenor saxophone 1948*

It wasn't the greatest name band in the world but it was a great band. I was working with Ronnie Pleydell at Brighton Aquarium and they had a big band policy one night a week. Teddy Foster came and must have liked what he heard or I must have looked cheap, I don't know which, but he offered me a job and I took it.

It was all road jobs, up and down the country. In fact I left him when he got a permanent job at Wimbledon Palais because I had no family at that time and I used to dread being in town. It was the one place I didn't want to be, because I didn't really have a home and I didn't have any friends, but while I was on the road I had friends in the band. When the band got to its London base, they dispersed so I was pretty miserable and I looked for another road job.

A feature of the band was they didn't have trumpets, they played what they called trumpet cornets. I was never sure what that instrument was. It was smaller than a trumpet but bigger than a cornet and produced a slightly different sound so it gave the band a slightly different feel to it. I think Albert Hall was the lead trumpet at that time. There were some great players in that band: Jimmy Staples was on baritone, and that was where I first came across Derek Humble.

We travelled on buses, the cheapest buses he could find! It would take the best part of a day even to get to Birmingham. One particular trip will always stay in my mind, the day we were working in Torquay, and when we finished we left overnight for Aberdeen in the most appalling bus which had a kerosene heater bolted to the floor. We travelled for something like two days to Aberdeen sleeping on the bus. We even changed lead trumpets at Newcastle, dropped one off and picked up another, I remember that very clearly!

We finally got to Aberdeen about six-thirty and we were due on the stand at seven. It was an absolute nightmare. We went directly from one job to another. That journey I'll always remember because that was way before motorways or anything like that. You never went any faster than the slowest thing in front of you!

Because we paid for our own digs we stayed in some pretty appalling places, and as for transport cafés, it's a miracle I'm still alive eating in those places! But life was great because for me that was family, that was something I didn't have at that time, so it was a lot healthier than joining a street gang or something like that.

I don't think Teddy Foster was generally liked from what I could gather, but I got on fine with him, I thought he was a good guy and he liked the way I played so that made him a good guy! He gave me plenty to do which I enjoyed. In those days leaders were pretty easy going, they weren't the martinets they had been prior to the war. Teddy would shout and scream if you were late or something like that but he was pretty easy going. Then later, as you moved a little more up the social scale, the bandleaders became a little more demanding. I think Teddy Foster was always happy to have the guys he had because he didn't pay a whole lot of money, although I could save some money in those days which was amazing.

RONNIE HUGHES *Trumpet 1948*

I was in Archer Street one day and someone said, 'Teddy Foster's looking for a trumpet player and he's going mad because he's auditioning guys and none of them are any good. Do you fancy it?' I had my trumpet with me so I went down and played for him and was grabbed and I was first trumpet with Teddy. He wouldn't let me play any jazz. 'Oh no, you're not a jazz player, you're a lead trumpet.' But of course when I left him to go with Ted Heath, Bobby Pratt was there and Stan Roderick and I took Dave Wilkins's place, so it was mostly jazz solos from then on.

Teddy was a Nat Gonella-type showman and he used to play this one number, 'St. James' Infirmary Blues' and we would have real fun with him, going for the notes if we didn't think he was going to make it. He would turn around and say, 'Who did that?' and all the trumpet section would be giggling. He would do the Nat Gonella or Louis bit with the gravel voice. Yes, he was a character.

I can always remember my first week's wages when I joined Ted Heath's band after Teddy Foster; the difference was ridiculous, it was about five times as much! Mind you, if we were playing a palais we would be on thirteen to fifteen pounds a week and that was a lot of money compared to the average wage in the country, but when I went with Ted Heath it was a different ball game entirely.

PETE MOORE *Piano 1948–49*

Teddy always used to say, 'I lost three hundred quid tonight,' or 'I lost five hundred quid tonight,' and I would look at the crowd in the dance hall and think 'Christ, he couldn't be losing money, the place is jammed!' What he actually meant was he made three hundred quid or five hundred quid less than he thought he was going to make. So that to him was losing. Typical of Teddy.

I'd been down to Archer Street and happened to see Basil Kirchin who told me Teddy's regular piano player had got sick and they needed a pianist quickly. Saturday night I was playing in a pub on the sea front with a jazz trio and on the Monday I was doing a broadcast, it was as silly as that!

We were at Wimbledon Palais for about three months then we went on the road for four months and then down to Brighton Aquarium for five months and back on the road again.

PETE WARNER *Tenor saxophone 1950*

A friend of mine was depping with the band and Teddy was having trouble with his rhythm section and a couple of the sax players, one of whom was Dave Lindup. I think Teddy had got wind that they were leaving so he sent me a telegram. I had to go to Brighton Aquarium for an audition with a quartet from Coventry. We played a few numbers for Teddy who sat there listening and so were the rest of the band, looking at each other wondering what was going to happen. It was quite embarrassing really as we knew what Teddy wanted to happen. Well, I was the only one who got the job in the end.

Teddy was one of those bandleaders who made you or broke you. Forget about the money side of it, he either set you on your way or you gave up and went back home and never appeared in public again. It was a wonderful band as Derek Humble was on lead alto – you can learn so much sitting next to someone like that and Pete Moore playing wonderful piano, he was playing like Erroll Garner at the time. Basil Kirchin was on drums, so it was a swinging band. World-class. The arrangements were great because people like Roland Shaw were doing them. I'd never played arrangements like them before. You really felt as if you had arrived.

Everybody dreads their first broadcast, wondering whether you're going to run when the red light goes on! It was May Day 1950, Maida Vale 3, we've all got the parts up and on goes the red light. Teddy beats the band in and the brass have got one number up and the saxes have got another one up and so Teddy had to stop the band. There was a long silence with much fluttering of paper before we started again. Not only was I dying of nerves but that was breaking point! Anyway, I got through my first broadcast.

FREDDY STAFF *Trumpet 1951–52*

I was with Ivor Kirchin's Band at the Royal, Tottenham, when Teddy Foster was looking for a lead trumpet as Pete Winslow had left. I think he was going with Geraldo. Basil Kirchin brought Teddy Foster in to hear me and I was chatting to him and I said, 'Look Ted, I've only got a range of a top D for a start. If you're doing Woody Herman, you can forget about me, I haven't got that range.'

He said, 'My arrangements will build your range. We'll put the odd E flat in here and there and if you miss, it doesn't matter, I'll build you,' and he did.

I hadn't done any real solo work out the front and Teddy wanted me to do some Harry James stuff.

'I can't, I'm terrified, I'm all right in the section,' I stuttered.

'I'll stand by you.'

My first trumpet solo was that theme from the film *Young Man with a Horn* and we were at Newcastle and the whole of the George Evans Band were in front with George and I'd started with them at the same time as Don Innes. I came down the front for this solo and as I started up Ted actually had his hand on my back. It was marvellous for confidence and once he knew I was under way he walked away and smiled. I thought a lot of Teddy for that.

Whenever an American band came out with a new idea, Ted would do it. Like when the Herman Herd were under way Ted would play Herman's music. I was there when the Billy May thing started and all the saxophones moaned like mad, oh no not all those slurps!

That was also the period when Basil Kirchin went to Ted Heath for six months and Ted Heath was very cruel because he knew he was getting Ronnie Verrell. It was very, very sad because Basil was a great drummer. When Basil came back to Teddy Foster, he still played great but he never made it the same in the business again. It broke his heart. He was a great drummer, he was good for the job, but Heath wanted Ronnie Verrell.

DEREK HEALEY *Trumpet 1955*

We did a 16-week Moss Empire tour with Teddy Foster and Al Martino, that was fun, and I'll tell you who used to do all his running around for him, Derek Nimmo. He must have worked for the office who put us on the tour. We were somewhere every week for 16 weeks – fantastic.

Teddy would be nasty to people he didn't think could play, but if he thought you could play he was great. I used to sing in those days, comedy songs and things like that, and we had Annette Kluger and were on this tour with Al Martino doing Glasgow Empire, and they're a real rough audience there. Teddy was always famous for his bald head and that night he had a wig on for the first time ever. We used to do 'St. James' Infirmary', he'd play the trumpet and I'd sing, and I remember him whispering in my ear just before we went on, 'If you move my wig you're sacked!' He was a lovely man, Ted.

The worst part for me wasn't getting the job, but leaving a job. I would dread telling the bandleader I was leaving, I don't know why. I used to think I was letting him down and things like that. So we're at Green's Playhouse with Teddy Foster and I was leaving to go with Geraldo and I'd got to give two weeks' notice. I put it off Monday, Tuesday, Wednesday, Thursday, Friday. Get to the Saturday and I don't know how I'm going to tell him. The lads knew I was going to do it but I didn't know how to face him. Anyway, Teddy got the needle with the trumpets on the Saturday night and Green's was packed, as it always was in those days, and he comes over to the trumpets and he says, 'Trumpet players, I've shit 'em,' and I said, 'Well you better shit yourself another one because I'm leaving and going with Geraldo!' That was my way out!

BARRY ROBINSON *Alto saxophone 1957*

When I came out of the Royal Artillery Band, Butch Hudson, the trumpet player who had left the army just before me, was with Teddy Foster at Tottenham, and their lead alto had been rushed to hospital so I got a call to go in. Teddy asked me how much I wanted for the day, an afternoon and evening, and then said the alto player who was ill was going to need all the money he could get. So I quoted some ridiculously low fee and of course when I joined the band everybody laughed and I realised I'd been ripped off!

The significant thing I do remember about Teddy Foster is that he was the only bandleader I've ever worked with who never counted anybody in. It was just an up beat and everybody knew the tempo and how it went. I always thought that was very impressive on the stage when at the end of a number his arms came down and we started the next one.

We were at Tottenham for Mecca and there were quite a few hooligans in the band and one Saturday night in the band room somebody obviously cut their hand and they wrote on the wall a message to the manager of Tottenham: 'You wanted blood, now you've got it!' The next week the band got the sack!

When he took the band on the road, I only lasted a few weeks. My father was a trumpet player and he was obviously dead keen for me to get on and work with a professional band, especially with a name like Teddy Foster. But he drew the line when on one of the dates we got on the coach at Baker Street at eight o'clock on a Saturday morning and drove all the way down to the Rhondda Valley, did this gig, drove all the way back and arrived nine o'clock Sunday morning. Twenty-five hours and he gave us three pounds because he said the venue could only afford a seven-piece band but he thought it would be good to keep the band together! Even my father, who was dead keen for me, said, 'Right, that's it,' and I left.

ROY FOX

1901–82

Theme 'Whispering'

Roy Fox came to Britain from America where he was known as the 'Whispering Cornetist', having developed a highly individual style of playing with a mute. He fronted a band at Hollywood's Coconut Grove, and with the advent of the 'talkies' became, coincidentally, musical director for the film company that bore his name.

In 1930 he was booked for an eight-week season at London's Café de Paris, and when he was appointed musical adviser for Decca Records, was granted a work permit on the clear understanding he would form a band of British musicians. Roy Fox and His Orchestra opened at the Monseigneur in 1931. Immaculately dressed in white tie and tails with his gentlemanly American accent, he was an instant hit with London's high society. He would voice over the introduction of his signature tune 'Whispering', played by Lew Stone on the celeste, saying, 'Hello ladies and gentlemen. This is Roy Fox speaking. The boys and I now have the pleasure of playing "Whispering".'

The engagement lasted less than a year as he was taken ill and spent three months in a sanatorium in Switzerland. Lew Stone took over the band in his absence, and when on his return Roy Fox fell out with the Monseigneur management, Lew Stone took his place, and although he could have insisted on taking the members of his band with him, he re-formed taking his new line-up into the Café Anglais.

In 1938 Roy Fox took his band on what turned out to be a disastrous tour of Australia and, with war threatening, he returned home to California. When he came back to these shores in 1945 it was to open hostility from bandleaders and musicians alike who felt he'd deserted the sinking ship in time of need. He never regained his popularity and in 1953 retired to become an agent. He spent his final years in Brinsworth House, the Variety Artists' Benevolent Home in Twickenham.

BILLY AMSTELL *Alto/Tenor/Clarinet 1931*

I got the sack from Jack Harris at Grosvenor House and was snatched up by Maurice Winnick, but I was only there for a week when Roy Fox got the Monseigneur and they did a deal. I was released and at 19 I was the first alto in Roy Fox's band.

Roy Fox was a hell of a nice guy but I wished he didn't play that trumpet! The first time I heard him it was terrible; it was shocking. He had a mute in the trumpet and he had a felt over the mute and it sounded like a nanny goat or a pregnant cow, but he was a nice gentleman and he paid me well. My brothers were slaving away in a workshop for £2 10s a week and there was I getting fifteen quid!

The Roy Fox Band was good. There was Nat Gonella and Lew Stone who sat at the piano; I never heard him play but he did the arrangements. Typically English, I tell you it was like a bloody butcher's shop. Over in America you had guys who, if they sat there, had something to offer and they could play. Not here. Lew Stone, good arranger, but did you ever hear him play? No? Nor did anybody else. I can't help being forthright. The inner core of the band was like a small committee, they decided what tunes to play etc; and when Roy Fox got ill, this little group didn't welcome him back and Lew Stone took over. It was the only choice they had; he was the arranger so he took over.

Nat Gonella and I used to go to the 43 Club, Mrs Merrick's at No.43 Garrick Street. It was the only place to go and have a blow. We'd go down there around two, two-thirty, any night we fancied, maybe not the night when we'd been recording during the day. It was lovely and she was a lady. She came from the upper class and I think both her daughters married titled men, but she had an eye to business. 'Are you here again?' she would say. 'Yes, Mrs Merrick, can we have a blow?'

One or two well known musicians married a couple of the girls from there. They weren't tarts but these good-time Charlies, the chinless wonders, used to come down there to have a drink with the hope of having one of the girls. But there was no hanky panky, or if it went on I didn't see it. These young geezers used to throw white fivers around, dance and get amorous, but there was nothing doing. The girls were as straight as a die; it was great fun. It was drinking and dancing, mostly drinking. They were called bottle parties. They had a fleet of young lads on bicycles who would go out and buy bottles as the club wasn't allowed to sell liquor on the premises. Certain places were licensed to sell alcohol 24 hours a day so the boy would go out on the bicycle, buy a bottle and bring it back to the customer. When they finished drinking they would put their name on the bottle and mark it so that they'd know no one else had been drinking from it, but sometimes when the good-time Charlies came the next night the drink would be below the mark!

I met several well known musicians at Mrs Merrick's, Teddy Brown, Manny Klein, Coleman Hawkins. There were never any raids on the club. I don't know what it was but Mrs Merrick had an 'understanding' with the chief copper at Savile Row whose name was Sergeant Goddard. I can tell you all this because they're all dead! She was never raided. All the other clubs were 'dives' and they were raided, but Sergeant Goddard was doing very well for himself and so was Mrs Merrick.

The lonely guy in the Roy Fox Band was Al Bowlly. People have called him a womaniser and a drunk but he was never like that. He was a nice clean-living guy and he used to go to the YMCA in Tottenham Court Road and meet Joe Crossman and they would keep fit. When we finished work at the Monseigneur, Nat and I would take Al with us. He didn't play or sing at the club but he came because it was company. He either comes with us or he goes back to his 'bed-sit' in Gower Street. The girls would say hello but there were no fans or mass hysteria, no hero worship. He was just an ordinary guy and he didn't drink. He would sit there with a lemonade. He didn't smoke, he was not a womaniser, not worldly, just a very nice guy. He was not all what they made him out to be later.

Al didn't like Mrs Merrick and Mrs Merrick didn't like him, so Nat Gonella and I would sometimes take him to a night club called the Bag O' Nails in Kingly Street, not far from the Palladium. We could go in and play. Nat would play, I would play, the American guys, whoever was over here, would play and Al would sit and hold his lemonade, and it was there he fell in love with one of the hostesses, Freda Roberts. She was beautiful, she had long hair like Rita Hayworth. She fell in love with him and he fell in love with her, they got married and it lasted two weeks!

I was only with Fox for about four and a half months because Ambrose sent for me.

WOOLF PHILLIPS *Arranger*

I was in the office at Campbell Connelly's one morning and the door opened and 'God' came in. He said, 'Hello, is Sid [Phillips] here?'

'No.'

'Did you hear Roy Fox's band last night? They played my new song like this,' and he sat down at the piano and rattled off this tune. 'It's a ballad, it goes . . . The Very Thought of You . . . Could you tell Sid to make certain the staff arrangers do it as a ballad?'

'I will,' and that was the one and only time I met Ray Noble!

HARRY GOLD *Tenor saxophone 1932–37*

I started to play tenor before I joined Roy. Ivor and I and Les Lambert had formed this vocal trio which later became known as the Cubs. Ivor used to do the vocal arrangements, I would do the band parts, and the style was based roughly on the Rhythm Boys and the Boswell Sisters: a mixture of the two styles. I sang the top harmony; you wouldn't think so to listen to my voice now, would you? We were very good and very technical and we used that team as an act with Jack Padbury's band. Up to then I'd been playing alto, clarinet, baritone and the odd bit of oboe but, when we got that job, the leader was an alto player so of course I said okay I'll change to tenor.

When Roy lost the band at the Monseigneur, he came into this restaurant where we were playing to listen to us. The bandleader took one look and said, 'I hope he's not going to pinch you boys,' and of course he did. He did the very same thing with the brass players in Billy Cotton's band. So we went en bloc to Roy Fox and I felt so sorry

75

for the man but obviously we had to look after ourselves.

It was a dance band of course, with some jazz people in it, and we also travelled around the country playing the variety theatres. He always dressed very well. An American, but he only wore English-made clothes, very smart and a gentleman in every sense of the word. But there was another side which you could describe as a gentleman rogue. You could understand some things, like he wouldn't allow drinking on the stand, and neither do I! We had to have a new uniform every year which we had to buy ourselves; we had a month's holiday without pay and the new uniforms always coincided with coming back from the holiday so that meant a bit of expense when you hadn't got it! Every year the uniform was different. One year it would be what we call bum freezers and we'd have a meeting to decide on what colour they should be, but he had the final word obviously. They had to be made for us, especially for little people like me! I still can't get clothes off the peg, I have to have them made. Luckily for me, my father was a tailor. I paid him of course, but it was next to nothing. Sometimes when I fancied something I would go to Bond Street to have a suit made and pay the tremendous sum of thirty pounds for that.

Before we went on tour we were working in the Café Anglais and the Café de Paris and later on the Kit Kat, and we got fifteen pounds a week which was good money for those days if you remember that a bus driver would have got £2 10s a week. One day while we were at the Café de Paris Roy Fox announced that we were going on tour. Some of us received that message with mixed feelings. Opinions were divided so we had to have a meeting and we said it wasn't all that great. It was going to cost us money to stay in digs although he would pay for the travelling of course, but we agreed that we would have to ask Roy for extra money. Humming and hawing we finally decided three pounds extra would cover it, so when we went on tour that was eighteen pounds a week. It wasn't bad as you could get good digs for two pounds a week, and if you wanted to splash out you could pay three pounds and that would be really great!

There was the question of your family, but we got back into London every so often. The life was enjoyable in variety and Roy's band was extremely popular. Wherever we went we filled the theatres, and when you get that it's really something. Bands like Roy Fox would not only top the bill, but take over the bill so that apart from a front of tabs act, either a comedian or juggler or something, we would work the whole of the second half. This meant that the lesser acts weren't seen as much and, apart from fans of the band, people stopped coming to see variety shows. That was the beginning of the end of variety in my opinion.

Ivor Mairants and I left Roy for the same reason. Every year we were called into his dressing-room one by one and told that we had to take a cut, and I wouldn't take a cut and Ivor wouldn't take a cut. But gradually pressure was being put on and we had to give something so as I used to do two arrangements a month for which I got paid, I said I'd do one arrangement a month for free. I can't remember exactly what Ivor did but he wouldn't take a cut, that's for sure. Then Roy introduced an 'all-in' contract where you could do recordings, a broadcast, the odd dance, all included, and that's when I decided enough's enough, I'm off.

The interesting thing is that as soon as the announcement was made in the *Melody Maker*, I got a phone call from Freddy Gardner to say he was starting a job with Bert Firman in a restaurant and they were looking for a tenor player, was I interested? Of course I was interested, never mind the money, I'm interested, I want to get back home! The same week I had a telegram from Jack Payne asking if I would like to join him, but he was going on tour so I said no thanks, I was going back to London. Once you get known, you see, you get offers.

PRIMROSE *Vocalist 1937–38*

I won a year singing with the Roy Fox Orchestra as a prize in a talent contest at Glasgow Empire, and when I first joined the band I travelled to London all by myself and nobody met me at the station. It was terrible because there I was all by myself at King's Cross and not too sure where to go! I remembered they were going from a bus station somewhere and I eventually found it.

The first gig was a Sunday night concert and Roy Fox was charming to me. He was very debonair and a very nice man. He was married to a Ziegfeld Follies girl and she was very kind to me too. I remember her as very glamorous in black velvet and silver fox. The first really nice dress I ever had was a Grecian-type dress, all pleated with things hanging from the back. It looked good on stage because I had very long dark hair in those days. The first song I sang with Roy Fox was 'Once in a While'. I remember I was only paid a few pounds a week. There were no good wages then, and if you got as much as eight pounds you were really wealthy.

I had to have a chaperone because being only 16 I was under age, and I shared her with the other girl vocalist, Mary Lee. She was the star and then there was Denny Dennis; he was with the band and we all stayed in theatrical digs. It was a good life and I enjoyed it.

I stayed with the band a year as that was the prize I'd won, and during that time we were on the Mecca circuit topping variety bills at all the Empires, and often playing ballrooms after the theatre. We travelled by train and Roy Fox travelled in his white Rolls-Royce. When I left him at the end of the year I went on the Mecca circuit singing with the resident bands at different ballrooms like the Fountainbridge Palais in Edinburgh and the Locarno in Glasgow, and that's where I was found by Jack Hylton.

IVOR MAIRANTS *Guitar 1932–37*

I started my professional career at the age of 20 by being recommended to Percival Mackie's band where there were five of us who remained friends – Maurice Burman, Jack Nathan, Harry Gold, Les Lambert and myself – and eventually we all went into Roy Fox's band at the royal command!

Roy Fox was very suave; in fact when he came into the Princes Restaurant in Piccadilly where the five of us were working, he was tall, handsome and wearing the best suit you've ever seen, sartorially perfect, and it was a foregone conclusion that we'd go with him. We were in Jack Padbury's band, and although we gave him a watch, he still cried when we left! This was when Roy Fox formed his new band in 1932 because he'd left the Monseigneur. We opened at the Café Anglais. They built a special stand for us and we were very big time. It was the first time Roy Fox had broadcast with the new band and it was the first time for the five of us that we'd gone into regular broadcasting. We had the singing trio the Cubs, which was my invention. Harry Gold was the top voice, Les Lambert the bottom voice, and I sang the melody as it was easier!

We broadcast once a week around ten-thirty on Wednesday nights for an hour. Ambrose was Saturday night, Harry Roy was another night, and so on. There were no more than one or two microphones.

Then we also went to Paris to broadcast on Radio Luxembourg. I remember we went on two eight-seater planes. It was in the winter and very cold.

From the Café Anglais we branched out to the Kit Kat which was under the Capitol Cinema in Lower Regent Street, and this was really big stuff. Roy Fox made some additions to the band including Peggy Dell on vocal and piano, so we had two pianos with Jack Nathan also doing the arranging for the band. Jack was really the musical director as far as that went. The Kit Kat wasn't a club it was a restaurant, and the people who came in were good, middle-class people and on Sundays we got all the dancers and a big Jewish crowd. It was extremely popular and people came for two reasons: one to look at Roy Fox and his wonderful tails, and two, to dance to Joe Loss who was the second band there. He'd come from the Astoria. We worked from nine until two in the morning but we had long breaks because there were two bands. This meant there was time to go and do a variety show at one of the Gaumonts, although sometimes it was touch and go whether we got back in time.

As well as showing films, cinemas would have three variety shows a day and very often it was a band show. Roy Fox became famous because he not only broadcast but he would also appear at cinemas like the Odeon, Marble Arch. During the summer when the Kit Kat was closed, he found engagements abroad and we ended up with a fortnight in the Casino at Deauville where we played half an hour on, half an hour off. It was marvellous! I called it furniture music: we were just the furniture while the people danced.

We stayed at the Kit Kat for a year and then we went to the Café de Paris. Now this was really upmarket socially and the Duke and Duchess of Kent would go there; I remember she used to limp a little bit. Sophie Tucker was there for a month in cabaret and we accompanied her along with her pianist Ted Shapiro who wrote all her tunes. What a wonderful accompanist he was. When she rehearsed you would think she was really crying when she did 'My Yiddisha Momma'. It was the most wonderful experience to hear this wonderful lady with this tremendous voice and expression. It seemed spontaneous but it wasn't spontaneous, everything was rehearsed. Noël Coward was also there in cabaret for a month and he was a tremendous artist: all those wonderful songs of his. Everything you've ever heard Noël Coward do, he did at the Café de Paris. Everybody came to hear him, you couldn't get a table.

At the Café de Paris we heard rumours that we were going on tour. Nobody wanted to go on tour! This was a cushy job: you were in town; you could do a few sessions; we didn't want to go on tour. But the inevitable fate struck us the same as it struck all the other bands. Roy Fox wanted to make money and sell his records. The publishers were very important people as they paid for the arrangements, the house in Hampstead Heath, a Rolls-Royce, you couldn't say no to that and it was all part of the side benefits for a bandleader who broadcast regularly.

The first singer with Roy Fox's band was Jack Plante who had a very high voice and sounded like a woman, then in came Peggy Dell and she sounded like a man! Denny Dennis was the next male singer and he was very good. The tricks we would play on Denny Dennis! Horrible tricks. Two of the main 'lumberers' in the band were Les Lambert and George Rowe, a trombone player. They had a bet on that they would be able to sell Denny Dennis anything as he was so curious about everything. They decided that Les would stand in front of an open window with no top on, take an ordinary hairbrush and tap himself on the chest saying that this expanded it and was good for the circulation and the voice. He did this as Denny Dennis passed by the open door and of course he asked what Les was doing. 'I'm a trumpet player,' says Les, 'and I've got to have a good expanding chest and to do this in front of an open window you have to have a special brush.'

'Can I get a brush like that?' asks Dennis.

Les turns to George. 'What do you think, shall I let him have this brush?' 'How much do you want for it?' says Dennis.

'Oh ten shillings,' says Les. Now ten shillings was a lot of money but Dennis gave him the money and Les sold him the brush and won the bet!

We kidded Dennis that if he sang a semitone higher than the accompaniment that this would increase his range, and he got Jack Nathan to play in one key and he sang a semitone higher! He used to trust me and much later on he confided to me that he knew I wasn't one of these leg pullers, but I was! We were very cruel!

As the diamond bracelets on Mrs Fox's arms increased in value and in number so Roy Fox came to believe he wasn't making enough money in the theatres! As he had to have more money for bracelets, the place to get it was off the band's wages, so he asked everybody to take a cut. Now Harry Gold, Les Lambert and I went in as a trio and we weren't going to take any cut so we agreed that we would accept the same wages but not take a cut. That was 1936. In 1937 he tried again but this time I could see the band was on the downward road because things weren't going as they should have done, so in August Harry Gold and I left. We were both presented with a gold watch by Roy Fox and the band and that was that.

I must say one thing for Roy Fox. While I was in the band, I had to go to hospital where I stayed for nine weeks while they decided whether they were going to operate or not, and he sent me my wages every week for nine weeks. He was all right. He was interested in golf and backing horses and he confided to me in his later years, just before he died, that he'd never read a book. The only reading he ever did was the betting forecasts and he betted every day.

ROSE BRENNAN *Vocalist 1946–47*

I was just coming up to 14 and doing a radio programme in Ireland, the big fish in the small pond. There was a huge theatre in Dublin, the Theatre Royal, which was ciné-variety and held nearly three thousand people. Roy Fox came to take over as MD and the bandleader there was very much a featured part of the show as the orchestra was on stage.

All the headlines in the papers were about Roy coming over and how he was looking for a singer. It just happened the chap I was doing the radio show for told Roy about me. He listened to the broadcast and I got the job as the resident singer and was with them for about 18 months. Looking back on it I wasn't nervous because I always lacked ambition and I lacked nerve. I had very low self-esteem and a huge inferiority complex because I was always fat and nobody went on diets in those days. But one thing I never doubted, I was good at what I did. The audience lets you know and I've stopped more shows than I've had hot dinners!

Roy Fox was one of the most elegant men I have ever seen, the epitome of gentlemanly elegance. He had a fund of stories about when he started with Bing Crosby and Paul Whiteman, and he told us about the society scene in the '20s and the importance of remembering that when you went out on stage people saw you before they heard you. Your appearance was paramount. He told us he would roll up at the

Café de Paris in his chauffeur-driven Roller, the valet would take his coat, and he would walk down the stairs at the Café de Paris. 'I never went to work, I appeared,' said in that beautiful soft American accent! 'I would conduct for a while and I would speak to those I wanted to speak to and they queued up to speak to me because in those days we were like gods.' Of course he had the pick of the society women and he used to get the Prince of Wales coming in. But the one thing of that period which he said he never found again was that even the music had an elegance. He would say, 'With Cole Porter you had elegance; the dancers were elegant and of course my band was elegant.'

His clothes were always immaculately cut and I think he must have spent all his money on them.

LENNIE BUSH *Bass 1951*

I knew Victor Feldman and he knew Maurice Kinn who had an agency before he owned the *New Musical Express*. He was the brains behind Roy Fox's band and they'd organised it to be this certain combination: trumpet, tenor saxophone, vibraphone, bass, piano, drums, guitar and four violins plus three singers – two girls, Judy Joy and Janet Webster, and the male singer Tony Mercer, who eventually became a big wheel in the *Black and White Minstrel Show*. Very good singer, Tony Mercer.

We went out on tour, three or four jobs a week, dances. Victor Feldman was on vibraphone and he was the musical brains behind the band. All the arrangements were done by Victor and so it was like a little bebop band with a string section. Very good it was. Martin Aston, a friend of Victor's, was the drummer, there was a guitarist called Ray Dempsey, and the piano player was Bert Annabel; Jo Hunter was on trumpet and Tubby Hayes was in the band.

Roy Fox was a nice man but looked incredibly old to me as I was only 23. He'd been very big in the '30s but it had all fizzled out for him during the war. He was an old man running a band of young blokes but he had this girl, an actress, and she was much younger than him. One day we came downstairs in the hotel to get on the bus and he was limping. 'What's wrong Roy, have you done your foot in?' And he said, 'Yeah, you know what it's like when you're playing around with your girl.' It was ridiculous this old man playing around with this actress! He was a tall man, terribly dapper, and he wore tails with the band in dinner suits. 'Whispering' was his signature tune in the '30s, and the strings would play that while the bebop band played 'Grooving High'.

I was in the band for almost a year and then Victor decided to leave to go to Bombay because he wanted to see India. I left because Victor left and then there was a complete change. Roy got rid of the fiddles and had a saxophone section; Benny Green was in it. I don't know how many brass he had but he went out on the road with this more conventional band. We started rehearsing and I knew it wasn't for me.

GERALDO

1903–74

Theme Opening 'Hello Again'
Closing 'The Clock on the Wall'

Gerald Bright was 19 when he started his bandleading career with a five-piece at Blackpool's Hotel Metropole. In 1924 he moved to the Hotel Majestic at St Anne's-on-Sea with his Majestic Celebrity Orchestra and built up quite a reputation over the next five years with his thrice-weekly broadcasts on the BBC station 2ZY in Manchester.

In 1929, deciding it was time to move onward and upward, he took a trip to South America to study Latin American music and, firmly convinced that the tango could become the new rage in London's West End, sold the idea to the Savoy Hotel. He dressed his newly formed band in exotic costumes, dropped the Bright, and Geraldo and His Gaucho Tango Band opened at the Savoy in August 1930 where it was to remain for the best part of a decade. Its crowning accolade came in 1933 with an appearance at the Royal Command Performance at the London Palladium.

With the start of World War Two the tango band made way for what was to become the most popular dance band in the country. Geraldo was appointed Supervisor of Bands for ENSA and his was the first band to go overseas to entertain the troops. He became musical director for Herbert Wilcox at Elstree and Pinewood and conducted 'Lights Up' at the Savoy for Charles B. Cochran and 'The Fleet's Lit Up' at the London Hippodrome for George Black.

The second half of the '40s saw the Geraldo organisation stretching out in every direction. He became one of the biggest fixers in the country, booking musicians for the Cunard line, something he continued to do up until 1971. Musicians were only too eager to work the Atlantic crossing in what became known as Geraldo's Navy, because it gave them a chance to hear the American jazzmen in New York.

Geraldo was never one of the boys – he was a star. When introduced to the customers in a ballroom in Redcar by bandleader Charles Amer, riotous applause followed his fewer than a dozen words: 'Ladies and gentlemen, this is Geraldo, good evening and goodnight.'

HARRY HAYES *Alto saxophone 1938–42*

When I joined Sidney Lipton's band George Evans was there and we sort of inspired each other. He used to write things for the saxophones and I used to play them. Then two years later we were doing sessions with Geraldo and he asked George and I to go to the Savoy.

When the war started Geraldo became the BBC Dance Band and we used to do nine broadcasts a week from places like the Paris Cinema and the Criterion for the princely sum of thirteen pounds a week! It was quite a big band with eight brass and five saxophones and a battery of vocalists including Dorothy Carless and Beryl Davis – she was a good singer, bit of a naughty girl but a very good singer! George Evans used to sing too and he wrote Gerry's signature tune 'Hello Again'. Ted Heath was in the band at the time.

One day we'd finished the rehearsal at the Criterion Theatre at midday and still had an hour before the broadcast. There was racing on that day from Ascot which was a rarity in the war, so I popped out the back entrance in Jermyn Street and went to the bookmakers along the road. Betting shops were illegal in those days, you could only bet by credit. There were about eight fellows in there all punting and suddenly the police arrived and they took us all off to Savile Row police station! So there I was in a cell with the time for the broadcast approaching rapidly . 'I've got a broadcast.'

'Shut up.'

So I missed the broadcast and I was in there until six o'clock. I thought, 'How do you explain this away?' I pondered all night and the next day rang Gerry's secretary in his office at the top of Bond Street. 'How is he today?'

'He's furious with you, absolutely furious, he hasn't stopped talking about it.'

'You'd better put me through . . . hello Gerry, it's Harry.'

'Where were you then?'

'Well I walked up to Piccadilly Circus and a fellow came up to me, obviously an army policeman with a red cap on, and asked for my pass. I was in civvies and had nothing on me so he took me to Savile Row police station and kept me there 'til six o'clock.' There was silence, and then, 'Oh, that's not bad,' and he rang off. I rang the secretary and she told me he'd rung up Savile Row and asked if they'd had a Mr Hayes in and they'd said they had but didn't say what for, so I got away with it!

Opposite the theatre was the Ritz Dance Hall and the bandleader there was Ivy Benson. We became great friends, Ivy and I. I thought she was marvellous for a girl! When I was teaching afterwards in Soho, I used to give all my girl pupils to her. She would ring me up:

'Who have you got Harry?' 'Well I've got a good baritone player coming along.' In the end I think all my girl pupils were in the Ivy Benson Band!

When we were doing the broadcasts with Geraldo we would sleep on the floor in the Paris Cinema because of the air-raids. The night the Café de Paris got hit – I was in Wardour Street just around the corner in some gambling club when the bomb fell and went through the roof, terrible noise. I rushed around and saw it all and saw the people lying there with 'Snakehips' Johnson.

We did a concert in Bristol and the brass section started messing about so Gerry said, 'Cut it owt, cut it owt.' They still kept messing about and he kept saying, 'Cut it owt, cut it owt,' and for weeks after that the whole band was going around saying 'Cut it owt, cut it owt!' He was a real cockney and marvellous to work for. He was knowledgeable and knew good players. Unlike Ambrose who after an audition would send the chap off and say to the band, 'Well, was he any good?'

I'd joined the Guards in April 1940 and Gerry ended up with eight Guardsmen in his band. That finished at the end of 1942 because the Guards wouldn't allow us to stay in the band.

IVOR MAIRANTS *Guitar 1940–51*

I joined Geraldo at Maida Vale and I'll never forget that rehearsal for my first broadcast. Gerry just beat straight in, never a count in with either his foot or his hand. So we start 'In The Mood' which I'd played many times with Ambrose in the usual tempo, and it was much faster so I didn't play, I just sat there holding the guitar.

'What's the matt-a?' He always said 'What's the matt-a'

'I can't play it at that tempo, I'm not used to it.'

'What tempo do you play it at?'

'Are you asking me?'

'Yes.' So I played a few bars and he started the band again. This showed me I was the boss regarding musical knowledge and so on. That's how we stayed. My relationship with Gerry was very good indeed and I used to take liberties, but only because it was going to improve the band.

I got on very well with him but it wasn't the same as getting on well with Ambrose who I admired as a bandleader, or perhaps Lew Stone who was easy going but knew what he wanted. I could see this was a different kind of character. Geraldo was never one of the boys and never one of the people. He was always very polite and very correct but didn't have the warmth. He had the finest orchestrators, the finest musicians and the finest band in the country without any doubt.

We used to play opposite Glenn Miller in the Queensbury Club. He would do a broadcast from one side of the club and we would do one from the other. Half an hour each so we became very friendly with the boys. We thought the Miller Band was great.

We were playing Newcastle Empire when peace was declared and Ted Heath had written that song 'Lovely Weekend' with Moira which Geraldo had played and broadcast. Ted had got quite a lot of royalties from that but he wanted to start his own band and decided this was the time to do it so he gave Gerry two weeks' notice. Geraldo was fuming and told him to leave there and then and he had to pay his own fare back. The petty things that happen. That was the start of Ted Heath's band. When Geraldo hated, he hated, but there was no reason to. Everyone has to get on and Ted took a big chance anyway.

I heard that Bill Finegan had left Dorsey to come to Paris to study under Nadia Boulanger. I told Geraldo I thought this was a wonderful opportunity to get him and Tad Dameron, who was also in Paris leading the Miles Davis Band, to do some arrangements. He was doubtful at first but agreed to my going over to see them. When I asked Bill Finegan about arranging for Geraldo he said he'd have to hear the band first and how much was he going to pay? I told him the usual rate for an arrangement is fifteen pounds. Well, eventually Geraldo went to thirty-five plus fares and hotels. You see, where he was going to improve the musical situation he didn't mind spending money at all. He had plenty of it of course, but he spent it very well.

We were in Blackpool for the summer when Bill Finegan arrived at the Winter Gardens. We were on the stand doing our last session so he had a good opportunity to listen to the band although there were 10,000 people dancing around. When we were playing 'God Save The King', we looked up and there he was in the balcony asleep while everyone was standing up!

The first arrangement of his we played was 'The Continental' which he had done for Dorsey, but we were the first to play it here. The first one he did especially for us was 'Comin' Thru The Rye'. Geraldo couldn't even conduct it, it was so contrapuntal; it was a wonderful creation. It was the most startling forward arrangement we'd ever heard in this country and I don't think anything like it has been done since. Geraldo was mystified and Bill Finegan conducted it for the whole day. He got on well with the whole band but his favourites were Laddy Busby, Eric Delaney and Jack Collier.

When Tad Dameron came to London he walked into the Maida Vale studio with this arrangement and Geraldo told him to take over while he went into the control room. Tad was wearing a sky blue suit, unheard of in those days. Smart as anything. Half the band accepted this as normal but the other half, including Laddy Busby, Les Carew and one or two of the trumpet players, not Alan Franks, bristled. They couldn't stand this black man with the smart suit coming in and usurping everything. The hackles were immediately up in half the band. Gerry listened in the box and didn't know what was going on. Eventually we broadcast that arrangement but there was great dissension in the band, in fact some of them wanted to leave. You can't believe the animosity because of his colour. He did one or two other arrangements and then Gerry could see it wasn't for us because you couldn't get the band to play it, it would cause too much dissension.

I stayed with Geraldo eleven and a half years. I kept trying to get out but I couldn't leave. We were earning a lot of money and even when the nine broadcasts came down to a few less, we were still doing a lot of work.

HARRY GOLD *Tenor saxophone 1942*

Geraldo never rehearsed as he expected you to read perfectly first go, and if you couldn't read you were out immediately. Sometimes we'd rehearse things for a recording or broadcast but even then there were times when he played numbers he hadn't rehearsed.

I was the first tenor and the other tenor would take all the parts, whether first or second, that had all the solos in. That really annoyed me. I didn't want to have rows with the guy, and eventually I went to see Geraldo.

'Look Gerry, I'm not happy, anything with a solo is taken from me. I don't mind sharing solos, that would be fair enough, but I want some solos.'

'Okay, I'll have your name or initials on the parts for any new arrangements.'

The solos still went to this guy and I felt really fed up with this, and also some of the guys would never speak to me. Geraldo wouldn't speak to me, the bass player wouldn't speak to me, I can't explain why, a very strange band. Then came a Sunday concert and one of the parts on my stand had a fabulous tenor solo at a terrific rate. That part was left and I had to read the solo at sight; every note was written but I've always been a good reader. I saw this mass of notes and I thought 'Here goes,' and I played it faultlessly.

I realise now why that part was there – he thought I'd make a mess of it – and from that moment on they all started to speak to me! The bass player came over and said, 'That was very good.' Oh, I'm now one of the band am I? Once that happened I realised that this guy on tenor was trying to work me out so I thought to myself nobody has ever worked me out of any band, I've always left the band when I wanted to, so I went to Gerry and gave him a fortnight's notice.

'Why, why?'

'I'm not happy, let's leave it at that. You promised me the solos, they don't arrive, so I'd rather leave.'

NAT TEMPLE *Alto/clarinet 1941–46*

We were due to broadcast on a Sunday morning from the Paris Cinema and the second alto was Carl Barriteau, a very fine musician in Ken Johnson's band working at the Café de Paris. A bomb hit it smack on, killed lots of people, and obviously prevented Carl from coming to the broadcast, so I had to do his part as well as my part and we just carried on as we knew something had gone wrong.

Harry Hayes got taken away by Military Police at that time because he was in uniform, in the Welsh Guards, but with the collar undone and he went out from the Paris Cinema for a breath of fresh air and was arrested. That was another broadcast where we had to double up. The audiences for the broadcasts would often include Military Police, and although the guys would have permission to play with the band, they would quite often put on false moustaches or wear somebody else's civvy clothing.

We had people in that band who could read anything, anything at all. We had a girl vocalist, Dorothy Carless, and she had no conception of time so was always late, but she'd walk in, pick up a sheet of music, a number she'd never seen, and read it perfectly. Perfect readers, good technicians, it was a quality band.

Geraldo had an enormous number of contacts. He knew how to pull strings and that is a very valuable attribute. He played piano but not very well, and in spite of his reputation he was the shyest person imaginable. When he went on stage he would never look at the audience. He'd go to the microphone to announce the next number and all the audience could see was the side of his face, he would never look at them. He belonged to the type of bandleader who were always smartly dressed, like Roy Fox and Sidney Lipton.

It was when I was with Geraldo that I started thinking about forming my own band. He wasn't too pleased, but it's a natural course of events.

DOUGIE ROBINSON *Alto saxophone 1943–55*

I went into the airforce at 17 and was there for a few months before they decided they could win the war on all fronts without me so out I came and up to London – the new kid on the block. Gerry needed a new lead alto player and in I went for Harry Hayes. I think it was a case of where angels fear to tread. That's how it started and I was there for 12 years!

That band did nine broadcasts a week and George Evans would come in with a pack of arrangements which we'd go through briefly, have a break, and then the red light would come on. That's what I was flung into at 17! George did a lot of the arrangements at that time and I liked his writing very much. Gerry wasn't at all dictatorial and he would leave it to the arrangers to rehearse the band. Gerry would do a lot of his own announcing and at the end of the broadcast he would say, 'The clock on the wall says Geraldo that's all.' He would announce 'the latest British "it"!' The comics of the day used to say Geraldo was the first one to drop his aitches, the H Bomb! He would say things like, 'Can't you play that more betterer?' Strangely enough his twin brother Sid didn't talk like that. They certainly didn't look like each other: Sid was short and fat, Gerry tall and elegant.

We had a black singer, Archie Lewis, who had a very commercial voice and he was so popular it wasn't true. It was the same with trumpet player Eddie Calvert, who was in Gerry's band. It was Wally Stott who wrote him a few bars solo on a number and he happened to do this on a theatre date and the crowd went mad for this trumpet solo. You could have got somebody else to stand up and play much, much better and it wouldn't have produced any reaction. So I guess it must be the sort of common touch, whatever that may be.

Gerry was one of the old businessmen and dashed around in a white Rolls-Royce, but as far as the music was concerned, he left the musicians alone. All he did was give the down beat, never anything else, just a down beat. That took a bit of getting used to, and when I left the band it took a bit of getting used to not coming in on your own when somebody counted four!

After the war he went to America on holiday and saw Duke Ellington's band rehearsing. He watched Duke searching for the right tempo and he came back to the studio and said, 'I think I'll count a few bars so we can get the right tempo.' The stick flailed through the air and we all looked at him in amazement and at some hidden signal we came in. But that was the end of that, it never happened again. From then on it was back to what was almost like a rapier thrust. He was never particularly good on tempos but the rest of the band knew the tempos and it seemed to work.

Gerry would write letters to give you the sack saying, 'I'm thinking of making a change in my orchestra and your services won't be required after . . .' But if you gave your notice to him he didn't like that. I gave him three months' notice when I left and he didn't speak one word to me after that, not a word. But I had a great regard for the man, especially musically, because he left us alone.

BILLY AMSTELL *Alto 1944–45*

Geraldo looked like a million dollars and frightened the life out of me. I had a little solo to play and he said, 'Look 't it' I couldn't believe my ears. There was this immaculate, well groomed gentleman, I'm cockney but he knocks me into a cocked hat! 'Look 't it, watch it, what.' I couldn't believe it.

Geraldo was a very ambitious man and he decided he was going to have the best band, and he did until Ted Heath came along. I had about a year and ten months' pleasure, not only musically but socially too. We had so much fun, we used to 'lumber' each other, and the greatest guy I ever knew was Maurice Burman. He was an organiser, a 'lumberer', a good musician, a great flair for music, a drummer, and yet to hear him play trumpet cornet you'd think it was Bix. Lovely player, and we used to have jam sessions in the band room. Dougie Robinson would play clarinet and I would compete with him on clarinet, and the gentleman of the band was Phil Goody, extremely good flautist and a gentleman. It was a good band.

I left Gerry. He didn't want me to leave but I did, and I went back to Ambrose and we opened at Ciro's.

WALLY STOTT *Alto saxophone 1944–48*

It was the summer of 1944 and the band was at the Palladium. They'd just come back from a Middle East tour for ENSA and I joined them a few weeks before D-Day. I was so thrilled because I'd been a fan of Geraldo's band for the past four years, listening to all their radio programmes, and I had total admiration for some of their stars, particularly Harry Hayes's alto playing and George Evans's arranging and singing.

I'd been playing lead alto for Oscar Rabin for a couple of years but I didn't want to tour any more; I wanted to stay in London to write arrangements but Oscar and Harry misled me by means of a codicil to my contract. It had a hidden clause saying I had to go back and play in the band on tour if there was a crisis. Of course, eventually there was a crisis and I refused to go so they got an injunction against me preventing me from playing anywhere. My solicitor said, 'Well you'd better not play, you'd better not work for anybody,' and for about eight or nine months I didn't dare. Then the buzz bombs started and the second alto with Geraldo came from Leeds and he wanted to go back so I was invited to come into the band. I told Geraldo I was under this injunction and I wasn't allowed to work, so he said, 'Look, leave this to me,' because he was in charge of music for ENSA and a powerful man. I think he also had some sort of control over who broadcast and I think he had immense power over other bandleaders.

So I joined the band and that was quite a nerve-racking thing. We seemed to live at either the Paris Cinema or the Criterion Theatre, and if they had a broadcast at eight o'clock in the evening, you'd turn up there at half past six, they'd run through two numbers, and then have a break, so if you were coming in from outside when did you get to rehearse? You ended up sight reading on the air, and these things were 'live', they weren't pre-recorded. In every other band the bandleader would say, 'One, two, one, two, three, four,' but with Geraldo, everything was on the down beat; when that stick came down that's when you started playing. It didn't matter whether it was 'Skyliner' or 'Sing, Sing, Sing' or 'In The Mood', you played when the stick came down! That was sort of scary but very thrilling too.

I joined the band on second alto and Dougie Robinson was on lead. Ted Heath was in the trombone section and he used to do a funny thing. He would sit behind me and when there were four bars to go to a solo I would hear this sound like a xylophone and it was Ted with his teeth out. Whenever he had a solo he whipped out his teeth and would play on his gums.

Ivor Mairants's guitar did strange things. I remember being at Alexandra Palace for TV with Geraldo who was doing his own announcing. He would stop the band then turn around and, in a very deliberate ploddy way, walk to the camera to announce the next number, and while he was out there you heard a voice from Ivor's speaker saying,

'This week in Parliament, the member for so and so . . .'! He once flew through the air at the Paris Cinema. He plugged his guitar in and did something strange, electrically speaking, and he went past me! After that they put up a plaque in the Paris saying you can't do whatever it was Ivor did!

Later on the Geraldo band became bigger and the personnel changed a great deal. I'll never forget how we got four trumpets. We went to Germany to play concerts for our boys on the Rhine for Christmas and New Year 1945–46 and when we got there the first evening we didn't have a concert so we sat in the visitors' mess and had drinks and chatted. Freddy Clayton was very young and I suspect he was too young to be let out of England or something like that, so there was a young man who had come with us on trumpet I'd never seen before, or so I thought. He came and sat next to me and said something rather enigmatic: 'You won't tell them will you?'

'I beg your pardon?'

'You know, what happened, you won't tell them will you?'

'I haven't the faintest idea what you're talking about.'

'You know, in Oscar Rabin's band at Glasgow Empire.'

'What happened in Oscar Rabin's band?'

Now something had happened but I'd totally forgotten about it because that was like another life. Then he reminded me.

I was with Oscar Rabin's band at Glasgow Empire and the week before we'd been Band of the Week at Weston-super-Mare broadcasting every day and this young man had been introduced to us as he was going to join the band on trumpet.

'Oh, I heard you on the radio last week.'

'Did you, what did the band sound like?'

'Terrible.'

Then somebody tried their luck:

'Did you hear my trombone solo in . . .' I forget what number it was and the reply was the same and he was murderous and had the most awful things to say about everybody. About three minutes into this conversation I saw a deputation going out of the door to Oscar and Harry to tell them if he joins the band we all leave! He was with us for about half an hour and we never saw him again. Now here he was with Geraldo in Germany so I assured him I wouldn't tell anybody about it. Every night we went off somewhere in a bus to do a concert on a base and it was always the same format: after the concert the bus driver would allow us an hour to go to the Sergeants' Mess or the Officers' Mess to be entertained and then we had to be back on the bus.

For the first 15 minutes he'd have the lights on then he'd put them off, thinking maybe everybody would sleep. We used to play childish little games in those days and this particular game was all the rage at the time. The older musicians and the singers would sit in the middle of the bus and there'd be young musicians at the front and young musicians at the back, and as soon as the lights went out, out came the elastic bands and there would be catapults firing over the people in the middle. This would be going on in the dark and one night this young trumpet player was hit on the ear and he said, 'I know who that was, if I'm hit again I shall be back there,' and he sounded very, very drunk, slurring his words. I was sitting near the back with Dougie Robinson and I wasn't playing this game at all. He was hit again immediately and he came looming out of the darkness, and to my horror I saw he was holding what looked like a German service pistol which somebody had probably given him in the Sergeants' Mess. He pointed this thing at my heart and said, 'I'm going to kill you now,' and he was totally drunk.

I thought this was a very serious situation and my friends behind him would take it away from him, but nobody did a thing, nobody moved a muscle, everybody was frozen, fascinated with what was going on. Eventually the gun got very heavy and it went lower and lower and he turned around and slumped back to his seat.

When we got back to England he was supposed to be out of the band, but I liked the way he played and as we had a recording the day we got back I persuaded Geraldo to let him stay, and I wrote something for him. He played it so beautifully on the record, Geraldo said he could stay in the band and he'd have four trumpets. That was Eddie Calvert.

I was being asked to write arrangements and I'd heard amazing things about Peter Knight, how he could sit in a corner and write without a piano with the band playing in his ear. I once did that at the Queensbury Club while we were rehearsing. It was 'Blue Skies', and because the band was interfering with my thought patterns I just did very simple things that I knew would work and it worked a treat because it was simple. I discovered the thing to do is to write something simple that swings and stay out of the way of the band, let the band play, so that was a lesson.

He was a very stiff sort of man, Geraldo, and he sized people up very quickly. People were either geniuses or fools, one category or the other, and if you got in the wrong category he had no respect for you at all. If you were in a category he respected, you could get away with almost anything. He was a pianist who could not memorise anything and certainly couldn't improvise anything so he always had to have the music, and of course that led to his downfall. When we did our band show on a concert, one of our numbers was Jerome Kern's 'Swing Time' which was a jazz waltz, and it was a piano duet feature with Sidney Bright, his brother, who was our pianist in the band.

There were a lot of practical jokers in the Geraldo band, and some of them used to go on stage in the darkness when it was being set up, and with a razor blade and a pen they'd change a lot of the notes on Geraldo's part. They'd scratch them out and write others in, and whatever they wrote in he would play! He'd be playing this thing and realising it was all wrong and had been changed and he would be swearing. He didn't really use vulgar language, he wasn't that kind of man, but he was swearing as best he could in his own way under his breath so the audience couldn't hear.

He loved to conduct classical music, and say we did five broadcasts in a week, which was fairly normal, at least one or two of them would be with a huge augmented orchestra and we would do Elgar or Debussy or Eric Coates or *American in Paris* or something like that. He'd love doing that and he was really in his element. I found myself arranging for a symphony orchestra, a swing band, something in between and occasionally a choir, and all kinds of things. That was the most wonderful experience and other wonderful things happened. For instance, about a year after the war ended Robert Farnon got out of the Canadian army where he'd been conducting the Canadian Band of the AEF and, needing a solid sort of job to start himself off, he came and worked for Geraldo and he wrote arrangements for us as a professional arranger, of course. Then, with the war over, Geraldo decided to take his wife, Plum, to America for a long holiday so that he could see what was going on in America in the music business, and he left Bob Farnon behind as our conductor. Bob conducted us and wrote wonderful arrangements and that was just a windfall for me. He was only with us for about a year and then he went off and started to write film scores and get his own broadcasts and things.

I'd learnt to write by a very illegitimate sort of method. When I joined Archie's Juvenile Band at 15, I'd never thought of writing music

Ambrose (Billy Amstell)

Above: Ambrose in Cannes 1937 (Billy Amstell)
Below: Ambrose Orchestra on a film set (Billy Amstell)

Above: George Elrick (centre) (George Elrick)
Below: Ivy Benson Orchestra Villa Marina, Isle of Man 1956 (June Pressley, second from left; Sheila Tracy on right; Paula Pyke, drums; Robey Buckley, trumpet, centre)

Above: Ivy Benson Orchestra, Douglas, Isle of Man 1956 (Sheila Tracy, trombone, left; Robey Buckley, trumpet, centre; Ivy Benson, clarinet)
Below: Ivy Benson with Ken Mackintosh

Above: Ivy Benson with Carmen and Guy Lombardo 1952
Below: Eric Delaney Band (Bert Courtley, Albert Hall middle tpts, Jimmy Skidmore left of saxes, Jack Seymour bass) (Eric Delaney)

Above: Tony Mansell, Cleo Laine, Frank Holder and the Johnny Dankworth Orchestra
(Frank Holder)
Below: Frank Holder and John Dankworth (Frank Holder)

Above: The Cubs – (left to right) Ivor Mairants, Les Lambert, Harry Gold (Ivor Mairants)
Below: Roy Fox Orchestra with Mary Lee (Ivor Mairants)

Above: (left to right) Bernard Rabin, Teddy Foster and Maurice Kinn (Diane Rabin)
Below: Roy Fox Orchestra (Ivor Mairants)

– it had never occurred to me. I noticed that whatever theatre we were in, within a few hours the pianist, Eddie Taylor, would put his wind-up gramophone on the bench and start playing a Tommy Dorsey record, but he'd only listen to about three bars then he'd switch it off and start writing things down. I asked him what he was doing and he said, 'I'm trying to write this arrangement down so we can play it.' I asked him if I could help but we didn't write a score we just wrote parts and there were parts all over the floor. That's how I learnt to arrange and I'd never had a lesson in harmony or anything like that because I'd more or less taught myself to play the saxophone and the clarinet. It wasn't until a couple of years later, when I was playing in another band and was doing some sort of show in Blackpool, that somebody asked if I copied parts. I said I did and he said, 'I'll have a score for you tomorrow.' 'A score, what's a score?' I'd never heard of a score and I was amazed to see this master plan of the whole thing!

Having got into Geraldo's band and started to write for strings, which I particularly wanted to do, I thought if I was going to learn more I'd really have to go and study rather seriously. Somebody told me about this marvellous little man, a Hungarian composer called Matyas Seiber, and I went to him. The first lesson will amuse you because he said, 'Now I believe you've been writing music so I think I must find out what you already know. Why don't you go to the piano and play something, something that you've written or something that you have in your mind to write.' Being a great fan of the Stan Kenton Orchestra at that time, I played a sequence of chords rather like *Artistry in Rhythm*. When I stopped playing there was a silence. 'I think we'll start at the beginning,' he said. I felt very crushed by that! He gave me some very simple exercises to do, harmonic exercises which anyone who knows anything about harmony could do, and it drove me crazy. It was so boring, so simple that I didn't go back for another lesson, I couldn't face it, it was like pulling out teeth.

As a couple of months went by I thought this is silly, if I'm going to make any progress I'll have to do this, so I went back to him and did all those things and I wrote these exercises that aren't supposed to have consecutive fifths or parallel octaves and all those sorts of things. I used to spend hours making sure there weren't any of those nasty things in the music and then he used to find them one after another!

We spent the whole summer of 1948 at the Winter Gardens Ballroom in Blackpool and I just hated being away from home all summer. So on Sundays I would rent a plane to fly to London; this was long before I had a pilot's licence. We'd fly down to Hendon which the pilot would be looking for with a map on his lap, and I'd get the tube to Shepherd's Bush where I was living at the time. Then Monday morning I'd get the train so I was only home for 24 hours, but it was worth it.

Freddy Clayton would go with me and sit in a little seat behind us which faced sideways in the Auster aircraft. I'll never forget the day we started off and it was very rough and right in front of us was a huge barrier of storm clouds. The pilot said, 'I don't see how we're going to get through,' and I shouted to Freddy, 'I don't think we're going to get through,' and Freddy was throwing up by this time, he was very, very ill. 'We're not going to go on we're going to have to turn back,' and no sooner had I said that, the pilot saw a gap in the cloud and he went through, and when we were landing at Hendon Freddy Clayton tapped me on the shoulder and said, 'I'll be glad to see the Tower'. He thought we were still going back!

Oh, I hated that whole summer away from home. This was why I'd left Oscar Rabin's band, I didn't want to be on tour, I wanted to be in London, and so I left Geraldo but I carried on writing arrangements for him, particularly for *Tip Top Tunes*. That, I thought, was the end of my playing, but in 1950 I deputised with the band on some broadcasts we did from the Piccadilly Studio, playing baritone because Phil Goody played flute.

Leaving Geraldo at the end of 1948 and not going to Blackpool again in 1949 meant that I wasn't a regular member of the band when Bill Finegan was arranging for them, but I played all the Bill Finegan arrangements when I deputised on baritone and he is a wonderful arranger.

WOOLF PHILLIPS *Trombone/Arranger 1946–47*

I joined Geraldo as an arranger. Wally Stott was playing in the band and the three of us, Bob Farnon, Wally and myself, were the three arrangers. If anything happened then I would play in the trombone section, and one day Jock Bain wasn't well so I walked in and played that Bill Harris thing, 'Bijou', with no rehearsal.

There was a programme called *Romance and Rhythm* with a choir and a big orchestra which was just music, no announcing. I did a big thing for that and this particular night they had Irving Berlin as the guest, which was marvellous. I started writing on the Monday and by Thursday I couldn't see straight! I had done about 268 pages of score with the choir, singers and so on and at the end of it Irving Berlin came over to me and he said, 'I must congratulate you, sir'. He called me sir – thank you – I was 25!

ERIC DELANEY *Drums 1946–54*

I have a lot to thank Ivor Mairants for because he told me that Geraldo was looking for a drummer and got me along to do an audition on a Saturday morning at Cripplegate Studios. Geraldo had gone to America and Bob Farnon was fronting the band and I was shaking like a leaf – the great Bob Farnon. Afterwards he said, 'Would you like to stay on and do the broadcast?' 'Yes please' I ran to the phone and phoned my mum and dad and told them to tune into the Light Programme! After the broadcast finished I got the job.

Not many weeks later I came into the studio for one of the broadcasts and this gentleman walked in and Ivor introduced me to Geraldo. You seldom spoke to Gerry, you had to go up the office to speak to him. What a gentleman's band that was. I saw a photograph the other day and I can remember that photo being taken, a BBC picture at the Paris studio. It was taken during the coffee break and the most noticeable thing about it is the whole band had ties on and we were all so smart.

We did late-night sets at the Winter Gardens in Blackpool. The doors closed at ten-thirty and everybody went out into the foyer and you hung around for half an hour until they opened the doors and you paid to come in again from eleven 'til two. We did one season up there when, not only did we do the ballroom every night, we did a broadcast every day. We did our *Tip Top Tunes* from there, *Music Through the Shows*, the dance band broadcasts, all from the Co-op building I think it was. We did the *Charlie Chester Show* because Charlie was in one of the shows. Every day for the whole season, imagine how much money we earned! It was marvellous. That was work!

You don't leave Geraldo; he'll get rid of you but you don't leave him. He said very little when I left, barely looked me in the face. It was obvious it was coming because for the last four or five years with the band I was starting to use the two bass drums with all the tom-toms on top, and of course all the arrangers, including Wally Stott and Alan Roper, were writing for all these drums.

One day the tymps were at the side of me in the studio and I had some wire brushes and I was playing on one of them, and I think it may have been Don Lusher standing in the corner who said, 'That sounds good.' I thought, 'I'll do this, I'll play the tymps with the brushes, no one's ever done that before.' And that became the big thing of course. 'Roamin' in the Gloamin' and 'Truckin' – two more hit records played with brushes. Then even bigger than that was 'The Manhattan Spiritual'.

DON LUSHER *Trombone 1951–52*

I saw the Geraldo Band when I was in the army, just before we went over for the invasion. They came to play for us at West Ham football stadium where we were hemmed in and I was fired with inspiration and that was really ludicrous because I made up my mind there and then that I was going to be like one of them and probably play with that band. I mean I might have got killed and I wasn't a very good player in any case. Ted Heath was the lead trombone and I didn't know Ted Heath from Adam in those days, and the band was full of that type of player.

In 1951 I got a call from Jock Bain who was with Geraldo saying I could join them if I wanted to, but I was under contract to Jack Parnell so I turned it down. Then eventually when the job with Jack ended – he was going on the road and I didn't want to go – I asked if the job was still there and it was. I think somebody had to be got rid of which wasn't very nice, but I had my interview with Geraldo, which was terribly impressive in the office at 73 Bond Street.

Not long after I joined we did a Mecca tour, all the Mecca ballrooms, some in London, some outside London. Six days a week, afternoon and evening, and the places were packed. I remember going to the Locarno in Glasgow, I think it was, and the queue of people for the afternoon session was unbelievable! Every Monday night we'd do a 'live' broadcast, and very often a Sunday concert.

The first date we did on that tour was Streatham Locarno and two or three of us went to walk through the main entrance to the ballroom and the big bouncers, in evening dress even in the afternoon, asked who we were and what we were doing. We said we were Geraldo's band and they said, 'Not this way, round to the back door.' When Gerry got to know about this, there was a band meeting at teatime and he read the riot act. 'My musicians go through the front door anywhere.' And I immediately admired him!

The band was delightful. Super trumpet section, magnificent saxophone section. Jock Bain was the lead trombone, I was on fourth trombone, and there was Maurice Pratt and Jack Thirwell. Eric Delaney was in the band while I was there.

While I was with Geraldo I got a call from Ted Heath's office saying they were doing a Stan Kenton programme and needed an extra trombone and could I go and do it? So I did, and then I had another call to do something else and I did that and then Wally Smith was off with bad cold sores and I was asked to go and dep for a period. Well I couldn't because I had things on, but I did go in a couple of times for broadcasts. Then the call came from Ted saying he would like me to join the band and would you believe I said, 'Well yes, but I'm very happy where I am with Geraldo.' Now Geraldo and Ted weren't the best of friends as I'm sure you've gathered! I didn't join then and when he asked me again, I said I would consider it. It sounds terribly big time now but I truly was very happy in Geraldo's band.

When Ted called me this time he was quite terse on the phone: 'Listen, I'll give you 'til after the weekend to think about it. I want you in the band but if you're not going to come, I want to know because somebody who has already been with the band is willing to come back.' That was a very big name and that shook me so I asked Jock Bain what he thought I should do and told him what Ted had said about features, playing first trombone and the money and all that business. Jock said, 'Well you won't get any further with me here in Geraldo's band so you must go, but everything he has told you must happen.' So I decided to give in my notice to Geraldo. I had to go up to the office and he said, 'Where are you going?' And when I told him Ted, that was the enemy, and he called him everything from a pig to a dog and then didn't speak to me for the next two weeks! Eventually I went back and did a couple of sessions with the band and he was all right.

Strangely enough when I finally gave notice to Ted and told him I was going to Jack Parnell's television band, he went crazy and he didn't speak until I left!

SYD LAWRENCE *Trumpet 1951*

We went to Holland and played at this lovely place for a dinner/dance and we opened up with a number and everyone is eating so nobody is dancing. Gerry goes to the microphone and says, 'Ladies and gentlemen, we've come over 'ere to play for your dancing so when we play the next number I want to see all your faces on the floor!'

I wasn't with him long. It was the one band where I was handed my notice and I never really found out why. It wasn't because I couldn't play otherwise I wouldn't have got the job. Missing a broadcast might have been something to do with it.

We were in London recording *Calling All Forces* at the Playhouse with Pet Clark and the Memory Man, Leslie Welch. It was a whole day thing and the next day we were in Manchester, in the studios in the morning at ten o'clock for a 'live' broadcast, and in the afternoon we were doing one of these all-Britain contests in Belle Vue. So it was a busy day and that meant the band had to travel overnight. We'd travelled down from Scotland the day before and I hadn't had a proper night's sleep. My wife Kath was in hospital having a baby so I was on my own. I got home from London to the flat in Kenton at teatime and I had to go to sleep. I set the alarm and it either didn't go off or I didn't hear it. The train was leaving at midnight and I woke and sat up in bed and the room was black and I didn't know where I was, I didn't know who I was, and then it hit me. I got into my clothes and ordered a taxi to take me to Edgware Road to see if I could get a lift, and the taxi dropped me off by the police station. By this time it was one o'clock in the morning. I popped into the police station and explained to the copper that I had to get to Manchester for 10 o'clock in the morning and asked him if he could stop somebody and get me a lift. He stopped a lorry, an awful bloody wagon with a great big spare tyre in the back which I had to sit on. After several hours, he pulled up and said, 'Okay guvnor this is as far as we're going'.

'Where are we?' Well, we were on the outskirts of Birmingham and they dumped me in the fog and I had to wait until a bus came in the morning. I had to phone the studio and ask to speak to Mr Geraldo.

''allo . . . oh, where are ya? Get 'ere as quick as you can for this a'ternoon.' He got a deputy from Manchester for the broadcast.

It was about that time I think some of the lads in the Geraldo Band were a bit envious of the Ted Heath Band because Ted had got the stars and they wanted to get some jazz going. Whatever I was, I was not a bebop player. So I don't know whether I got my notice because I missed that broadcast or whether I got worked out of the band for a bebop player, which is what I think happened because Jimmy Deuchar took my place. But Jimmy Deuchar only lasted six weeks because he wasn't a big band player and he must have got fed up. There was loads of lovely melodic jazz in Gerry's pad which Alan Franks used to play. Then another lad went in and he stuck it for two weeks.

I got a lift home with one of the guys one Friday night, I won't say who it was, and he said, 'By the way Syd, you'll find a registered letter in the morning with your notice.' Not very nice. You never spoke to Geraldo; none of the lads seemed to speak to him. I didn't like him, you couldn't approach him. A very successful man of course, and always had a fine band.

I'd been down south for far too long and I wanted to go back to my roots. I had my sights on the BBC Northern Variety Orchestra so I went back to Chester and played in the little ballroom I'd played in before. I was doing all right but I decided to take a day job with Hoover, servicing washing machines and cleaners. I was picking up twenty pounds a week at this job plus my gigs, and this was in the '50s. I went to this house and knocked on the door and this young housewife opened the door and she was in a kind of kimono. It was my first call and around breakfast time and the radio's on and it's George Elrick with *Housewives' Choice*. There's me with the lid off and I'm cleaning the Hoover with this brush, there's dust flying all over the place, and suddenly George Elrick says, 'We've got a record of Geraldo and His Orchestra' and I look up and say 'I used to play for Geraldo you know,' and she looked at me very strangely this woman. I could just imagine what she'd tell her husband when he got home: 'Some jerk cleaning my Hoover this morning told me he used to play for Geraldo!'

DEREK HEALEY *Trumpet 1955–58*

When you went to the office in Bond Street, there was the outer office with Miss Hill the secretary and she put you in touch with Mrs Raisin who was his personal assistant, and then you went into Gerry's office which had a white fluffy carpet and he was sat at a huge desk two feet higher than you were. Bob Efford went to give in his notice and, businessman that he was, Gerry bamboozled him so much that he stayed on for less money!

I remember when I first joined the band, I'd just come down to London from Bolton Palais where I'd been playing with Teddy Foster. I was only 20 and the Geraldo trumpets were Ronnie Hughes, Stan Reynolds and Leslie 'Jiver' Hutchinson (Elaine Delmar's dad). I heard they wanted a lead trumpet so I rang Gerry's office and Miss Hill said to make an appointment to go in to see them. When I finally got through to talk to Gerry he said, 'I can put you in any of these Howard and Wyndham Theatres for pantomime or perhaps you'd like a job with my bands on the boats?' 'No, no I want a job with the London band,' which of course was lead trumpet! I had to go to Lowestoft to do an audition and I thought, 'Well, he won't ruin his band by letting me sit in the middle so I'll be on the end and they'll throw me the odd number and see what I'm like.' But when I got there the empty chair was in the middle and that was it, get on with it, and I played all the leads all night and got the job!

I remember doing a 'live' broadcast of *Tip Top Tunes* which we did for an hour every Monday night. Harry Roche, Frank Dixon, Maurice Pratt and Tommy Cooke were the trombones and me and Stan and Ronnie and Harry Roche were in the Grosvenor pub around the corner having a drink and a laugh. We hear this broadcast coming over the radio with the *Tip Top Tunes* signature tune. We all looked at one another and said, 'Jeez man, that's us!' We ran out, ran up the stairs of Aeolian Hall, about three flights, into the studio and finished up playing the last eight bars! And all Gerry did was put his tongue out at us! He never bothered or anything. He was great.

Gerry was such a gentleman. We did the *Sunday Night at Blackpool* television shows and had to travel through the night from Torquay as it was the only way you'd get there. Gerry would have a chauffeur but he would drive and the chauffeur would sit in the front seat and sleep! I had no car in those days, I'd just come down from Bolton so I couldn't afford a car and Gerry used to take me with him. We would get up there and he'd go to the Imperial, have a shower, and come into the pit at the Blackpool Opera House at nine o'clock in the morning having driven from Torquay, looking immaculate with a hairnet on so that the earphones wouldn't spoil his hairdo! And we, all young men, were absolutely shattered, having travelled overnight. I don't know how he did it.

He was like a father to me, Gerry. He was one of the nicest guys I've ever worked for. For me it was the pinnacle, apart maybe from when I went to Jack Parnell's Elstree band years later. It was the best band I'd ever been in.

BOB EFFORD *Tenor saxophone 1956*

I joined him when Keith Bird left the band. That was a great musical experience. Saxophone-wise it was the best time I ever had, the best section I ever worked with and the writing was quite the most exciting saxophone writing I ever came across. Wally Stott of course used to write for that band, and they also had some Sauter–Finegan stuff and it was a really good band.

I rather liked Geraldo; in fact I've been fortunate in that way, I've liked all of my leaders. I guess if I didn't like them I wouldn't have worked for them. He had some endearing traits; he would stand in front of the band dressed in tails, with a baton, mouthing the words 'Don't follow me', which was pretty good I thought! He gave the band full rein. He knew his own musical limitations although I'm sure he was capable in his own way.

I believe he'd been quite a well known accordionist at one time and he could play the piano after a fashion. But he knew he didn't know too much about the kind of music his band was playing, so he would just ask his musicians and the end result was he had a very good band because he didn't make any of those decisions himself, he just let the guys tell him what was best.

We seemed to broadcast all the time, it was just one broadcast after another. There was a problem at one time with the trombone section. I can't quite remember how it came about but Harry Roche was leading the section and he and Gerry must have clashed head to head, which they did on numerous occasions, but always patched it up. On this particular occasion we turned up at the Aeolian Hall with three trombones instead of four and, Harry being the lead chair, nobody else would sit in it because they didn't want to get into the middle of the confrontation. If you remember the opening theme of *Tip Top Tunes* it was played on four trombones, so it was played without the melody! I do remember that very clearly.

Although I didn't actually leave Gerry, it got to the stage where the band was getting less work and he couldn't afford to pay retainers so there wasn't actually that much to leave when I joined Ted Heath. I don't even remember whether I actually gave notice.

RONNIE HUGHES *Trumpet 1955–58*

I loved him. He was a joy to work for. The thing about Gerry was he always let you play the way you wanted to play and that's the way it was with him. He never bothered you, whereas with Ted if I played something and he didn't like it, he would say so.

It was a very much more relaxed band than Ted Heath's and it was always a great band to play in. We did something one night with Gerry which I'll never forget. On *Tip Top Tunes* we used to do a salute to the bands and on this particular night it was Woody Herman and his arrangement of 'Muskrat Ramble' – very difficult. By the time we'd finished rehearsing all the string things, there wasn't any time left so Gerry said, 'Boys I want you to go up and have a listen to this record of Woody Herman, we're playing this tonight.' We listened to the record and played it 'live' on the air without any rehearsal and it was fantastic; it was incredible. We'd had a look at our parts in the corner by ourselves, but we didn't actually rehearse it.

I did Gerry's very last concert in Eastbourne, and I think he died shortly after that.

ROSEMARY SQUIRES *Vocalist*

In 1955 I started doing 'Tip Top Tunes' and that really put you on your mettle. You did your own spot and then you had this medley and I forget how long it lasted. One tune going into another, beautifully arranged and you had to have a good ear for pitch and key changes and it was done 'live' before an audience, usually at Aeolian Hall. In 1959 the BBC decided to take 'Tip Top Tunes' on the *Queen Mary*, 'Top Crossing' and that was a 13 weeks series recorded with Jimmy Grant the producer, Brian Matthew the compère and Geraldo's full band but no strings.

Geraldo was married to one of the Cunard family and she was a very old-fashioned lady with a high choker around her neck with a little bit of lace. Charming to the nth degree. I met them on deck one morning and he said 'Come and walk with us' so we started strolling along the deck and an elderly gentleman and his wife, very elegant, came towards us and Gerry said 'Oh Rosemary you must meet Sir Archibald McIndoe'. He was the famous plastic surgeon and before he could introduce me Sir Archibald looked at me and he said 'I spy a Gillies nose' and Gerry looked at me and said 'I don't get it'. Now Sir Harold Gillies had trained him and he had done my nose in 1957 and Sir Archibald had recognised Sir Harold Gillies' work. Isn't that amazing on the deck of the *Queen Mary*?

Geraldo was a great one for going down to the gym. He liked to swim and do exercises. Although he never had a sylph-like figure he was immaculate. Every hair was in place and he was in every sense a gentleman.

We had first class accommodation and we ate in that wonderful first class lounge with that gorgeous panel at the back and it was lovely. We had Gracie Fields on our outgoing journey and Desi Arnez. We had a lot of stars coming and going because that was the way they travelled. We got Gracie up to sing a couple of songs. I always remember she had a great pair of legs!

What an experience that was! We did the recordings in the first class lounge and we had special permission from the Captain for the engineers to drill holes in the parquet flooring to put the mike stands in so they wouldn't shake or wobble. Most of the passengers were American and they'd never had anything like that before!

It was a foregone conclusion that any band on board always gave a show to the crew down in the Pig and Whistle, as it was called, – right down in the bilges or scuppers. My dress was an ankle length one, all satin and they got me a chair but the water was slapping around my feet. So I had to sit with my feet propped up and my dress wrapped over my knees so it wouldn't get wet. We recorded a short broadcast down there and this little steward kept coming up and saying 'I'd like to sing a song'. And Gerry was saying 'Get orf, get orf'. Well the band started laughing and Ralph Dollimore, who was on piano, laughed until he cried and Gerry said 'It's not funny' and he said to the little steward, 'No, I'm afraid we have everything set out as this is a proper broadcast.' Then the crew all shouted 'Go on let him sing, be a sport, don't be rotten'. So this steward came up all done up with eyelashes and powder and everything and sang one of these grey haired mother songs. Gerry said 'Don't you record that on pain of dismissal'. But they did and they kept the whole tape and somewhere, someone's got a tape of that!

NAT GONELLA

1908–

Theme 'Georgia'

Nat Gonella played with the bands of Billy Cotton, Roy Fox, Ray Noble and Lew Stone, as well as leading his own enormously popular small group the Georgians. Heavily influenced by his idol Louis Armstrong, his trumpet playing and singing delighted audiences worldwide for more than half a century. With his trumpet finally put back in its case, he is often to be found singing in his local jazz club in Gosport, Hampshire.

NAT GONELLA

When I was 17 I was in a revue, *A Week's Pleasure* with Gracie Fields, and for four years we travelled all around and the last night we were appearing at Margate. I had no job to go to and this drummer who was playing at a dance hall down the road came in to see me, and asked me if I'd like a job with his band.

'But you haven't heard me play yet.'

'Yes I have, you can hear you down the end of the street!'

So I finished on the Saturday night and started with him on the Monday and I was getting seven pounds a week so I was doing well.

When I was with the revue I would listen to Louis Armstrong's recording of 'Wild Man Blues' and I used to try and play his chorus, and then the clarinet had a chorus after that and I thought I'd like to do that as well so I got a clarinet and learnt to play it.

I was playing with this dance band and someone recommended me to Billy Cotton so I went with him and there were three trumpets. At the Locarno Ballroom in Streatham, everybody was dancing and we were playing nice melodic numbers and I started playing a bit of jazz, having heard Louis Armstrong's records, and I think that's how I got the job, being a hot trumpet player. I would get featured on these Armstrong solos so Billy had me out front of the band on this night and I copied Louis Armstrong word for word and played the trumpet like him. When we got to the end of the number there was a long, high note held for six bars and I was very confident but when I went for this note I missed it. I struggled for it again and I missed it again, and I struggled for it about three or four times and finished up with tears in my eyes as I went to sit down. That was my first experience of doing a solo out front!

Billy Cotton was very easy going and very friendly and he had other interests because he was a racing motorist. He was a man of the world, he wasn't an evening dress man, and he would mix with everybody. Very easy to get on with.

We had an exchange between Billy Cotton's Band from Ciro's Club in London and the band at Ciro's Club in Paris, and that was a coloured band. When we were at Ciro's in London we had to play very quietly because society people wanted to hear themselves talk. Anyway when we came back from Paris this coloured band had been blowing their brains out and got away with murder and we got sacked straight away as we weren't as good as they were!

We weren't doing very much and we were offered a job with Roy Fox who was opening a new restaurant in London and we took it en bloc, the three of us, trumpets and trombone. Billy was a bit vindictive about that – well you couldn't blame him, losing his whole brass section all at once. So of course we went with Roy Fox and had a very successful time with him.

The main thing I used to do was go to the night clubs and play jazz. Invariably it would be the piano player who was in charge of the band and he'd say 'We're going to play "Sweet Sue",' and I'd say I didn't know it, and 'Well you will do by the second chorus,' and we learnt to listen with the ear. You got used to hearing chords and that was a great asset for playing jazz.

The Nest was our number one night club; marvellous place that was. In the Nest they'd be on the floor doing a shuffle-like dance and there'd be Armstrong, Cab Calloway or Duke Ellington and quite a few British bandleaders on the floor and I'd be playing trumpet. Some of these lads would come in a bit late, in evening dress, having been on a society gig and they'd go down to the end of the ballroom, put two tables there, and go back the other end and run and dive over the two tables. The Nest was what they called a 'bottle party' which meant you bought a bottle and had to have it stored.

I met Louis Armstrong in 1932 when he first came over here to the London Palladium, and my brother and I booked seats every night for the whole of the first week, both houses. The first night it was packed and we were in the front row, dead centre, as we wanted to see everything that was going on. When we looked around about halfway through, there were only about twelve people in there, twelve musicians, that's all. Everybody walked out; they couldn't understand it because he came on half bent down, sweating with a handkerchief round his face, and they thought he looked like a gorilla walking on the stage. The second week we had a rovers ticket so you could go where you liked for the same price, so we sat on the floor looking down the aisle at the stage and when anyone walked out we tripped them up because we were so angry that people didn't stay!

I met him that first time because I was in Archer Street, 'the street of hope' as we called it, and Boosey and Hawkes were just around the corner and someone told me Louis's trumpet was there being cleaned. I knew the manager very well so I went round to Boosey and Hawkes and asked if I could deliver it for them. I went to this little hotel in the Strand because they wouldn't have coloured people in the big hotels. I think Duke Ellington was the first one they allowed in to the Dorchester. But this one, where Armstrong was staying, was only a small hotel and the doorman said he would take it up but I told him I had to deliver it personally. Then Louis's manager came down and said he would take it up but I wouldn't give it to anybody until I was up those stairs and delivered it to Armstrong personally. That's how I met him and I told him how good I was! I chatted with him for some time and of course we were great pals after that. I think seeing him that first time after carrying his trumpet around was probably the greatest moment of my life. I couldn't believe it because he was like a god.

My first band in 1935 was a jazz band and we were all interested in the same kind of playing. We opened at Newcastle Empire and I was on a percentage of the takings and we did very big and I got about £400 as I only had five fellas to pay. I had three more weeks, Nottingham, Liverpool and Birmingham, and after that they wanted to put me on wages. 'No, I'll stick to percentage if you don't mind!'

I've been very lucky really, I've played jazz, dance music, modern music – which I call headache music – bebop. Harold Hood was on piano in my first band, he's the boy I found in the Nest Club; Al Bowlly was on guitar for recording and Pat Smuts was on tenor sax. We had Bob Dryden on drums, he was the first band I'd played with before I went with Billy Cotton. The bass was Tiny Winters and that was it, a five-piece and me. Jimmy Messini was guitar and singing.

Smoking pot was pretty open at that time because Louis Armstrong always smoked it, but I didn't see very much of it. I saw more over here than in America. A couple of my band musicians smoked it at one time when we started the modern music and I changed my band. They tried to get the girl vocalist smoking it as well and I went in one night and there they were with a bowl and long pipes like the Chinese. 'You're only playing half a chorus tonight, what do you want to start getting high for?' It was a dance and we played arrangements so half a chorus was about the most they did.

Of course my drummer, Phil Seamen, was picked up several times. I gave him his first job as a drummer with my band. I had him when he was a young man and I knew his mother and father very well. He hadn't ever had a drink until he'd been with me for just over a year and it was his birthday and somebody enticed him to have half a bottle of beer and he got high on that, walked backwards and fell on his drums. From that moment on he started drinking and eventually got into drugs. Several of my musicians were like that which was a shame, but you couldn't stop them.

I went to New York to record for Decca in 1939 and went to the Cotton Club and Cab Calloway's band was there. I was with Tommy Farr the Welsh heavyweight fighter, who was over there fighting Joe Louis. He'd been in the Cotton Club the night before and any celebrity they'd call onto the floor. They called Tommy on again and he said, 'Now I sang here last night but I'm going to introduce you to a very good friend of mine.' When he introduced me the brass section stood up and one passed his horn to me to play on. I did 'Old Man Mose' and there's not a lot of people who can play that. I did a couple or three numbers but that was one of them. It was marvellous! Cab Calloway couldn't talk to me as he wasn't allowed to come across the footlights because all the people on stage were black and the clientele were white and it was like that in those days. Tommy Farr had a gangster as a bodyguard that night; his manager would have seen to that. I was in the manager's office at the Cotton Club and he was chatting to me, wanting to book me somewhere, and this gangster pulled a gun on him because he was offering me work. It sounds silly now but at the time it was exciting because if that gun had gone off I don't know where I'd be now! It was a very exciting evening. The Boswell Sisters were in the audience and the Green Sisters, who were just starting at that time. It was a marvellous atmosphere.

I went to the Onyx and lots of places. I depped for Bobby Hackett one night when he had terrible gumboils in his mouth – I think that was at the Onyx Club but it's a long time ago. I remember the trip going over; we went in a German ship and I got quite friendly with the captain. All the passengers were Jewish getting away from the Nazi regime in Germany. I was in first class and there were only about ten of us, all the rest were in steerage.

I went to this very big hotel in New York where Benny Goodman's band was playing and I saw Lionel Hampton standing at the lift and I'd met him in London about three months before. I asked him why he was waiting and he said he was waiting for the bell to ring to let him know it was time for him to go upstairs to play. He wasn't allowed to sit on the stand with the band. In those days that was the way it was – amazing.

LENNIE BUSH *Bass 1948*

I used to go down Archer Street looking for work and to see my friends. Kenny Graham was a friend of mine and he was in Nat's band and he said Nat needed a bass player and was I available that Friday, so I did this gig at the Aquarium in Brighton, which was a dance hall. Phil Seamen was the drummer and it was the first time I'd met him as Phil never used to come down the street. It was quite a small band because every now and again Nat would get bigger than a six- or seven-piece band when he got a job for a bigger orchestra. All the band were tearaways. They were a funny lot; Phil Seamen always liked a drink and he smoked pot and the guitar player Roy Plummer used to drink quite a lot.

It was the first time I'd met Nat Gonella who I'd seen when I was just a lad, working the theatres. A lot of his work was in variety theatres. Anyway, I did the one night and I got the job. He said, 'You might as well stay if you want to.' We toured, a few one-night stands and every now and again a week in variety with his New Georgians. On the variety dates it was a quintet with Roy Plummer who went to Australia and a pianist called Denny Termer and there was a singer as well: Helen Mack. We used to do all these funny tunes.

Nat was a fantastic player. Kenny Graham did a bit of writing and he got him interested in bebop and we would do things like 'Grooving High'. Nowadays he denies he ever liked bebop, calls it rubbish, but he was mad about it at the time and we used to play a lot of bebop tunes. He would sing 'Georgia' of course, and his act in variety theatres was really geared to ordinary people, not jazz lovers. Every now and again if he had a job where he needed a male singer he would drop me and there was a fellow called Brian Dexter who played the bass and sang and he used to do it. I was with him on and off for a couple of years.

During the war Nat was married to Stella Moya, and when he was away in the army she had affairs with all sorts of people and he found out and they broke up. I think she must have taken quite a lot of money with her because after that he never seemed to have much and he'd made a lot in the '30s – a fortune.

When I first met him, he was married to Dorothy and they lived on the main Edgware Road in Edgware with a damn great dog called Georgia and an American convertible car. They were nice people. He was a lovely bloke, one of the nicest blokes I've ever worked for actually.

TED HEATH

1902–69

Theme 'Listen To My Music'

Ted Heath's start in the music business reads like a film script: an out-of-work trombonist busking in a London street, heard by Jack Hylton who offered him a job in his band at the Queen's Hall Roof, one of London's earliest dance venues. He went with Hylton to the Kit Kat, was with Ambrose at the Mayfair, Sidney Lipton at Grosvenor House, and in 1939 joined Geraldo, who little suspected that his new trombone player would one day become his most serious rival.

During his five years with the band Ted Heath and his wife Moira wrote 'That Lovely Weekend' which Geraldo agreed to broadcast provided Ted paid for the arrangement. It cost him eight pounds but it was money well spent as the song became a hit and spent weeks in the charts, as did their second song 'I'm Gonna Love That Guy', which Betty Grable sang in the film *Call Me Mister* and it was in the American Top Ten for 14 weeks.

The band's famous opening theme, 'Listen To My Music' was written by Ted Heath originally in the key of D Flat as a practice piece, long before he formed his own band. Today it still heralds the band's every appearance on stage, although now in the brighter key of D.

JACK PARNELL *Drums 1944–51*

My first job had been in an agent's office, Leslie McDonnell, MPM Agency, so I put Ted in touch with Leslie McDonnell and he got him the Hammersmith Palais on a Monday night. In those days poor old Ted didn't have any authority over the band. He was a trombone player and a bloody good one, but to us he was a sideman we played with on different sessions. Ted was a beautiful, sweet trombone player, doing all the Tommy Dorsey-type solos very well indeed and he really wanted a sweet band. Kenny Baker and I wouldn't let him have that. It's true! He'd say, 'Okay number 44,' and Kenny and I would say, 'Oh no we don't want to do that, 68,' and we would play 68! That was the way it was and it was quite a few years before Ted established discipline in the band. It was a really wild bunch of egotistical so-and-sos.

Around that time a guy called Sid Gross was putting on jazz sessions at the Adelphi in the Strand and the theatre was packed. There was Stephane Grappelli, George Shearing, Kenny Baker, myself, just this gang of guys doing jam sessions on stage. I told my uncle, Val Parnell, about this. 'They're packing them in, they're doing real business on a Sunday. Why can't we try it with this new band?' He agreed to give it a try and we did the first Swing Session. So now we had the Palladium Swing Sessions and the Hammersmith Palais once a week and this started to build the reputation of the band. We were also getting broadcasts and Pat Dixon was tremendously helpful.

The next big thing was when Toots Camarata came over from America to do the music for the film *London Town*. Money was no object and Camarata wanted the Ted Heath Band as a nucleus to the orchestra. We were all put on a retainer of fifteen a week, and that plus the Hammersmith Palais, was a lot of money then.

It was tough for Ted as he was spending a lot on the library and the band was expensive as he had top musicians. He was having a struggle and he financed it on a couple of hit songs he'd written with Moira, but I think all that went and it was quite a struggle for the first two or three years. Then it slowly gained momentum, the business became good, and he brought in good singers. He had Paul Carpenter to begin with, who gave the band a bit of Americanism with his announcements, and he could sing very well before the bottle got him. I started singing with the band right at the very beginning as I'd always sung a bit. Somebody like Bobby Pratt who was quite a good drummer would go and bang the drums. Reg Owen would do these long introductions to my songs to give me time to get down from the drums to the microphone, and another interlude for me to get back!

After about 18 months the band began to get very big indeed with the kids; it was like the Beatles of the time. I remember going to Liverpool Empire to do a Sunday concert and the police were controlling the crowds outside the stage door. We looked out and there was just a sea of faces. I was very bad when it came to dealing with the fans. I could never understand how people appeared to idolise you, it was beyond my comprehension and it irritated me. I never idolised anybody apart from Buddy Rich! I would sign autographs reluctantly saying, 'I'm too busy, I've got to put the drums away.' I was terrible, an awful person, but that was the way it was.

Paul Carpenter had started to go off to do film parts so Ted brought in Lita, followed very quickly by Dennis. Bands have got to have focal points and it's always the singers. Playing good solos is not enough and Ted realised this. Eventually he had Dickie, Lita and Dennis, so now the band was really well rounded; it had got everything and it was on top of the world.

We were on the road permanently, mostly by coach although Ted used trains at the beginning. Ronnie Scott was in the band and Ronnie was Ronnie and he couldn't be bothered to get up in the morning and catch trains so he used to fly at his own expense. This irritated Ted, he didn't like it at all, this guy getting up at half past eleven and going down to an airport and getting a plane to the next gig while we were all huddled up in the cold in a coach or a train. One day Ronnie didn't make it, there was fog or ice or something, and this was Ted's opportunity to sack him. We all protested because Ronnie was our pal and I was always the spokesman, the rabble-rouser in the band. Ted had more trouble with me than anybody. 'If he sacks Ronnie we're all going to leave, right?' Everybody agreed so we all marched towards Ted's dressing-room and I thumped on the door.

'Come in.'

'Ted, if you sack Ronnie we're all going to leave, aren't we fellas?'

I turned around and there wasn't one guy there, not one! So he sacked Ronnie and got Tommy Whittle in.

I was unbelievably fiery and temperamental in those days and if there was any trouble it was with me and I think Ted was very pleased to see the back of me although in another way he wasn't. It was one of those off-on relationships. I can remember having a terrible row with him over something, probably nothing, where he didn't speak to me except through Les Gilbert:

'Tell him so-and-so', 'He says so and so','Well you bloody well tell him', and it used to go on like that! He was a father figure and I was just a rebel, I was that kind of a guy; I wanted everything my own way and when I gave in my notice I think he was pleased! But I really did love Ted although I did my best to push him out when I had my own band, but that's this game isn't it? That's competition.

KENNY BAKER *Trumpet 1945–50*

Ted was brilliant to work for. Lovely man. We were lucky in the beginning because he relied on the musicians. I think he knew that we all wanted to make it good. None of us played about. I was a bit irrepressible and used to do silly things but I'd never mess the parts up. I'd always stand up in the right place, I'd always play right, I'd always get the right music, I'd always make sure the phrasing was right. I started writing and doing some arrangements and also ran the swing group. That was Ted's idea, he said it would break up the band a bit.

The singer with the band at the start was Paul Carpenter, when he was sober! I'll tell you a funny thing about Paul which he never knew. He would sometimes miss a bar but the band all went with him. 'He's done it again!' and we followed and he never knew! That's where the band was clever. The other thing we did with Paul, which was my idea, we would get to this big ending and as he hit his last note we'd put it up a semitone so he'd finish and the band would come in a semitone up. Dead right, nothing wrong and he'd look round and you could see on his 'chops', 'there's something funny there'. The next night we'd do the same thing on another song and put it down a tone and Ted didn't mind because we never messed it up. We played it right but in the wrong key and Ted was happy to let it go.

At the beginning Ted was very shy and that's why he got Paul Carpenter in to do the announcements and sing. Paul was a brash Canadian. 'Hiya folks, this is the Ted Heath Band and we're going to play you 30 minutes right off the top.' He did all that patter and Ted just conducted, never said a word, not at the beginning.

We were coming back from up north and putting all the

instruments into storage because we were going on holiday for a fortnight. We got to King's Cross and standing on the platform was a big trolley with a load of fish, and a dead fish head had fallen out. Right next to it was Charlie Short's bass and Stan Roderick said 'I got an idea' and he gets this fish head, all slimy, slippery and wet, and stuffs it in the bass f holes. Dear Charlie comes up, gets his bass, and puts it in the left luggage and it's there for a fortnight! When we all came back to go to work again we're at the Ritz Ballroom, Manchester, and he opens his bass and there's the most awful smell. He spent the first session with a long coat hook trying to get this fish out. He didn't find out for a week who did it and then chased Stan all around the bandstand!

Things like that happened with the band, it was lovely. I remember walking along the road with Ronnie Scott one day and you know how he loved to tell stories and was a bit of a practical joker. He was passing a butcher's shop and there was a big tray of old bits of meat and gristle and knuckles with sinews chopped up so he went up to the butcher and said, 'Can I have one of them?' He gets hold of one of these things and it's the end of a big shin of beef with all the sinews and blood hanging. He pulls his coat down and stuffs it up his arm and he's got this thing sticking out as though he's lost his hand! He goes up to a dear old lady walking her dog and says to her, 'Look what your dog has done to my hand.' She nearly had a fit! It looked terrible. That was Ronnie Scott!

Ted was always very approachable. He'd never shout at you, but say, 'What's the matter son, have you got a problem?' and he'd always talk. He might come up and touch your hair and say 'It's getting a bit long you know, make sure you have it cut.' He was very fussy how you looked on stage.

When I left the band I said to Ted, 'I like the band, it's lovely, but I want to go on. I never get any of the dots out unless you get a new score and I've got to learn it. I know all the charts, I'm playing the same solos and I'm getting rusty on sight reading.'

'What do you want to do?'

'Do you mind if I leave?'

'I'd rather you didn't. Is it the money? I'll give you more.'

'No, it's not that, I must do something different.'

'Will you give me three months' notice?' Which I did, and I'm very chuffed to say he did try to get Maynard Ferguson to replace me. Maynard was then with Kenton and I think he politely turned it down.

NAT TEMPLE *Alto/clarinet 1945*

Ted was scratching around for work and he was given a 'Music While You Work', which meant he had to do exactly what the producers of that show required, which meant no jazz. Not under any circumstances do you depart from the melody, and no vocals. Sitting in Ted's band was a gentleman called Kenny Baker well known for his fantastic ability to extemporise and play jazz. He was 'it'. Ted took him aside and warned him about this. 'You've got 16 bars to play Kenny and I don't want any notes that don't belong to the melody, you understand what I'm saying?' Yes, he understood, and come the broadcast Kenny starts with about two notes of the melody and then it was gone, it could have been anything. Ted gave me a lift home from that broadcast and he was fuming. 'That little b— he'll never work for me anywhere. Never. He let me down!'

I'd joined Ted Heath when he first started his band, and when Geraldo got to hear of this he didn't like the idea of Ted stealing some of his men. He told those of us who were playing for Ted Heath, and I was one, we either went with Ted, who had very little work, or stayed with him with nine broadcasts a week. Take your choice, you can't have both. So I left Ted Heath and returned to Geraldo.

TOMMY WHITTLE *Tenor saxophone 1947–52*

I got a call to go to Wimbledon because Ronnie Scott hadn't turned up. I didn't know the job was in the offing, which is just as well because I would have been scared to death to do an audition. I did everything that was required, stood up in the right places, played solos, and didn't have time to feel nervous. I remember Harry Roche coming and talking to me afterwards and saying he hoped I liked the trombones, as if I had time to listen to the rest of the band! A few days later I was offered the job and Ted said it would be a three-month trial but he never told me I'd got the job and I was there for five and a half years! That was just like a dream come true to me and I was tremendously excited as the Ted Heath Band at that time had such esteem. When I got my first week's pay packet I thought I'd arrived!

Ted decided to have a kind of a stage show when we were booked for a week's variety at Golders Green Hippodrome. The saxophones had to do a number with Lita Roza, playing American instruments. There was Henry McKenzie – I think it was his first day on the band – me, Leslie Gilbert, Reg Owen and Dave Shand, and we all had to go out on the stage and dance a samba in a circle shaking these things with Lita in the middle singing 'Enjoy Yourself It's Later Than You Think!' Can you believe it? For a start musicians are the world's worst dancers, it's a well known fact, and apart from that none of us wanted to know about taking part in anything like that. It was a dismal failure and I don't think it lasted the week.

I got on well with Ted but you had to toe the line all the time, playing-wise as well as general behaviour. It was just accepted you had to be well presented and so on and so forth. I left Ted because I wanted to further my solo playing. When I gave in my notice he said he thought I was doing the wrong thing, and in a way he was right because very shortly after that the band went abroad to Australia and to America and I missed all that. But then I joined the newly formed BBC Show Band as featured soloist and that was fantastic as I was on the air every week.

JACKIE ARMSTRONG *Trombone 1947–53*

I joined Ted at Hammersmith Palais and you couldn't get on the floor when he was there on Monday nights. The place was crammed with everyone standing and gaping at the band. Nobody wanted to dance, they just wanted to listen and look.

When Harry Roche, who was the lead trombone, asked me if I would be interested in doing an audition for Laddy Busby's chair as he was leaving, I was petrified. I mean this was a big-time band – untouchables. I'm not good enough for that, I thought, do us a favour! He told me that Ted liked the way I played, so I thought I might as well do the audition as I had nothing to lose. Afterwards, when Ted said, 'You've got the job boy', I was still in two minds whether to take it as I was very happy with Lou Preager's band, earning twelve pounds a week. But I did join Ted and it was probably the best decision I ever made because there I was in a trombone section with Harry Roche, Jack Bentley and Jimmy Coombs in what was soon to be the top band in the country. Not only was I a featured soloist but I was also quite happy to play the fool on stage. I would do anything to get a laugh. I used to play 'A Thousand Violins', which was a violin solo, complete with cadenza and so on.

Just after Harry left the band, Ted brought along an arrangement of 'The Touch of Your Lips' to a recording session. Now this had been done for Harry but you know what you're like when you're young, a bit brash, so I said, 'Yes, I'll have a go at it'. Of course it was all done on wax then, you couldn't drop in, it all had to be done in one take, and the very first take came off. That was it and it was a big success for me.

I was always given second-hand arrangements. We did a concert with Dennis Brain at Westminster City Hall and Ted had an arrangement of 'Sophisticated Lady' done for him. Later when we went into the studio for a recording session, he asked me if I'd like to do it on trombone. I've played those two solos to death and I still get asked for them today. If you played a jazz solo and Ted liked it, he would ask you to write it down and play it every night. Even on a recording he would want it played exactly the same way. Eventually the audience could sing your jazz solo!

Looking back on those six years with Ted, those were fantastic days. A Royal Command Performance, packed ballrooms, a sea of faces, it was a terrific show band.

HENRY McKENZIE *Clarinet/tenor saxophone 1949–67*

Ted was strict with clothes and I got the job because of that as I took Johnny Gray's place who had come in one night with one of those shirts without a button at the top and Ted said he didn't want him wearing a sports shirt, he wanted a proper shirt. The following night he came in wearing it again and Ted sacked him.

My first week with the band was a disaster because it was the first week's variety Ted had done and the band wasn't up to that sort of thing. Everything went wrong that week. We did a number when the smoke screen came on but it wouldn't stop so we couldn't see and people were shouting 'Fire!' We did 'A Thousand Violins' when we went out front with violins, but the manager put the wrong record on and we were all standing out the front laughing and people wondered what was going on!

The day I joined the Heath Band they had a broadcast that evening so in the morning the lead alto and myself went through the hard parts and in the afternoon they had the rehearsal. Then two shows in the evening which finished at half past ten, and we were broadcasting 'live' from Bond Street at 11 o'clock. I didn't know what had hit me!

After the Tommy Sampson Band it was a bit strict. With Tommy if you got to the coach call half an hour late it didn't matter, but when I first joined the Heath band I noticed the difference because I got there ten minutes late and the coach had gone! I got a train and made it in time. You could never be late for rehearsal, death was the only excuse! Compared with Tommy Sampson's band the money was great. I remember thinking I could buy a suit every week, whereas in Tommy's band you had to save up for a suit! There was a broadcast every Monday, Sunday concerts, and roughly about five or six one-night stands a week. We took broadcasts in our stride; they were 'live' and we just did them. The first Sunday I was in the band was a Swing Session at the Palladium and when you were new in the band you had to do a big feature, and I did 'How High the Moon' which went down pretty well. According to the write-ups, which I've still got, it stopped the show!

We did an Australian tour in '55 and that was a bit hectic right from the start as we had engine trouble all the way going out, and when we arrived in Sydney we didn't have time to go to the hotel, we went straight to the hall and the people were sitting in their seats. It was a case of leaving here, flying to Sydney, and going straight on the stand. We had a few days in each place but it seemed as if we were always pushed for time on that tour.

One of the things I remember happening on our first American tour was Miles Davis wanting to play with his group in Pittsburgh, and I don't think Ted was too keen on this. Anyway they got together to discuss how long he would do.

'How long will you be doing Miles?'

'I don't know man, I go on there and I blow.'

Ted liked to set programmes so that really upset his routine! Everything was decided beforehand and he stuck to that. We didn't alter one single thing on the whole of that tour. He'd worked it all out in his head before we went there.

One memory I have of Carnegie Hall, apart from being petrified because everyone in New York was there that night, was I'd broken my mouthpiece and had to play solos on a clarinet and mouthpiece I'd never played before. You hear so much about Carnegie Hall and when you find yourself actually there it's a bit frightening, but I think you reach a point where you say to hang with it, I don't care if they like it or not, just go on and play, and it was a big success. Whenever we finished a concert, Ted would always say, 'Thank you very much'. He didn't give you much praise. I can remember him saying to me after we'd recorded something and I went up to hear it, 'Very good isn't it? Are you pleased with it?' and that's about all he ever said.

I suppose if you were speaking to him you would call him Ted, but if you were speaking to someone else you would refer to him as Mr Heath, although I don't think I ever called him Ted.

RONNIE HUGHES *Trumpet 1949–54*

My first job with the band was New Cross Empire. There was no rehearsal and I turned up at the theatre at six o'clock and Bobby Pratt, Stan Reynolds and Stan Roderick were in the dressing-room and we went through the programme. I'll never forget playing that signature tune for the first time. Everybody sat on the stage waiting for this and when it came I nearly fell off my chair. I've never, ever heard a sound like that and I've played in quite a few bands. It was unbelievable.

The first number was 'The Bells of St Mary's' and it involves a lot of hat waving and bell notes which you have to read pretty carefully, so consequently the first show I've got my head down and I'm doing the best I can. Afterwards I'm walking down the corridor to the band room and Ted walks towards me. If he called you 'mate' it sometimes meant he wasn't too pleased with things. I didn't know that at that time and I couldn't believe I was playing in Ted Heath's band.

'Did you enjoy that mate?'

'Yeah, it was fantastic, it was really marvellous.'

'Well, second house, hold your trumpet up, I don't care whether you play or not.'

That was my initiation into Ted Heath's band!

We went into the studio at Decca to record 'Hot Toddy' and there's some music with sixteen bars of chord symbols which, as you know, you just make up as you go along. We must have done about five or six takes I suppose and every time I'd just play whatever came into my head. The first night after the record had been issued, we were playing 'Hot Toddy' out on a gig somewhere and I stood up and played something. After the gig Ted said 'Hey, listen mate, that 'Hot Toddy', I want you to play what you played on the record.'

'I don't remember what I played on the record.'

'Well go and buy the record.'!

He was wonderful although there were a few problems with my association with Lita before we got married. He was very much against it and it was a bit awkward at times. But I think he sort of liked me, and not many people know this but I actually took him out for the very last time in his life. He was a mad Fulham football fan, he loved Fulham, he really did. He'd go anywhere to see Fulham because when he was a young man he'd played on the pitch with Wandsworth Town Band. After he'd had his stroke we were doing a broadcast from the Playhouse at Charing Cross with Ralph Dollimore standing in front of the band. I was depping for Eddie Blair and Ted was sitting in the front with Moira, and after the broadcast he was talking to the guys and he said to me, 'Hello mate, do you still go to Fulham?'

'Yes, I still go sometimes.'

'I've got nobody to take me and I'd love to see Fulham.'

Now in those days Tommy Trinder and Chappie D'Amato were Fulham directors and Moira got on to them and arranged for us to meet them in the directors' box. When we got there all the roads leading to Fulham Football ground were closed off. I'm about to give up when this old cop stops me and I tell him, 'I've got Ted Heath in the car, he's not very well, we've been invited by Chappie D'Amato and Tommy Trinder and we can't get there.' The cop looked in the car and said, 'Hello Ted, wait a minute' and he got a motorbike cop who took us right down to the ground, helped me to get Ted out of the car, and we watched the match. He didn't really know what was going on but I took him to the match, I took him home, and I think that was the last time he ever went out anywhere. I'm quite proud of that.

LITA ROZA *Vocalist 1950–54*

After my divorce I was working in Miami and I'd saved up enough money to come back to England for three months. Reg Owen had told Ted about me so I rang him at his Albemarle Street office and he said they were working at Trentham Gardens and, as I was in Liverpool, would I go over to Stoke on Trent and have lunch with him and listen to the band that night.

You would have died laughing! They were staying at the Station Hotel in Stoke on Trent and of course you'd all been wearing utility clothes here and I'd just come off the boat in all these smart American togs, and I turned up at the Station Hotel in this bright red American P jacket and a brilliant white beret with my hair cropped like a man's. As I walked into the dining-room you could literally hear knives and forks go down. The boys told me later they thought I was a high-class, well-heeled scrubber that Ted had found! Obviously not, because he wouldn't flaunt me at the Station Hotel in Stoke on Trent! I heard the band and I thought it was terrific and I remember him saying to me, 'How would you like to sing with this band? We're doing a Swing Session at the London Palladium, would you come down and do an audition as I'd like to hear you?'

Now I'll tell you a funny thing. When I was coming over on the *Queen Elizabeth* from America, there was a group playing on board with Ronnie Scott. I was sitting in the lounge one night and Ronnie Scott came over and asked me what I was doing.

'I'm going to England to see if I can sing with the Ted Heath Band'

'You'll never sing with the Ted Heath Band, he won't have a girl singer.' I always remember that!

I sat in the stalls at the next Swing Session while they rehearsed and then I did a couple of numbers.

'How would you like to go on tonight?' said Ted.

'Lovely'! It's amazing how youth has such confidence. I sang 'I've Got My Love to Keep Me Warm', 'Tangerine', 'Don't Worry 'Bout Me', all with the small group. It was wonderful, wonderful. I got very good reviews and, according to the *Melody Maker*, I stopped the show.

Ted signed me up to his agency and I worked in cabaret, I worked at the Orchard Room with Felix King, I did other gigs, and I made odd appearances with Ted as guest star and he collected 10 per cent! For six months I did what I could have done anywhere with any agent, I put some songs together and did an act.

I was lying in bed very late one night and the phone rang and it was Marcel Stellman from Ted's office. 'Christine Norden has been taken ill, can you get down to Torquay?' Christine Norden was a film star and she used to sing occasionally with the band because Ted wanted some glamour. Marcel put me on a train in the morning and that was when I really started singing regularly with the band.

Dickie joined in 1949, I joined in 1950 and Dennis joined in 1951. We were all great chums. We used to call Dennis 'Sir Laurence' because he spoke a bit like Olivier. Stan Reynolds used to say, 'Here he comes, Sir Laurence!' In 1951 we did a tour of Germany and arrived in one place and there was no dressing-room. I was moaning, 'I'm fed up, there's no place to wash, there's no place to dress, how do you expect anyone to go on looking glamorous?' And Ted said, 'For Christ's sake' or words to that effect, and I said, 'Bollocks to you too.' I can't remember exactly what happened but they all froze and Roy Willox still talks about it. He and Henry McKenzie were tootling away and suddenly there was a deathly silence as no one had ever spoken to Ted like that, but I was having no nonsense.

Ronnie Hughes and I discovered each other at the Wimbledon Palais. We were coming back from a dance and were in Tommy Whittle's car in the back seat and our hands happened to touch and before you knew it we were holding hands. Ronnie and I started going out together and it made no difference to the band; I wasn't going through the sections and I'm sure that's what Ted thought I might do. After all, I was a divorced lady! Ronnie was the first boyfriend I'd had since I was divorced. One Sunday he rang me up and said, 'Ted has had a word with me and he wants me to stop seeing you and he's going to have a word with you when you arrive so I'm just forewarning you.' Nothing was said that day, but three months later he calls me in to his office.

'Have a seat.'

'No, I'll stand,' which puts him at a disadvantage as he's already seated.

He shuffles his papers, which was a habit of his, and said, 'I really think you ought to stop seeing Ronnie Hughes.'

'Why?'

'Because you could do so much better.'

'Have you got plans for me then?'

'I think it ought to stop.'

'Look Ted, first of all, if I do anything wrong on the bandstand, you can tell me; if I do anything wrong music-wise you can tell me; but you can't tell me what to do when I'm not working.'

'Well if it continues one of you will have to go.'

'Take my notice.'

'I don't mean that.'

'So what you mean is that Ronnie will have to go? If Ronnie goes, I go.'

'Leave it, we won't discuss it any more.'

I don't think anyone had ever stood up to Ted before. Everyone was so anxious to get into that band; it was the apex of a musician's career and they were literally queuing up. So Ronnie and I got engaged and we just kept going out with each other. The strange thing is that as soon as I left the band in 1954, Ted sacked Ronnie. He was a canny old bugger on the 'qt' with his 10 per cent and all that.

The great thing about the band was they were totally uninhibited with me. I never acted like a girl; as far as I was concerned I was one of the lads and as far as they were concerned I was one of the boys. Everyone accepted I was Ronnie's girl; anyway most of them were married.

Coming back to Aeolian Hall after a one-night stand for a nine o'clock broadcast, we would arrive about seven-thirty in the morning absolutely shattered and pile in to a little Lyons tea room close by. What the wives were doing there, God only knows, I suppose come to collect their husbands. I used to get nobbled every time. 'What was it like, what did he do, did he go back to the hotel after the concert?' I don't think any of them were into scrubbers, I really don't, so they didn't have to worry.

I was being offered various things and I didn't want to stay as a band singer, I wanted to go solo just as Dickie had done. I thought it was about time I went. Dickie left in 1953, I left in 1954.

DENNIS LOTIS *Vocalist 1950–55*

I came over to England from South Africa, not really intending to join a band because I was doing musicals and acting in plays and I wanted to be the next Jack Buchanan. But when I went to see one of the Sunday night Swing Sessions, I thought, God, I've got to sing with this band! I went to see Ted at the Decca studios and Frank Horrocks reluctantly played for me after the session was over. Ted obviously liked what he heard because he said 'Right you can join the band.'

That was on the Thursday and on the Saturday I did Shoreditch

Left: Geraldo rhythm section: Ivor Mairants, Sid Bright, Eric Delaney, Jack Collier (Ivor Mairants)

Centre: Geraldo Orchestra, Samson & Hercules Ballroom, Norwich with vocalist Carole Carr. (back row) Eric Delaney Ivor Mairants, Eddie Calvert, Derek Abbott, Freddy Clayton, Alfie Noakes
Bottom: Geraldo sax section Moss Kaye, George Harris, Dougie Robinson, Wally Stott, Phil Goody

Top: Jack Hylton vocal group: Jack Hylton (left), Pat O'Malley (centre), Billy Munn (right) (Billy Munn)
Centre: Jack Hylton Band and Liverpool footballers (Billy Munn)
Bottom: Rosemary Squires (right) and Gracie Fields (Rosemary Squires)

Above: Kenny Baker Swing Group (Charlie Short, bass; Jack Parnell, drums; Norman Stenfalt, piano; Dave Goldberg, guitar; Kenny Baker, Harry Roche, Reg Owen, Johnny Gray) (Kenny Baker)
Below: Ted Heath trombone section (left to right) Keith Christie, Wally Smith, Don Lusher, Jimmy Coombs; (trumpets at back) Bobby Pratt, Eddie Blair (Don Lusher)

Dennis Lotis (BBC Photograph Library)

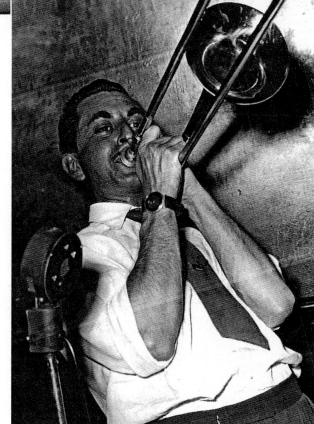

Above: Syd Lawrence Orchestra
(Freddy Staff second from left
trumpets; Chris Dean on right,
and Andy Smith on left,
trombones) (Freddy Staff)
Below: Vic Lewis
(George W Harrison)

Above: Larry Gretton, Rose Brennan and Ross McManus (Ross McManus)
Below: Oscar Rabin Band ENSA tour (Ken MacIntosh, standing front left; Oscar Rabin, Diane Rabin, Terry Devon, Harry Davis, middle row, centre)(Diane Rabin)

Above: Ken Mackintosh Orchestra (Ken Mackintosh)
Below: Harry Davis, Oscar Rabin and Ted Heath (Diane Rabin)

Top: Harry Roy Band and Janet Webb (Freddy Staff, trumpet second from right) (Freddy Staff)
Centre: Oscar Rabin Band (Bob Dale, Eddie Palmer, Diane, Harry Davis, Oscar Rabin, Beryl Davis, front row) (Diane Rabin)
Bottom: Harry Roy en route to South America (Stanley Black third from right front row) (Stanley Black)

Town Hall sitting next to Dickie and Lita, and the following Sunday I was at the Palladium – unbelievable. Dying of fright of course. I was on the stage where Sinatra had stood, all the greats – incredible. And that was how it started. Dickie was absolutely wonderful. Rena, my wife, came over just before Christmas and he said, 'Where the hell are you going to go for Christmas, what are you going to do?'

'I don't know Dickie, I guess we'll sit in my little bed-sit.'

'No you won't, you'll come to my house and we'll have Christmas together.'

You would have thought he would be reluctant to have another singer with the band but we shared rooms and he was a great friend. He was so dedicated to the theatre he could think of nothing else; what his next impression was going to be or his next joke. He was never one of the guys, as it were, but a lovely fellow for all that.

I sang the up-beat stuff; in fact I had quite a row with Ted one night. We did a six-month stint at the Savoy and I was in the Green Room playing the piano and singing 'Body and Soul' and he said, 'I don't want you singing those songs.'

'You hired me as a ballad singer and I'm singing all this crap like 'Feet Up Pat Him on the Bo Bo'.'

'Yes, you'll sing what I tell you to sing.'

'Well you can stick your job up your arse.'

I told Rena what I'd done and she said, 'You stupid fool, call him up and tell him you were talking tripe.' So I did and he said, 'Well I didn't think you were serious about it anyway.' He was very good Ted, I mean he lent me the money to bring Rena over; he was a good guy, I liked him very much.

The guys in the band were wonderful and I was very friendly with Wally Smith, he was such a funny guy, and Duncan Campbell. The things they used to get up to after the show I cannot tell you! Johnny Hawksworth was a pain in the arse quite frankly because he was always going over the top. He was a terrible extrovert, he should never have been a bass player, he should have been a featured artist. One day in Swansea he was standing in the middle of the square on a soap box spouting Marxism. Ted, who was with Les Gilbert, dragged him off saying, 'Get off, if you don't stop that nonsense you're fired.' They were great days!

The fans in those days screamed their heads off. They never danced, just stood around the stand gaping at us. We were in Reading

Town Hall and I was singing 'I'm in the Mood for Love' and they got me by my ankles and pulled me off the stage. It was like a tug of war as they were pulling me one way and Ted with his arms around my waist was pulling me onto the stand. They took my bow tie and my handkerchief, my shoes and socks, and I had to climb back onto the stage barefooted. They eventually threw my shoes up to me but kept the socks! I sometimes left the stage as Ted said I ought to do something really daring, like go and kiss the girls. Well one night at Wimbledon I went down off the stage and, oh my God, they tore my shirt to pieces! That sort of thing used to happen in Birmingham a lot and one night Dickie, Lita and I had to be driven back to the hotel by police because they would have broken the doors down. It was unbelievable.

The guys were all in love with Lita and they used to think Lita and I were a couple. The band all knew, of course, that Lita and Ronnie went out together. Ronnie and I had fisticuffs once, God knows why, I think it may have been about Lita. They were having a fight and I separated them and she scratched his face and he turned on me and said 'What do you think you're doing?' and wham! We had hardly any rows among that lot and you know how close you are in a band.

I was on the road with the band for four and a half years and I made a film with them, *It's A Wonderful World* and there was a French girl in it who all the boys thought I was having it off with – absolute nonsense of course!

I went back for the band's last American tour and Carnegie Hall was incredible. I had a twenty-minute spot of my own, singing what I wanted to do, so it was as if I was a featured guest artist. Everywhere the band went they got a wonderful reception.

DUNCAN CAMPBELL *Trumpet 1951–69*

I went in the band originally on third trumpet but Johnny Keating, who did most of the arrangements, would always put our names on the parts so that one minute you'd be playing lead trumpet and the next you wouldn't. It was a wonderful way to do it as it always sounded fresh. Not many arrangers did that. When we did the Palladium Swing Sessions it had to be new material every time and Ted would ring up and ask me if I had any ideas. Once I said, 'I've got nothing,' and he put that in the programme, Duncan Campbell . . . Nothing!

I did comedy vocals with Tommy Sampson and with Cyril Stapleton so when I went with Ted I think I started screaming something in one number and he said I was to do something in the show, and it went on from there. Hawksworth and I used to get away with murder!

We were in Newcastle and I didn't realise the top of the organ, which sank down below the stage, was glass and I stepped on it and went right through up to my neck. I carried on singing and everyone thought it was part of the act! People in Newcastle always remember that!

We played Bingley Hall in Birmingham for a big exhibition the whole week. A lot of families would come in so Ted couldn't play jazz all the time, and we had to think up things to do. I would be behind the curtain at the back dressed in tails and Ted would say, 'Here he is, the mad professor.' One night I opened the curtain, slipped on the stairs, grabbed the mike, fell on the floor and did the number like that. Ted said he would give me a pound a night extra to do that every time! That was a lot of money then, but by the end of the week I was black and blue all over!

Every year we had a dinner meeting and Ted would hire a big suite in the Savoy Hotel. At the end of the meal he would ask if anyone had anything to say and he would be listening to everything because he knew the guys had had a few drinks and would talk. He wouldn't say much but he'd be taking it all down.

We were at the Beach Ballroom in Aberdeen and I'd just come off the stand and I saw these three lovely girls standing there and I said to Charlie Pressley whose band I'd played with, 'Charlie, who are those three lovely girls?' and he said 'They're my daughters.' I thought, 'Which one shall I pick?'

The following year we were playing for the Chelsea Arts Ball on New Year's Eve at the Albert Hall. Ted Heath was in the centre of the stage, on the left was Ivy Benson, and on the right was Sid Phillips, and when it came to midnight Ivy suggested all the girls should go and kiss the boys in the Ted Heath Band and June rushed up to me and said, 'You've played with my dad, Charlie Pressley.' I knew she was the girl I was going to marry, and later when I got the ring we went straight to the Albert Hall and put the ring on there – isn't that romantic? In Scotland the Glaswegians always hated the Aberdonians and you had to marry a Protestant Glaswegian from next door! I phoned my mother and told her I'd found the girl I'm going to marry and the first thing she said was, 'Is she English?'

'No, she's Scottish.'

'Where does she come from?'

'Aberdeen.'

'Bloody worse,' and she put the phone down!

When June was in the Isle of Man with Ivy I would fly over from Blackpool which we used to do with Ted Heath every year. It was a little Piper aircraft and it cost five pounds return. That was a lot of money and I just saw her for half an hour, gave her a kiss, and flew back. I had to do that in case I lost her!

I remember when we played Torquay and the Benson Band were there, the girls all invited us to a party and we went along and being mad about music we all took our records. It ended up with all the guys sitting around the record player listening to records, and do you know what the girls said? It went all round the business: the Ted Heath Band are all queers!

JOHNNY KEATING *Trombone 1952, arranger 1954–69*

Early in 1952 there was a general reshuffle of the Ted Heath trombone section and at that time I was lead trombone with the Squadronaires but none too happy musically. With no regard for practical things like eating and so on, I upped and left. As fate would have it, during my last broadcast with the band I played a trombone feature which was heard by Ted Heath and, bingo, I joined Ted's famous and wonderful brass section.

Exactly a year later I got the sack! The death note was pushed under the door saying he needed someone, with more experience. Don Lusher was that someone and who could argue with that? But it more or less put paid to my aspirations as a trombonist, because after working with all those excellent musicians, enjoying the fun and the fame and the infamous perks that went with it, nothing could top that, so I returned to my first love, arranging.

I liked Ted okay but as a trombonist he made me very nervous. He would stand over you, or worse just behind you, when you were playing, watching your positions. Very spooky.

I'd only done two scores for Ted at that time, 'Eloquence' featuring

Roy Willox and 'Henry 9th' for Henry McKenzie, but 18 months later Ted's arranger, Reg Owen, was seriously injured in a car smash. At that time I was about to become Geraldo's chief arranger, a big assignment in itself, when I got a panic phone call from the Heath office asking me to do two quick vocal arrangements for the band's weekly radio spot. I was rather apprehensive about the whole thing, but I thought to myself, you just say one word about my arranging and you can stuff it! But he liked them, asked me to become his arranger, and upped Geraldo's offer, so there I was back with my dear friends. But this time I was in charge of not only myself but every note the band played, in fact practically the entire Ted Heath book from that moment on. I think the idea of the two trumpet features for Bobby Pratt and Bert Ezzard started with 'Memories of You' followed by 'Bill'.

When Ted was laid low with his first major stroke, instead of his secretary paying me for the first two completed arrangements for a forthcoming *Tribute to Al Jolson* album, Ted demanded to examine the scores. His verdict was I hadn't given them the due care and attention he deemed necessary and had instead rushed them through in order to get the money. He paid for 'April Showers' but refused to accept 'Sonny Boy'. Both scores were without marks of expression and the like, not entirely unusual for me, being eternally late with delivery, and this probably influenced his decision.

Three months later I put myself in the dire position of having to do eight arrangements, five vocals and three instrumentals for a broadcast just 24 hours away. Copyist Denis Raye was with me the night I attempted the eight. When starting score number seven and realising there was no way of getting to number eight, I opened the filing cabinet and pulled out 'Sonny Boy', gambling on the long shot that Ted wouldn't remember, and told one amazed and very sceptical Denis to copy it. The ploy not only worked but more than that, Ted liked it so much he played it twice a night for months, for him a most unusual occurrence.

DON LUSHER *Trombone 1952–61*

I left Geraldo after a midday broadcast, went to Ted, and rehearsed ready to do a broadcast with them that night! After that I went back to Gerry's band and said, 'I don't like it, the tone of the band is all

133

different,' so they said, 'You'll get used to it,' and somebody said, 'Well, you're going to get a lot more money than us!'

I actually joined the band at East Ham Baths which was an ordinary dance date and it was a cultural shock to me as we couldn't get on the stand for minutes because there were so many people. It was so exciting, the sound of the band was fantastic. I played two features that night and we came off and had the same problem getting back on the stand again. The next week, which was my first full week, we were top of the bill at Finsbury Park Empire with a Sunday concert at either end. We also did a Luxembourg broadcast, a BBC broadcast and two sessions at Decca. We always got paid in cash, and when I took this home, a lump came to my throat as I said to my wife Eileen, 'Look!' It was incredible, a pile of white fivers! We'd worked solidly, but the money I couldn't believe.

Before he formed his band Ted was in peak form as a trombone player and so at the start he had a number of arrangements written where he played solos and joined in the section. This was before my time but I gather it worried him; with the responsibility of the band he didn't have the time to practise. He would stand on the side of the stage with his mouthpiece buzzing, but it wasn't enough and he decided to pack in playing. He would play 'How High the Moon' in unison with the trombones and fling his instrument around in the air, that sort of thing, but he was never a serious player after that. It didn't stop him coming up to us and saying, 'Don't do that'. He was very critical not only of the trombones but every member of the band, but encouraging as well. He would say, 'Nice, nice that'. You just didn't do it your own way because he had a way of doing things. You could go into that band as a first-class player but if he didn't particularly like what you were doing, he'd tell you.

In 1955 we went around the world to Australia and New Zealand, back within the month, and the next year the start of a succession of American coast to coast tours. We had some time off in New York and went to Nola Studios on Broadway and there were three bands rehearsing: Basie's band just back from vacation, Woody Herman's band on the other side, and in the middle Ted Heath. We all had coffee and talked about money, and I think the Herman Band had the pin because we were getting more than they were!

We saw that the Dorsey Brothers were at the Statler Hotel so we said we were musicians from England and the head waiter came up and got us in. I expected a rather elderly trombone player-bandleader who would be off the stand as much as he was on and whispered the occasional solo. Wrong! Tommy was about six foot six, brimming with health, a silver crew-cut, he played all the solos, played all the lead, conducted like a military bandmaster, and the band was sensational. In the break Tommy and the band came over and chatted to us. Ronnie Chamberlain and I went on four nights to hear them, we were so hooked. We sat right in front of them and you could carry on a conversation, and one night they just plonked a microphone in the centre of the band and did a 'live' broadcast. Tommy Dorsey played 'Getting Sentimental' and when he got to the middle eight the NBC announcer started to introduce the band and Tommy didn't even step back from the mike, he just played that middle *subito pianissimo* until it was over and then he went up to *mezzo forte* again.

When we played Carnegie Hall, we were all extremely nervous because we knew that in the audience there were people like Benny Goodman, Gerry Mulligan and many more. If you listen to the recording which has now been reissued on a CD, you can hear the band is so tight it's incredible. I played 'The Carioca' and Ted set it off faster than ever before! The band went down so well, and the ovation at the end! We just stood there and Ted had tears running down his cheeks.

Ted kept tabs on us all the time. Sometimes on a dance date, the band would be a bit tired and there might be a few too many laughs and just for an instant get a little bit ragged, and he'd turn around to the fellas and say out the side of his mouth, 'Come along, come along, play properly, play properly' and that was it, no yelling and screaming. When we were recording at Decca we all used to go up and listen in the control booth and they'd play it back too loud and Ted would say, 'Nobody listens like that, think of the car radios.' Then he'd say, 'Can't hear the tune, where's the beat?' He'd have the score there and say 'Take that out, that figure clutters things up.' It was all absolute common sense.

I remember once or twice when we were recording the hits and the arranger would bring them in to Decca, we'd play them through and the band would go a into a quiet sulk.

'What's the matter, what's the matter?'

'Ted this is terrible.'

'This'll be a hit,' and it was!

He seemed to know what to play, what not to play, who to have in the band, who to hire, who to fire, and people did get fired, mostly to make way for someone else to come in. In Nottingham you had Ken Mackintosh with a fantastic band and Oscar Rabin had good players and Ted would be listening to those bands and out would come the old envelope or the paper and he'd make a note of who he wanted in his band. That sort of thing used to happen so you could be asked to leave to make way for someone else.

Ted was very good to me, he guided me on all sorts of things. He gave me a ticking off when I went out front, for looking too tense; he said, 'Let the shoulders go, you're in command.' He was right. He said to me in the car one night, 'Have you ever thought of being a bandleader?'

'Not really.'

'Wouldn't you like to be?'

'Yes, it would be marvellous.'

'I reckon we could fix that with you one of these days.'

I could pick the band but no one from his band, he would finance it completely, pay me a wage, and I would take the band on the road. He got me a short-term contract with Decca under Don Lusher and we recorded a couple of singles which never got anywhere but he said we'd persevere because he felt we could do something good. Eighteen months later the band manager said Ted wanted to see me in his dressing-room. He sat there in his underpants as he'd never sit in his stage clothes. 'I'm sorry to have to tell you we're going to have to shelve the idea of your band. I'm now struggling with this band; things have changed, the groups are here and it's not going to happen, I'm sorry.' And that was that.

You could do any studio work as long as it didn't interfere with Ted, and as I was doing very well I thought it was time to try to get in the studios full time. Jack Parnell's band was making a great deal of money at Elstree with big American shows, and also, of course, it was like a Ted Heath old boys' band, so I decided to go. The decision taken, I had to go through this outer office, the inner office and then eventually to Ted, and I thought gosh, I wish I wasn't doing this! When I told him I wanted to leave he said, 'You can't do that. Where are you going?'

'Jack Parnell's television band.'

'You won't leave, that sort of work will drive you crazy.'

Once I'd given in my notice, he didn't speak until I left, and furthermore the next date we did was at Sandown racecourse. I used to play a feature about two numbers in and when I started to stand up to get ready to go out to the front, he cut it out and went on to the next number. I didn't play a note that afternoon! But my time with Ted was a fantastic experience.

In the mid '70s Thames Television and Moira Heath asked me to front the band for a documentary on Ted Heath, and afterwards we were asked to do concerts, and I've been fronting the Heath Band ever since as well as my own band. Ted Heath taught me all I know, and not just about playing the trombone. If I have a position these days as a part-time bandleader it's all due to him.

RONNIE VERRELL *Drums 1952–67*

I got this call to go for an audition with Ted Heath as Jack Parnell was leaving. I went along to Hammersmith Palais where they were rehearsing for a broadcast that night. I had to sit on Jack's drums; he's a tall man as you know, and I could hardly reach the pedals. I saw Ted standing over me and I was so nervous, I can't tell you. They put this fast number in front of me and I read it okay. Anyway the verdict was – I don't know whether I heard it through Jack or somebody else – that I wouldn't get the job because 'he plays okay but he's got no personality'. That was it. I was totally destroyed, but at least I had my job with Claude Giddings at Gillingham.

Then I got this offer from Cyril Stapleton and went on the road with him for about three years and that gave me the confidence playing in front of large audiences doing drum solos. I thought, if Ted could see me now.

Anyway, in my third year Jack was ill and Ted Heath wanted me to do this *Sunday Night at the London Palladium*. We went through the rehearsal and Sammy Stokes, bless his heart, said he'd go over anything I wasn't sure of in the break before the show. That night I really gave it one because I was with Cyril Stapleton anyway and I couldn't have cared less. I did a drum feature and got tremendous applause so I got offered the job. The only snag was I was under contract to Cyril and if I wanted to leave I would have to give three months' notice. Ted said that would be all right, I was to give my notice in tomorrow and join them in three months' so I signed a contract there and then. I handed in my notice to Cyril and meanwhile Ted got Basil Kirchin to fill in until I joined. Basil became very popular with the band because he was very 'lairy' and when Ted would bollock him for something he would say to Ted, 'You're only getting at me 'cause I'm a Jew' and that would make the boys laugh! Things like that, and it was awful the way he got the sack. The band boy said in the coach one night, 'Oh, by the way, you're leaving next week, you're sacked 'cause Ronnie Verrell's joining.' I heard about this and knew he was popular so I phoned up Ted and said, 'Keep Basil on, I've seen him with the band and he's great. He's very popular with the guys and he's swinging the band along. I'll stay with Cyril.' And he said, 'You will honour your contract.'

One or two of the guys in the band gave me a hard time when I first joined. Things like, 'Oh he doesn't swing like Basil' said loud enough for me to hear. It was hard enough anyway playing with the Ted Heath Band and it was nothing to do with me the way Basil was treated. But after a while I did a number called 'Viva Verrell' with the drums down the front and it really brought the house down, and after that I had fifteen happy years.

What a band that Ted Heath band was. There'll never be another Bobby Pratt, he was a drummer's delight; he would phrase along with you. Dickie Valentine, Dennis Lotis, the glamorous Lita Roza – fantastic. It was full houses everywhere. I used to read in the papers such-and-such a band at so-and-so Empire with guests so and so. Ted Heath never had guests and we were always sold out. That's how good it was. I remember thinking I never wanted it to end.

We were the first British band to play in America and after three weeks on the road our last night was Carnegie Hall. People like Sonny Payne and Basie were sitting there and everybody was nervous. I didn't drink in those days, never touched it, but I said to Bobby Pratt, who always had some scotch handy, 'Bob could I have a swig of your scotch?' I had a large mouthful and we went on and I couldn't stop the palms of my hands from sweating with fear. The first number was 'King's Cross Climax' which started with a fast drum solo. It was as if my hands were greasy and I had to hold the sticks tight so they wouldn't slip out of my hands. I had to do it stiffly but I got through it and there was tremendous applause so I started to relax. As the evening went on I felt more and more relaxed as the band was going down so well. By the time we got to the last number, which I think was a drum feature, I really gave it one and brought the house down. We got a standing ovation for three or four minutes. When I looked at Ted after it was all over I had tears in my eyes for him. 'You did it Ted, wonderful.'

'Oh thank you very much, you all played very well.'

I wanted to cuddle him but he wasn't the sort of man you could do that to, he kept himself distant from the band.

He was one of those fellows who would never rant and rave, he would just come out with something subtle which would put you right through the floor. You wanted to be swallowed in a big hole in the ground. I'll give you an example. Duncan Campbell was playing this sweet solo at the Palladium and he did a couple of little fluffs and Ted, still smiling at the audience, sidled up to him and said, 'Shall I mind your boxing gloves for you?' and just went away and Duncan went as red as a beetroot. He's red anyway! And if Ted called you 'mate', 'listen mate', that meant up the office next Monday for a really good dressing down. But he did it all quietly and subtly and everybody respected him. He was the greatest ever, Ted Heath. There'll never be another or a band like that.

When I was playing in the band at Gillingham Pavilion we had a trumpet player come down called Denis Rose who we all idolised because he was the original bebop player, and he asked me if there were any bookies around. He wrote me out three horses and told me to back them on three doubles and a treble. 'I don't gamble,' I said. 'Do it, do it,' he said. He was such an idol to me I spent eight shillings and won three weeks' wages and that hooked me on gambling. The next day he showed me how to read racing form and it developed from there. I started playing cards when I was on tour with Cyril Stapleton and the Ted Heath Band. At night coming back in the coach we'd pack some suitcases in the aisle, put blankets on them, and play poker for money, all night. I was hooked on it and I had an account with a bookmaker and it was gambling, gambling, on everything. I became very anti-social. When the other guys were socialising I would be sitting in a corner reading the racing form. I missed a lot of things in my youth.

One day I was taken to the Sportsman Casino in Tottenham Court Road by Derek Watkins and Terry Jenkins for dinner with my second wife. After the meal they suggested we look at the tables so I agreed and thought it was fabulous and signed up as a member. I went on the roulette wheel and of course for the first three or four visits, same as the horses, I was carrying £600 cash around with me that I'd won in four visits betting in sums of ten shillings. I thought Hollywood here I come, but of course eventually I was blowing money night after night. I won't go into figures but it got so bad that Vic Flick the guitar player saw me on a recording session one morning, and bless him he saved my life. I'd been to two casinos the night before because cheques ran out at one, you're only allowed so many; I went to another, blew three more cheques, got to bed at five and I was on at ten. I looked like death. I felt suicidal at the time and I told Vic. He disappeared, came back and said, 'Right here's a phone number, phone them right now, right now or I'll kick your backside for you.' So I phoned them and they said, 'We'll see you tonight Ronnie.' Gamblers Anonymous, group therapy.

I thought I was the only one doing it and I was going mad but there were people there, anything from barrow boys to barristers with their bums hanging out their trousers, blown three houses, blown businesses, you name it. One of them said to me, 'You've got the same look I had when I came here eleven years ago. Look I've got eleven stars now which means eleven years without touching gambling. I'm going to pray for you tonight Ronnie, stick with it.' I didn't have another bet for months and months. I did break out again and I still gamble, but I've got it under control now because I think of those days when I was blowing all my money. I blew a fortune – you wouldn't believe it. I was earning fabulous money but it was going straight onto the tables. They say the more you get the more you want and I thought the money would be endless. There's always tomorrow when I'll earn this and get it back. Wrong! I advise everybody, don't start, don't start gambling because it can get hold of you like cigarettes.

KEN KIDDIER *Baritone saxophone 1955–69*

I got the job because George Hunter didn't want to go on the Australian trip. Maybe he had a premonition because on the way out we had engine trouble and had to spend two days in Karachi while they changed engines. Never mind, good place to get a curry, or so we thought. They fed us on roast beef, Yorkshire pudding and roast potatoes for two days. We never saw a curry!

We eventually get airborne again and we hit this colossal thunderstorm as we're coming in to land at Darwin. The steward sort of floats up to the ceiling, all the guys have got their heads in sick bags, everything's falling out of the overhead lockers, and Ronnie Verrell cuts his hand on an ashtray. We get through it and Colin Hogg, the band manager, comes along and sees an empty seat. 'Who's missing?' And at that moment a dazed, green-faced Danny Moss emerges from the toilet where his head had hit the ceiling. 'What happened?'!

Darwin was a very primitive airfield and we had to walk through what looked like the Everglades to reach these sort of wooden chalets on legs where we were meant to be staying when some guy shouts, 'Single file please.' 'Why?' 'Snakes.' You've never seen musicians move so quickly! That was our introduction to Australia!

RONNIE CHAMBERLAIN *Alto saxophone 1956–66*

There were a lot of soprano sax solos as Ted liked the sound of the soprano sax and I would catch him out of the corner of my eye looking at me as I struggled with all these solos. Anyway, a few months went by and after the American tour he came up to me one day and said, 'Well mate, are you happy?'

'Yes, I am.'

'So am I.'

That was it, I'd been accepted! I was there for ten years and we became very good friends. He used to like to travel with me in the car when we were doing one-night stands.

We had a lot of fun in America, and when Don Lusher and I had been down to the Statler for a few nights, Tommy and Jimmy called us over and Jimmy went and got his alto saying he wanted me to try it, so I blew his alto. Charlie Shavers, who was in the band, said he wanted us to go down to Basin Street, which was a jazz club, to hear Clifford Brown who was the rage at the time. He said he'd wait for us outside. Well Tommy and Jimmy started talking to us and they kept us there an hour, but when we went out Charlie was still waiting for us. What a wonderful man.

We were staying in some hotel in New York and it was horrible, so the Dorsey band said, 'You don't want to stay there, come and stay in our hotel, the President.' We moved in there and it was great. When we were going on the road and we had all this shopping we'd got in New York, they said, 'Oh don't worry just leave it all in our rooms,' and we did!

That first trip we went out on the *Queen Mary*, and although we were in cabin class we were given the privilege of using the first-class facilities on the proviso that we gave a concert in what they called 'The Pig', which was right down the bottom of the ship. Unfortunately there were a few of the guys in the band who suffered very badly from sea-sickness. In fact there was only one section left in the dining-room and that was the saxophone section! We felt very proud of ourselves. They had to give Bobby Pratt injections so he could play. I don't think the *Mary* was stabilised and it was quite awkward playing, but we did it. We had to do the same thing on the way back on the *Queen Elizabeth*.

We went on the road with Nat King Cole and he was attacked. It was horrible. We were booked to play in Birmingham, Alabama, and the guys in his trio were absolutely scared stiff saying, 'We don't want to go there man.' We did our show first and when Nat came on they insisted that the curtain was drawn in front of us so they couldn't see the white band accompanying this 'nigger' singer as they called him. That's how they talked down there, 'Are you with this nigger group?' We couldn't believe it. Leigh Young, Lester Young's brother, was the drummer with Nat and he was the MD and of course we couldn't see him through this curtain. It was absolute chaos and we just had to stop. In the end they relented and pulled back the curtain and big applause went up from the audience. Then there was a commotion and a guy came running down the aisle, jumped onto the stage and was on top of Nat and got him on the floor. The concert stopped immediately and we all went off. I felt really sick and went outside and puked, it frightened me so much. Poor Nat was in a terrible state and the audience were just as shocked as we were. In those days they had segregation with the whites one side, and the blacks the other side but the whole audience were as one, and afterwards someone stood up and apologised for the terrible behaviour to Nat and the band.

Bobby Pratt would never do a session without a bottle of scotch and when we were in America some of the states were dry and he would panic. We would have to stop so he could buy his booze before we got there. On the Decca sessions he always had this brown paper bag with the bottle. He said he couldn't play without it. After Ted died and Ralph Dollimore was fronting the band, we did a show with either Tom Jones or Humperdinck, and Gordon Mills who was their manager said, 'Get that man off, I don't want that man on stage.' Bobby came into the band room and said 'What's happening? Why doesn't anyone want me to play?' He felt he was being rejected. Of course it went to his liver and the pain got too much for him. Stan Reynolds went to pick him up one day, banged on the door, and could smell gas. He managed to get in and found Bobby with his head in the gas oven. He pulled him out and revived him but two or three days later he did it again and that was it. I think it was the pain and the fact that he couldn't play the way he used to play.

I took over the lead alto chair in about 1960 and I suggested Dennis Walton for second alto to Ted. We both had similar figures! I liked his playing and we both seemed to think the same way and so Dennis came with the band and was there until Ted died.

BOB EFFORD *Tenor saxophone 1958–69*

Ted was just the nicest guy; I never had any problems with him. I remember after I'd been with the band just a few weeks he asked me where I was living and I told him some apartment or other and he said, 'Wouldn't you like a home?'

'Well of course I'd like a home but I can't get the down payment together.'

'Go get one, I'll lend you the money.'

That just got me on the track straight away. I never knew whether he took it out of my wages or not because when I joined his band we talked about all kinds of things at the initial interview, and when I mentioned money he said, 'We don't like to talk about that. Trust me, you'll be better off than you've ever been in your life,' and I believed him. I went home and my wife said, 'Well how much are you going to get?'

'I don't know.'

'What do you mean you don't know?'

It really was ridiculous but it was true. At the end of the week he would come with these plain white envelopes and when you opened it up, there was always far more money than you had any reason to expect, so when he said he would take the loan out of my money, how would I know? It never seemed to be any less and if he was taking it then everybody else must have been earning a great deal because I still had these nice fat pay envelopes.

That just turned my life around and anybody who can do that for you, how can you possibly say anything bad about them? It was family, he treated his band like family. Rather like children, he was very patriarchal in that sense. He would throw Christmas parties and there would be no booze and you would play children's games like Stick the Tail on the Donkey! That'll give you a clue as to his way of thinking towards his band! It was just delightful, he was such a sweet man, and Moira too, such a nice lady.

I was on Ted's last American tour and I stopped the show at Carnegie Hall! I had a feature called 'Exactly Like You'. I wanted to do something I'd written myself that was based on 'Exactly Like You' but Ted wouldn't buy that. So I played the tune and I thought it sounded a little bit trite going out in front of thousands of people in New York and going da, da, da, da, da da . . . it seemed pretty dumb to me but anyway I did it, and of course after I got through the first chorus I could take off and start to blow. I don't know if I was as good as they thought I was or whether they were just amazed that some little English guy could come out and swing, but it got the job done anyway and actually stopped the show. I got a standing ovation and the show ground to a halt for a while. Very flattering. I owned New York for one night. Symphony Sid talked about me on the radio and the town was mine! I always remember Johnny Hawksworth saying to me, 'You should capitalise on that, go around some agents in the morning.' 'I've just joined the band, I can't do that.' It just shows what an English approach I had in those days. I'm sure John was right because you do only have New York for one night and if you don't do something about it, the night after they say 'Who?' It was a magic moment, it was really something.

That was a very nice period of my life and of course I never left Ted, he just died and that was that. I hung around in Britain for about ten years but I always had eyes to come to the States particularly as we had come here with Ted's band. Once I got everything straightened out to come over here, that's what I did.

JACK HYLTON

1892–65

Theme 'Oh, Listen to the Band'

Jack Hylton, at 5ft 3in, may have looked insignificant but he was anything but in the world of show business, a force to be reckoned with from the time he transcribed his first Paul Whiteman record to discovering or promoting such star entertainers as the Crazy Gang, Arthur Askey, Julie Andrews and Shirley Bassey.

He was relief pianist with the Queen's Hall Roof Orchestra when Paul Whiteman's recording of 'Ilo', the very first 'orchestrated' jazz that had been heard in Britain, arrived from America. It was to prove a turning point in his career. He copied the orchestration, made his first records with the Queen's Hall Orchestra, and was rewarded with 'Directed by Jack Hylton' on the record labels. In 1924 he formed his first touring band and in 1929 was the top attraction at theatres all over the country, travelling over 60,000 miles, giving 700 performances and selling in excess of three million records. He was much in demand on the continent and was paid £1,700 to play at a party given by the French car manufacturer Citroën who threw in a new car for good measure. Between 1927 and 1938 the Jack Hylton Band did 16 European tours and in 1930 visited ten different countries in as many weeks. In 1933 he was well qualified to promote and sponsor Duke Ellington's European tour.

Jack Hylton made his BBC debut from Savoy Hill in 1926 and was

145

the first band to broadcast to America in 1931, soon to become a well known name there fronting American bands rather than his own, due to union opposition. The outbreak of World War Two saw the end of the Jack Hylton Band but not the end of Jack Hylton who was now set to become one of the country's most powerful impresarios, not only in the theatre but in radio and the new medium of television. He employed some 500 people, worked an 18-hour day, seven days a week, and expected others to do likewise. The lad from Bolton liked fast cars, fast planes and women, and lived life at a hectic pace until the day he died.

BILLY MUNN *Piano 1929–36*

I came down to London in the autumn of 1929 and worked for a short while at the Café de Paris and went from there to the Hotel Cecil, which is now Shell Mex House. I then did an audition for Jack Hylton who was a big name and I was very frightened. In fact I'd had a letter of introduction to him before that and went to the stage door in Glasgow to meet him. When he came out I was so nervous I couldn't talk to him and I went away without speaking to him! But that was a year earlier and my greatest ambition was to join that band because it was *the* greatest band of its time, certainly in Europe.

I did the audition, got the job, and joined the band at Glasgow Empire. There were headlines in the paper: 'Local Boy Makes Good'. I was only 18 and all the band were my heroes. I suppose I got the job because I was handy, presumably cheap, that would have registered, and I wasn't bad-looking. Hylton had quite a good looking band by the way. The band always looked very nice and there was no one in the band you could call ugly. Dave Shand was a beautiful fellow.

Jack Jackson had just left and Bill Ternent was on second trumpet and he could play every instrument in the band. Whenever a man left, Bill would take over that chair until they got a replacement. Magnificent musician. These days with multi recording he could do a whole orchestra himself. He was there all the time I was with the band and he was chief arranger too. My other heroes were Poggy Pogson and Joe Crossman who joined the band a week before me, and Phillip Braun from France, who joined the band the week after me. They were my pals.

We were carrying five saxophones at the time as Joe had just joined and Joe had taken Pogson's book which I thought was tragic as Pogson was a better lead saxophone player than Joe would ever be. Poggy didn't like that very much. Johnny Raitz was on tenor saxophone but Johnny wasn't a jazz player. The trombones were Leo Vauchant and Lew Davis, and as Lew had been the only trombone player until Leo joined, he put Lew's nose right out of joint. The funny thing is that Lew did exactly the same thing to Ted Heath in the Ambrose Band. Lew became lead trombone in the Ambrose Band when he left Hylton and that put Ted Heath's nose out of joint! Ted Heath had a row with Ambrose, partly over that, and joined Sidney Lipton. Leo Vauchant's real name was Arnaud and he went to America when he left Hylton and later became chief arranger for Fred Waring's Pennsylvanians. Then he went to Hollywood and he arranged some of the great musicals; you often see his name on the credits. He was the best arranger I ever worked with; he was a pupil of Ravel – what more do you want? He played cello and trombone.

We had a whole team of arrangers, Bill Ternent, Peter York, Paul Fenoulhet, Phil Cardew, who was an outsider – he came in the band for a time – then there was Melle Weersma, a wonderful Dutch arranger who came along later. All Bill Ternent's arrangements were dead simple and dead routine; Peter York's were very academic, dead correct but no great thought behind them; I used to do some arranging and often wrote the last jazz chorus for Bill. The record of 'China Town' is my arrangement. All the arrangers, like Peter York, who was the second piano at that time, could conduct their own arrangements, deal with the fine points, correct any wrong notes and then let Jack do what he wanted with it. Billy could do it and Phil Cardew wasn't even in the band so he could do it, but Leo couldn't because he had to play his trombone all the time. He hated having to sit there hearing some of his best ideas being massacred. That's one of the reasons he left the band. Hylton held his work permit from France and put out an injunction against him working for anyone else, so that's why he went to America.

Sam Browne was the vocalist and he left about six months after I joined, and then O'Malley came in and he was with the band until the break-up. You know you can hear Sam Browne every week on the radio? He's on that 'Breakaway' signature tune on Radio 4 on Saturday mornings. That's the Jack Hylton Band and Leo Vauchant did the arrangement. They recorded it about a month before I joined and

Peter York is on piano. We used to play that on stage. Sam Browne couldn't read music but before a gramophone session recording all those songs, all new to him, he would say, 'Billy, play this for me,' and I played through the song on the piano once and he knew it, well enough to record it. That's not bad is it? Wonderful – that's a real natural musical gift.

We only used one 'mike' in those days by the way and Sam stood next to Jack and the 'mike', and I can't remember what the number was but one of the guys kept splitting notes so they had to stop the wax and start again, and those waxes were quite expensive. After this had happened three times, Jack turned around in a fury and kicked Sam up the behind and Sam had done nothing! Just because he was there, Jack kicked him! I was told that every time we stopped it cost a fiver for a new wax and that was a lot of money then. That made me terribly nervous. My first solo with the band was on my first recording session, a Phil Cardew arrangement of 'Hang on to Me'. I remember thinking of a nice solo to play, like Arthur Schutt would play it, the American pianist who was my hero. But I eventually played something that was more reminiscent of Fred Elizalde; jazz for a beginner! That was purely nerves. Terrifying.

On a session we'd rehearse and then go for a test which was played back to us. Now when they played back that test that ruined it, the needle cut the groove completely. You could only play it once and some of our best performances were on tests and couldn't be repeated. They would say that's fine and then we made the actual record and we made a minimum of three. We always did a minimum of three takes in case anything went wrong in the processing. I've got some alternate takes in my collection that weren't issued. They're quite interesting.

We were on 'all-in' salaries which included everything. We got nothing extra for recording sessions, that was all included. My weekly wage when I started was eighteen pounds, six times what my father was making, and I was only 18! My second year I got twenty and the third year was twenty-five, and so on.

I enjoyed touring, I loved all the continental bit. We were treated like the Beatles were you know. I remember we were doing a concert in Amsterdam and Phil Cardew had come into the band on saxophone. Harry Robins, Bill Ternent, Pogson and I were in a taxi and as we approached the theatre all these people were milling around trying to get into the theatre and Pogson says, 'What's wrong with them going on the road?' So he jumps out of the taxi holding his beloved oboe and cor anglais in a case and walks straight into the canal. It was smooth and shiny and he thought it was the road! We hoisted him out still holding his oboe and cor anglais and had to strip him off. Phil Cardew lent him his dress suit and Cardew played offstage in his underwear!

We were doing stage shows and concerts and we never used music – never. We were the only band who did that. We could do a show and concert tour without a note of music, all from memory. You'll notice that on pictures of the Hylton Band there are no music stands. When I joined the band that night at Glasgow Empire I was allowed the music for one night but it was on the floor and I was looking down at it. Playing dance band piano you don't need a terrific memory. We'd rehearse a lot and if we had a new number we'd go through it and through it until the slowest man in the band knew it backwards. The boys playing third and second trumpet on concert arrangements would have their orchestrations copied on to those band cards Boosey and Hawkes used to use and they would stick them inside the bowler hats. The bass and sousaphone player Clem Lawton had a bad memory and he used to copy the bits he couldn't remember on to matchboxes and hold them in his hand! Would you believe that?

I'll tell you a story about Clem Lawton. We did one of these so-called bloody comedy numbers with thousands of verses, 'He Played His Ukelele as the Ship Went Down' and we had a set on stage of an old-fashioned sailing ship and we had three-cornered hats. We did these speciality numbers all the time on the stage. That was the great thing about the Hylton Band. There was a storm and the drummer at the back would get sick and the thunder roared and the lightning struck and then everything would go quiet and we played behind Clem's sousaphone solo very quietly. He gets towards the end where he takes big breaths and we'd all take breaths with him, and he came to his penultimate note and Bishop, one of the drummers – we were carrying three drummers at the time, one playing tympani, one playing xylophone and one playing drums – stood up with a pair of bellows to pretend to give Clem air from the bellows for the last note. Mike, one of the other drummers, whispers to me, 'Hey Bill I've filled the bellows with flour,' and at that this great cloud of flour came out and Clem looked like the Abominable Snowman! Hylton was doing his nut, 'Who did that?'

We always had two pianos; it was the fashion, and the other piano player Freddy Bamberger was a great practical joker. You know the spike on a bass? Well while Clem was playing his sousaphone, Freddy undid the spike and pulled it out as far as it would go. When Clem comes to make a sudden quick change to string bass, he couldn't reach it and he's standing on tip-toes. Hylton's saying, 'Who did that?' while he's conducting. Hylton forbade Freddy and I to room together because we were good pals and incapable of not doing a practical joke if one occurred to us. We used to undo the beds of the boys on tour. We'd go into their bedrooms and take the beds to bits and lay them out in nice rows on the floor and when they came in at night after the show, they had to put them together again! Then we'd put the cabin trunks against the door so in the morning when they opened the door there was nothing but a wall of trunks and they couldn't get out. True!

We'd do double shows, like Holborn and Penge Empire. We'd finish the first half of the first house at Holborn, dash like mad into a coach that was waiting for us and drive straight down through the London traffic – they were terrible journeys – and got there in time to finish the second half of the first house at Penge. Everything was waiting for us. There were duplicate instruments, and we were wearing our band jackets. We finished the second half at Penge, and would then do the first half of the second house and straight on the coach again and back to the Holborn Empire for the second half of the second house. We doubled the Kit Kat and Brighton Hippodrome. There were taxis waiting for us at the Hippodrome in Brighton to take us to the station. We'd get on the train and be back in London in time to play at the Kit Kat.

I'd played trumpet in Glasgow but thought I'd never make a professional trumpet player, but after seeing Louis Armstrong I would try to play all his solos, and one night at a party I picked up a trumpet and did this impression of Louis for the boys, with the handkerchief and the mannerisms, and Hylton saw this. One thing about Hylton was that if anyone could do a party trick of any kind, he'd put it in and he was doing a show with Eddie Polo, *America Calling*, which was going to be the second half of the forthcoming Palladium show. He had the Nicholas Brothers over for that by the way – marvellous, and we did the Mills Brothers and I did my Louis Armstrong number.

You know how a gauze works in the theatre, if you light it from behind it disappears, but if you light it from the front you can't see through it. So by jiggering the lights you can fade the gauze in and out.

Jack had the idea as a finish to the show and we tried it out at the newly opened Piccadilly Theatre in Denman Street. Amy Johnson had flown solo to Australia, and when she came back she was a terrific heroine, the number one girl of the century. Lawrie Wright – his pen-name was Horatio Nicholls – was a pal of Jack's and he wrote a number called 'Amy'. Jack would announce to the audience: 'And now a tribute to our grand Yorkshire lass Amy Johnson.' Pat O'Malley would come downstage to sing the second chorus of 'Amy' and then they would drop in the gauze which had Amy's route from Britain at the top right-hand corner to Australia in the top left-hand corner. Then the band disappeared and the audience could see the map. The band porter, Harry Fisher, dressed in black and carrying this long black pole with a lit-up aircraft at the top of it, would come on behind the gauze with this aeroplane on a stick following the line of the map. We could see everything from behind the gauze of course, and we were playing snippets of various tunes from the various countries this plane was meant to be crossing. Once it got to the other side of the map, full lights, the back tabs opened and there was Jack's valet, Henry Taylor, in flying gear and goggles in a cockpit, waving from behind the band. The front tabs would come down and that was the end of the show. A marvellous finish, really effective.

Until one day the gauze didn't come down. Harry Fisher didn't know it hadn't come down so he came on with this pole, which of course everybody could see, and he's wandering around the stage looking for the line of the map. Meantime the brass have disappeared offstage because they couldn't play for laughing. Hylton by this time was blue with anger and the language off stage to the people who worked the switches was picturesque! This was a new theatre and this was all new gear. Anyway, we finished the number, the back tabs opened, and there's Henry waving to puzzled silence because the audience were still stunned by this man in black. Hylton calls 'Tiger Rag', which was our stand-by number, and as we start playing, down comes the gauze with the map and the band disappear completely! Hylton nearly had apoplexy.

Jack was working at the Alhambra in Leicester Square; I think he did about 50 weeks there one year, an all-time record. Horatio Nicholls had written a number called 'While The Sahara Sleeps' and they hired a camel and a camel beater from the zoo. Marvellous, except the camel used to make the most awful windy noises! They had this camel at the back of the stage with a sphinx on the backcloth and in front of that was the back tabs, so when they lifted, there was the scene with the camel.

They had a split rostrum which was on castors so it could be drawn off the stage, half one side, half the other. The idea was, Pogson came out and played the oboe and Hylton wearing a fez did a snake dance. This was in front of the front tabs. While this is going on they moved the rostrum aside then opened the tabs, and there was the scene with the camel. The bass player put two legs of his chair on one half of the rostrum and two on the other and he's playing away and suddenly there's a terrific crash from behind the tabs and there is the camel and there was the driver and there was this bass player on the floor trying to disentangle himself from the sousaphone!

We wore dinner jackets and white waistcoats but that was because Jack wore a black waistcoat. We had lots of outfits. Light green slacks and green pullovers with green and white shoes. We had maroon jumpers with a silver J.H. on them and white slacks and black and white shoes. He sent us to Savile Row to get suits for the film *She Shall Have Music*. They were made by Anderson and Shepherd, famous tailors in Savile Row, and I could never have afforded a suit like that. They cost £80 and about eight was the most I ever paid for a suit. Jack engaged Brian Lawrence, an Australian fiddle player and singer, for the film which we made at Twickenham studios. Or maybe it was the director who hired him to play the juvenile lead opposite the American girl June Clyde. When Pat O'Malley got to hear about this he stormed out because he didn't want to know. After all, he was the singer with the band and the film was about the band singer. Shortly afterwards Pat rejoined Jack and went to America with him and stayed there. This was the end of 1935 and we all went to America as soon as we finished the film. Actually, the film was finished without us with extras doing our parts in the long shots.

The Standard Oil Company wanted the band in America, but when we got there Petrillo and the union stepped in. Jack thought if he got the band over there that would be a strong card, but we stood around in New York for twelve days doing nothing. It was wonderful because we went everywhere, but we couldn't work so he sent us back. The American Union was like the Mafia and Jack, of course, had blotted his copybook by trying at one time to bar American bands coming into this country, and they remembered that.

Jack stayed because he was broadcasting for Standard Oil with American musicians and he had a band in the Drake Hotel in Chicago and one in New York, so how could he look after us in London? When we got back to town, Frank Barnard, the manager, said Jack had got some dates lined up for us in London until he got back. But he put us on an eight-week suspension and he shouldn't have done that because we'd been working 52 weeks of the year for years. Frank asked me to take over the band until Jack got back but I said I didn't want to do that. I said to let Sonny Farrar do it, the banjo player who fancied himself as a personality boy, so he did it. Then Buddy Rogers came from America and conducted the band for a couple of weeks – Mary Pickford's husband, a good looking lad. When Sonny took over it was no good at all and then we split up and all of us went our various ways. I joined Lipton straight away, but some of the boys stayed around and went back with Jack again when he re-formed after he got back from America at the end of 1936.

There was nothing wrong with Jack, bad-tempered sometimes but long-suffering as far as I was concerned. He stood for a lot of rubbish from me, turning up late and that sort of thing. I was always late for a gramophone session in the morning and that's bad because that costs money. I was living in Gower Street and I would get a taxi to Chelsea Town Hall where we were recording. One day I was three quarters of an hour late and Jack never said a word to me. They were playing a number and he was playing piano and couldn't make head nor tail of it and he said 'Come on Bill sit down, you've saved my bacon,' and of course forgot all about me being late!

Jack was a womaniser, and how! Mrs Hylton, Ennis, was a charming woman. He gave her a band which Bill Ternent found for her and it was said the only reason he gave her the band was so he could guarantee never to be in the same town as her! They fought interminably and the main reason was Jack's womanising. He met this beautiful girl in Budapest, Fifi, and eventually married her and she became the mother of his son. Ennis was having it off with Ronnie Scott's father Joe, who was a lead alto player. Ennis was a nice person and I think she rather fancied me a little bit, although she was much older than me. I wasn't bad-looking in those days! She was coming to one of our concerts and she asked me to go with her to keep her company. I think it was somewhere like Great Yarmouth and we went through Colchester and I'm sitting with her in the car. I'd never made a pass at her because I'd never thought about it and as we came into this market square there was a shop straight in front of us with the name F. Lucking, and we both started laughing!

WOOLF PHILLIPS *Trombone 1937–39*

When I left Joe Loss I went to Bournemouth for the summer season playing at the Pavilion. I met a lot of people and had many girlfriends; it was all very nice. One particular day a member of Jack Hylton's band came in, a fellow called Sid Millward who was a lead alto, a very good saxophone player. This was before all the comic stuff. I didn't know him and then I got a letter saying that Jack Hylton wanted me to join his band immediately. There was some difficulty over that but I got out and I went over to Jack's office the next morning and went with him in his Rolls-Royce up to Birmingham where the band was playing. Then on rehearsal I played something and everybody got excited, which was nice. He'd asked me how much I'd been getting and said he would double it, and that was before he knew I was a cricketer! Jimmie Reynolds, a Canadian, a great trumpet player, was there. Bruce Campbell was one of the trombone players and Wilbur Hall, who was with Paul Whiteman for years. He used to do tricks and wear big boots, a comedian as well as a trombone player!

We were playing all the big theatres, we were doing the *Rinso Radio Revue*, broadcasting like mad and recording for HMV. We were very busy. Jack Hylton was wonderful to me because he thought I was a little genius, first of all as a trombone player and secondly as a cricketer. He would tell everybody, 'He plays cricket for me and he played for Lancashire!' There were some quite good cricketers in Jack Hylton's band. He'd heard about me because the first thing I did for Harry Roy when I was 15 was to play cricket. They played against Eton College and Sid had told Harry that his young brother could play and I got a lot of runs. I was captain of North Middlesex for quite some years and I played for all the counties in charity games on Sundays. I played with Dickie Attenborough when he was hit on the head which stopped him playing.

There were a couple of people in the Hylton Band who were very bad drinkers but generally it was a good band and nice people. I remember once we were in Brighton and there was an act called Buck and Bubbles, very famous black dancers; they were in that film *A Song Is Born* with Danny Kaye. I was in the Brighton Hippodrome one afternoon and I saw one of them and said, 'How are you liking it here?' He said 'All right man but I can't get no tea,' and I said, 'But there are tea shops all over,' and he said, 'No, *tea*,' meaning of course marijuana!

We did the very first television show from Alexandra Palace. We came straight from the Holborn Empire, they put some stuff on our faces, and we were on. The first real public television show. We had to wear blue shirts because you couldn't wear white in those days. Yes, Jack Hylton's band was on the very first day of television.

On the Friday before war broke out we were playing at the Palladium and that was the day Germany invaded Poland. The evening show was sold out and 30 people came so 200 people on the stage did the show for 30 people in the audience. On the Saturday the Palladium closed. On the Sunday morning we played for the Scottish London Territorials in Trafalgar Square in the morning, and on the Monday at nine o'clock in Tottenham Court Road I picked up 'Stinker' Murdoch and we drove to Shepherd's Bush to make the film *Bandwagon* which Jack Hylton's Band was in with Arthur Askey and Pat Kirkwood. After that we did various things and went to Bristol for all the BBC broadcasts. Then one day I got my papers and I was in the army.

PRIMROSE *Vocalist 1938–39*

Jack Hylton came into the Locarno in Glasgow one afternoon where I was singing, and he also came into a night club in Sauchiehall Street where I used to sing on a Friday night, and that's when he asked me to join his band.

My mother and father came because I was very young and within two weeks I was down in London and my first date was the Palladium! We had like a circus with horses and soldiers and guardsmen and everything. It was marvellous. There were a lot of girl vocalists, June Marlow, Peggy Dell, the Henderson Twins; oh he had a colossal number of girls in the show. My stage dresses were made by Colin Beck who was a very big name in those days.

After the Palladium we played all the Empires on the Mecca circuit. I think I only made one record with Jack Hylton, 'Jeepers Creepers'. Bruce Trent was in the band playing bass and singing and he was very nice.

Jack Hylton always had a marquee at Goodwood and we were walking past and there he was standing outside eating bread and marmalade and all his guests were inside having champagne and the lot! He was a real north country little man. He was a bit of a Romeo on the quiet and I think June Marlow was his girlfriend at the time. She later married Joe Davis the snooker player.

Jack Hylton was marvellous to me and I was with him until war broke out and then he disbanded.

SYD LAWRENCE

1923-

Theme 'Evening Serenade'

Syd Lawrence spent twenty years playing trumpet for other people before forming what started as a rehearsal band in 1967. Nobody could have anticipated the tremendous success that awaited the weekly gathering of musicians in a Manchester Hotel. The big bands were finished, the Beatles and the Rolling Stones reigned supreme, but then against all the odds, along came Syd Lawrence and His Orchestra.

SYD LAWRENCE

When Alyn Ainsworth left the NDO and went to London, pop was taking over, and slowly these lovely arrangements disappeared into the library and we were playing blown-up pop numbers. A pop number is okay in its own environment, a four-piece group with a twangy twangy thing is fine, but what's a big band going to do with it and who's going to listen to that? The kids aren't, because they're going to like the original version.

This bothered me, particularly when we found ourselves playing this stuff. We did this awful beat show every Monday night with an audience full of kids all waiting for the guest groups. They booked the Beatles before they were famous, but by the time the date came around they were up here and the police were everywhere!

I'm sitting on the bandstand one night and I thought, God Almighty, I wish we could play our own music we grew up with. Wait a minute, if I can't do it for a living I'll do it for fun, and the one thing I could do was provide the music. I picked on Glenn Miller because that name had kept cropping up, and when I thought of Glenn Miller I didn't think of 'In The Mood', I thought of all those beautiful slow arrangements that Bill Finegan did. I asked the corner men of the NDO, the lead trombone, the lead trumpet and the drummer and so forth, if they would be interested if I brought in some of the good semi-pros who'd never had a chance to play in sections. They recommended certain semi-pros, good players, so I got this band together in a pub in Didsbury and we played upstairs in what would be their private function room. I paid 30 shillings to hire the room. The musicians' wives started coming and then the wives' friends started coming and then the friends' friends started coming and people could hear the band in the street and were coming in and asking what it was all about. As the weeks went on the room was filling up until the landlord thought he'd better open the bar, and then suddenly the room is nowhere near big enough. So we had to leave and go to another place, much bigger, and that filled up. I still couldn't pay the guys union rate because we were only charging 2s 6d to get in.

Finally we went to the Mersey Hotel which has a huge ballroom, and then I get a phone call from a producer with Granada: 'I was at your concert last night and liked what I saw and heard and I'd like to do a programme for Granada.' The cameras came in to the Mersey Hotel and they made this fifty-minute programme, but we never heard any more about it.

Below the ballroom was another room where they would book a cabaret act to appear, and one week it was Les Dawson. I knew Les because I'd worked with him with the NDO and he popped up on the Tuesday night and listened to the band. We got him on the stage and he cracked a couple of gags for the audience and the place was heaving. A week later Les comes in on the Tuesday night with another gentleman, a producer from Yorkshire Television. Les was doing a series called *Says Les* and normally the orchestra wouldn't be seen on the screen but they decided to put our band on the screen and that was it. We were away on TV, and a few months later Granada phoned and said, 'Syd we haven't forgotten you but we were a bit restricted with shots and we'd you like to come in again and re-do some. You won't need to blow a note, all the guys need do is mime to the tape and we'll have a guy going around the back of the band with a camera on his shoulder.' That programme went out at eight o'clock on a Saturday night on the network. Wouldn't people give their right arm for that now?

As well as the Les Dawson shows, we did quite a lot of TV, and in November 1969 I decided to go on the road. I had a lot of thinking to do as, don't forget, I was earning £17 10s in the NDO. The BBC wouldn't let me do the first series of *Says Les* so they got Dave Lee to conduct for me. It was the Syd Lawrence Orchestra, but they wouldn't let me front it because I was contracted to the BBC. When Les got the second series the producer said to me, 'Either you front your band or else we'll have to get somebody else.' So I took a chance and gave my notice in to the Beeb.

I always remember the union gentleman, who was quite a character, saying, 'So you're going on the road are you? How long are you going to give it then, a couple of years?' How could he have known what was going to happen? Nobody did. Petrol was cheap, people had cars and they paired up. We couldn't have a coach because we weren't based in London. I think I was probably the first band to have people picking each other up in cars and travelling in twos, threes and fours. There was never any problem finding players, there isn't to this day. There are some fine young players about.

It was a lovely feeling to have written the music and as a transcription you knew how that music had been played, so you wanted to repeat that performance, the urgency of it, the dynamics, the *vibrato*, the tightness. Tight is the magic word for a band; you ask Ronnie Verrell all about the word tight.

Three years after our first get-together we did the Royal Command Performance from the London Palladium and it was magic. What used to terrify me was if I had to speak at the microphone. You have to be somebody else to be able to do that. I was lucky because Kevin Kent, my singer, was a compère and he could talk and crack a joke. So I just stood there and tootled and never said a word and he did all the talking. One night, after a couple of years, we went to Nottingham and there's a bloke who's a real big band fan, Manfred Desseau, who was delighted when Ken Mackintosh formed a band and was in the Palais there. He came to my concert in Nottingham and asked me to go and have dinner with him and his wife afterwards. We were sitting at the table and he said, 'Syd, do you realise you stood on that stage all night and never said a word? You're going to have to start speaking.' And you know, it hit me right in the face as nobody had put it quite like that before.

So Kevin then started to do a few little gags and bring me in on them until the crunch came and he left. Then it was all up to me and it took a while to break the barrier down. There's a barrier in front of most people for speaking on a stage isn't there? It's an art and most people can't do it, they're terrified, and I was one of those people but I had to do it. Slowly but surely I lost the fear and loosened up, particularly when you start getting applause, it helps to relax you. I wasn't a great compère but we managed okay and people say they miss me out front! Especially some of the things I said! Like the night in Dublin when they had this scaffolding on the stage. I was there with the promoter when they were putting it up in the afternoon. 'What the bloody hell are they doing, what about tonight's concert?' There was all this scaffolding and it was for the show that was going to be on all week so there was no way they were going to shift it. I was furious. It was the Olympia and it was packed out. 'Good evening ladies and gentlemen, it's lovely to be here in Dublin, but I'd just like to apologise for the erections behind me.' The band exploded, and after about two or three seconds I realised what I'd said! Then there was the other one in the Usher Hall, Edinburgh. We'd been going year after year to this beautiful hall and I always introduced the members of the orchestra and Andy Taylor, our lead alto player, is an Edinburgh man and it's always nice when you hit their home town. And year after year I'd said, 'Here he is folks, born in Edinburgh, Andy Taylor.' Applause, applause. Second year, third year, fourth year and so on, and then, 'Here he is folks, Andy Taylor, still born in Edinburgh'!

In the earlier days the drinking could cause a problem but I think I got around it one way or another. I had to make one or two changes because of it, but I can understand why there is a problem because that's the kind of job it is for heaven's sake. They've travelled for miles and miles and what else do you do when you've got a couple of hours to kill? The pub across the road is the obvious place to go. But the odd one would perhaps overdo it and it would show and it would embarrass me terribly on the stage.

After years I found out what my name was: the buggers were calling

Above: Harry Roy sax section. Harry Goss, Joe Arbiter, Nat Temple (Nat Temple)
Below: George Evans Orchestra. Don Innes (piano); Grace Cole left, Freddy Staff second from right
(tpts); Bill Geldard second from left, Gary Brown right (tbns)

Above: Disc jockey Christopher Stone (centre) with his wife and bandleaders (left to right) Bill Harty (drums), unknown, unknown, Lew Stone, Christopher Stone and wife, Caroll Gibbons (half hidden), Harry Roy (laughing), Geraldo, Ray Noble, Henry Hall, Jack Hilton, Jack Jackson (at back), Ambrose, unknown (Joyce Stone)
Below: George Evans Orchestra and the Ivy Benson Orchestra, Palace Theatre, Grimsby, 1951 (Bill Geldard)

Above: Lew Stone Orchestra at the Monseigneur, 1932 (Nat Gonella, third from right, front; Al Bowlly, centre front, guitar) (Joyce Stone)
Below: Nat Gonella (left, front); Lew Stone; Stanley Black (behind Lew) (Joyce Stone)

Ray Noble 'borrows' some of Lew Stone's orchestra for an engagement in Holland, 1932. (from left) Tiny Winters, Nat Gonella, Al Bowlly, Mrs Ray Noble, Ray Noble, Harry Burley, Lew Davis (Joyce Stone)

Bottom right: Tommy Sampson Band 1948. Rosemary Squires, Johnny Hawksworth (bass), Ken Goldie, Wally Smith (tbns), Henry McKenzie (second left saxes) (Rosemary Squires)

Left: Lew Stone (Joyce Stone)

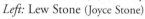

Cleo Laine and John Dankworth

Joe Loss

Above: Joe Ward's wedding, Isle of Man, 1951. Rose Brennan in hat behind the bride,
(Rose Breenan)
Below: Eric Delaney, 1996

Woolf Phillips,
California, 1996

Bob Efford,
California, 1996

Ronnie Verrall, 1996

Beryl Davis, 1996

me the Führer! That was my name, but not nastily. Apparently I was strict but I was respected for it, that's what they kept telling me. I was strict only because I wanted the band to sound good. If anybody relaxed or did something daft, I would say something.

I've missed one side of it terribly. I've missed going on the stage. I've missed sitting in dressing-rooms. I can see dressing-rooms all over the country and I know exactly what they look like, I've been in them so often. What I couldn't do now is the travelling, I really couldn't do that now, and also it isn't fair on your wife to be away all that time, all those nights, year in and year out.

I never regretted forming my own band, I absolutely loved fronting it for 20-odd years, seeing the adoration on people's faces and meeting them in the interval. It brought people together who would never have met. There are people in this country today who have got great friends who live close to them or miles away and they are friends simply because my orchestra was in their town.

ELEANOR KEENAN *Vocalist 1972–76, 1977–78, 1981–85*

Before I joined I went to Pete Smith and asked him to do me an arrangement of 'The Trolley Song' for Syd's band. I remember taking it to the first rehearsal and giving it to Syd and he looked at me and said, 'I do the arrangements in this band.'

'Pete Smith's very good you know,' I countered.

'Yes I know how good he is, but I usually do the arrangements.'

So he vetted it and changed a few things to make them a bit more Miller, I think, and that was the very first solo song I sang with the band. From then on, anything that I really desperately wanted to do I would have done anyway because I was doing some broadcasts at that time so they were always handy.

Syd was a bit of an ogre. He used the singers basically for the vocal group and I think, if he'd had a choice, he wouldn't have had a female singer. I felt he had this idea that a woman's place was in the home; I got the vibes, like 'when is she going to have a baby and leave me', sort of attitude! Over the years we became very good friends although we had our rows – many, many rows! I had to suss his mood out before I'd go in and suggest a new number or suggest a pay rise, which I did very often! He would always have to think about it. I would tell him how I had to service my car and pay out money for all the dresses I had to buy.

He was funny about clothes. He had his likes and dislikes. He liked low-cut, slinky outfits and that really wasn't me. I was never a low-cut, slinky person. I was always a ballroom, big-skirted, long-sleeved type. Occasionally I came up with something that he really liked but on the whole he didn't really like the clothes I wore, even though I spent a lot more than the average girl singer.

Although I was with the band in total for eight years, I did leave twice, first to join an all-girl group, Three's a Crowd, and the second time to go on tour with Roger Whittaker. Even though we had our ups and downs Syd always asked me back and I've always enjoyed it.

Chris Dean was the lead trombone when I came back for the third time after Angela Christian left. Apparently when he saw me he said to Andy Smith, 'Who's the bird?' And Andy Smith said something like, 'No chance mate' because I was known as 'concrete knickers'! Anyway, Chris and I started travelling together. There were four of us in the car, Bernard Bean the bass trombone, Steve Wilkes, Chris and me. That was good fun and we were a good team, taking it in turns to drive. Chris and I got quite friendly, then it got a bit more serious and we were trying to keep it a secret from the band but you couldn't keep many secrets in that band 'cause it was like a family. Everyone got to know everyone's problems. We were working in Bradford one night and Chris and I had travelled up together and we thought it was a nine o'clock start. We went in to the band room and left our stuff and decided to go and have a Chinese. When we came back to the theatre I said, 'Gosh, they must have two big bands on tonight,' and Chris said, 'Mm, that sounds very like Jeff Hooper' and then we said 'Oh, it is Jeff Hooper!' We both had to sneak on to the stage very sheepishly and Syd was not at all happy. I think that sort of let the cat out of the bag, everyone knew then that we were a pair! Freddy Staff nicknamed us 'The Royals'.

ANDY SMITH *Trombone 1974–*

We did a Dixieland number every night which produced one of Syd's classic announcements: 'Now for a completely different sound. Six of the band's members will come out at the front and entertain you!'

I was sacked nine times, a band record! I sit at the end of the section next to the saxes and in front of the drums so I was in the firing line, and whenever Syd started shouting I would get the full onslaught. I'd stop playing and say, 'For Christ's sake stop shouting' 'Don't you shout at me,' he would say, and so it would go on and eventually I'd be fired! Then I would go and say I was sorry and he'd say, 'Do you want to stay in the band?'

'Of course I do Syd.'

'Well at least you were man enough to come and apologise.' He always said that to me!

FREDDY STAFF *Trumpet 1976–92*

Brian Rankine was leaving and Syd rang me and asked me to dep for him in Coventry. He was astounded that I sight read the book on the concert. 'Of course I sight read the book, I've been playing the bloody stuff since I was 15!' So I depped with the band here and there and then he said he'd have a jacket made for me and I was in.

A normal concert should be about an hour each set but Syd would do an hour and twenty, and sometimes we'd be sat there for maybe an hour and forty! Unbelievable, and the theatres were moaning about the overtime and how they wouldn't make money out of the bar. Don Banks always had a few pints inside and there was one night when he actually said to me, 'I'm sorry Fred, I'm actually doing it,' and I could see this little trickle running towards the mutes behind these big music stands we had. That was a tremendous laugh among the guys because it went right round the band immediately without Syd even knowing! The following day we were at Blackpool for a concert and Bill Turner and I went out to search for a little tiny po with Blackpool on it. Before the concert started we put it in his mute bag so he's getting all his mutes out and here's this little po. It must have put it in his mind because, believe it or not, that night he did it again!

It almost happened to me at a concert in Hornchurch when I'd gone to the pub to have a drink with my sister. I rushed back and forgot to go to the loo and in the signature tune I'm in trouble but think I can control it. Well an hour passes, we're into the hour and fifteen and about to play 'Leave Us Leap' with a drum solo coming up and I know roughly how long that is. I whisper to Ronnie Verrell to give us a couple of extra bars and my cue will be the tom-toms! There's a complete blackout so I go off the side of the stage, round the back of the screen, and as I get there the spotlight goes straight on Ronnie. I'm trapped because the stage is set up for a play with tables and chairs and there's no way out. I'm running backwards and forwards and everyone can see this little shadow running round and round like Tom and Jerry! I was in a panic by then because there was no vase or anything handy. In the end I find a door, thinking if the tom-toms start now I'm in trouble. But I made it, dashed back on stage, and as the lights went up, I'm playing!

We were in Dublin, a very important concert, and all the dignitaries were in. We never used to rehearse in those days, only for broadcasts, and when we arrived the stage was set for *West Side Story* with all the scaffolding. Syd's already told you about that, but we were hardly able to play the first number for laughing and it took a while for Syd to know why. He couldn't think what it was he'd said. That was just the start and at the end of the evening the mayor comes on and says, 'I'd like to thank Sid Phillips for this wonderful concert'! Syd's neck goes red as he wasn't at all friendly with the mayor and he didn't want to be in Ireland anyway because it was just after Mountbatten had been killed. To cap it all, as the curtain comes down it drapes round his neck and he's dragged to the floor with this great big heavy curtain round him. The last thing we heard was him kicking his dressing-room door and screaming, 'Never again!'

Don Banks and I used to room together because he could stand my snoring. We went to the Arab Emirates with the band, and arrived in Dubai late at night. It was hot and sultry and we went straight to our room, and when morning came, I opened my eyes and told Don to pull back the curtains so we could see what it was like outside. He pulls them back and says, 'It's dull, it's going to rain'. 'How can it be dull and going to rain? We're in Dubai.' I had a look and sure enough the whole place is dull and misty, so we put on our raincoats and Don's got his umbrella. Down we go in the lift and we're walking through the foyer with people in their shorts all staring at us. We open the main doors and there's this blazing sun and we realised that it was smoked glass in the hotel rooms! That's true. Because of the heat and the sun all the windows of the hotel were smoked glass and there we were thinking we'd come all that way with our swimming costumes and it was raining!

Because Don Banks lived up north, my driving companion down south was always Bill Turner. Bill was a great driver regardless of what he drank; he was a safe driver. We were returning from a concert at the Dome in Brighton and we'd had a couple of pints after the show and Bill's driving so it's my turn to have a kip. I'd dropped off when Bill said, 'Fred, something funny has happened. Have a look,' and we were under the wing of an aeroplane!

'We're in an airport.'

'I know'.

Somehow coming down the back doubles through Feltham before the M25 was built, he'd taken a left turn and gone straight into the air cargo of London airport!

How we got in with the security I don't know, so we drove out and I dropped off again. I opened my eyes and noticed a pub on the right-hand side we'd just passed.

'Was that pub called the Airman?'

'Yes that's the Airman pub.'

'It was on the right-hand side, you bloody fool, we're on our way back to Brighton!' True! That was Bill's driving: no sense of direction, but he'd get you there!

I was the band union steward and I had a bit of a disagreement with Syd at one stage and we didn't speak for a year! When it was all over the old man called me into his room, put his arm round me and said, 'We're still mates aren't we?'

'We can be.'

'I'll tell you what,' he said, 'it's the best you've ever played this year you bugger!'

I always arranged my own trumpet solos but Syd corrected them! He got new equipment and was hearing things he'd never heard before. We'd be rehearsing 'A String of Pearls', if you please, because he'd found two different notes! Inside parts that nobody else would have heard and he would spot it if you played the old note when you didn't get the parts out! He was spotting things all over the place on the Miller things and was driving us crazy!

I left the band the same day as Jeff Hooper, New Year's Eve 1991, and in 1992 we started *A Swing Affair*. When Syd decided to retire none of us thought that Brian Pendleton was the right man for the job and I saw a recipe for disaster. We saw the red light and decided to go.

No matter who's in a band, as far as the public is concerned if the band leader is there that's the most important thing. Syd proved that when they all left him in 1974 to form the Millionaires. They thought they'd dropped him in it and he was finished; great mistake because Syd had the name and people didn't go and see the Millionaires, people came to see Syd Lawrence.

I'll never forget Teddy Foster saying to me once, 'I don't care who I've got in my band, I am Teddy Foster,' and it's so. It didn't matter who Glenn Miller had in his band, people went to see Glenn Miller. And that was the trouble when Syd had gone because people wanted to see the old man out front. It's true you know.

GARY COX *Tenor saxophone 1976, 1980–81, 1985–94*

The first time I joined Syd I lasted four weeks. I couldn't stand all that touring, I'd never been used to it. I only got home about twice in those four weeks so I finished and told him I couldn't stand the touring. What Syd said is not really repeatable! 'But you've only just got here, what do you mean you want to leave?'

The next time I got a message from him was in 1980 and he said to come up to his cottage for a chat, so I went up to the cottage and there was a huge knocker on the front door, like a lion's head or something. My first instinct was to get hold of this knocker and I gave it a few heavy thumps on this oak door. I hadn't seen him for four years and he opened the door and he didn't even say hello or anything. He just pointed to this bell and said, 'What do you think that is? Kath's just fallen off her chair with the noise of that resounding through the cottage!' So I got a bollocking the first time I saw him after four years! I went back with him again and this time I stayed for just over a year.

When I joined him again in 1985, the touring was much less as the band were doing about four nights a week and I could cope with that. You got home every night and you could have a bit of a rest. Steve Shaw and I used to travel with Syd and he would talk all the time in the car. I remember one day when Steve and I were just sitting quietly thinking, and we'd been going for about half an hour when he suddenly slammed the brakes on and shouted, 'It's like a bloody morgue in this car!'

Syd would drive us to the gigs, but because he'd like to have a drink in the interval Steve would drive us back, because even if he'd only had one whisky he wouldn't drive. He liked Steve to drive because he was young. He had a thing about anybody a bit older driving, so he didn't trust me! The funny thing was Syd would drive down and the petrol would cost x pounds then we'd go back at night with Steve driving and we always had to fill up when we got to the garage near Syd's house, whether it was three, four or five in the morning, and this one time it cost a pound more and he was really racking his brains. 'How can it cost fifteen pounds to get there when I was driving and sixteen to come back exactly the same route?' Anyway, the conclusion he came to was that Steve had a leaden foot. This happened a few times where it cost more to get back than it did to get down, and he wasn't happy about that at all, he was always on to Steve to keep his foot off the accelerator!

Syd was very good in front of the band although he was a hard taskmaster and could be a bit bad-tempered at times if things weren't absolutely how he wanted them. He would play Bobby Hackett-type solos and did them very well. But the things he said on stage! We were doing this Old Soldiers reunion and they were all sending up requests. One was signed from a Gordon Highlander, and Syd reads it out: 'This request is from a Mr A. Gordon Highlander.' You know 'Story of a Starry Night' from Tchaikovsky's 6th Symphony? He announced: 'Now ladies and gentlemen we're going to play a thing that was originally written by Tchaikovsky and then Glenn Miller got hold of it and turned it into a beautiful piece of music.'

It was the same programme practically every single night. All the Glenn Miller stuff, 'Little Brown Jug', 'Chattanooga Choo Choo', and I just grew to hate them. After eight years it got to be very frustrating for me because I didn't get a chance to play anything. Sixteen bars was considered to be a long solo. I got the odd things but maybe he thought if he let me play some solos he'd have to pay me more money or something. I think that might have been behind it.

I heard that one or two people were getting a lot of money so I thought I'd ask for more.

'Any chance of a bit more money Syd?'

'Oh no, there's no more money for that chair, you see it's the chair that gets the money it doesn't matter who's sitting on it. It wouldn't matter if Stan Getz was sitting on that chair he'd get the same. In fact I don't think I'd pay him as much as I pay you.'

There was no answer to that!

RONNIE VERRELL *Drums 1980–*

When I was with Cyril Stapleton, Syd Lawrence was the young trumpet player, and as soon as I heard him play I thought that's the bloke I want to sit next to in the coach, he plays my sort of music. Marvellous, beautiful, like Bobby Hackett. I sat next to him and we would play cards and I roomed with him.

I didn't see him for years and I heard he'd got his own band but I never bothered to go and see it, I was too busy. I heard he played Glenn Miller and I didn't want to go along and see a night of Glenn Miller! Then I got this call. 'Hello Ronnie.'

'Hello, who's that?'

'Syd Lawrence. Look Ronnie, I want a sensational drummer, do you know anybody?'

'Well all the good drummers I know will be doing sessions.'

'Could you help me out? I know you're busy. How are you fixed next Sunday?' So I helped him out that Sunday and 16 years later I'm still helping him out!

I loved the band. It was so tight and good and it was great after years and years in the studios suddenly to be playing to a 'live' audience and play how you want to play to a full house and being appreciated. I'm a great admirer of Syd Lawrence. The boys will tell you they used to call him the Führer because if he got angry his eyes were like a madman's. He'd turn around and give some of the guys the most terrible bollocking ever. If you were called to his room the guys would say you'd been summoned to the bunker! But although some of the guys didn't like him because he used to get so angry very quickly, they respected him as a musician, as I do. But I like the old boy, I love the old guy, I really do. I forgive him for a lot of his little frailties, we're all human. He's a marvellous musician and he's the best 'taker down' of a record in the country. Absolutely perfect, and he'll spend hours getting it right. It's very hard to hear everything on a record but he'll get it and he'll sort the chords out.

His wife didn't want him to go on the road any more so he sold the band, but he still occasionally turns up and it's great to see the old guy when he comes on with that smart suit of his, trumpet in his hand. He gets a tremendous reception because the public loved him and they still do.

What I'm in now, is like a family. I've been with these guys for so long I've got my pet players in the band and we're called the whoopees; we're always out drinking and last to bed, but they're great players. Andy Taylor the lead alto, Andy Smith and my dear Ken Williams, who I was with for 16 years. I'd never known him before and he became one of my greatest friends. He died of cancer at 51 and I haven't got over it yet, he's irreplaceable.

The journeys are quite hideous but we usually share cars, sometimes I drive and sometimes somebody else drives. The mileage on my car in four and a half years is 150,000, that's bearing in mind without the times I'm on the road with somebody else. If I'd done it all in my own car it would be 250,000 by now. It's quite arduous.

JEFF HOOPER *Vocalist 1981–92*

I was working at the Double Diamond Club in Caerphilly when Syd came along to do a concert and I was out front compèring and singing. Eleanor Keenan, bless her, said to him, 'You're looking for a new singer, there's a guy here'. He took one look at me and said, 'He's too young, he'll never know the songs.' I was only 17 at the time.

A few whiskys later he decided it might be a good idea to give me a short audition so he called me backstage to his dressing-room. He got his trumpet out and said 'Do you know a song called 'At Last'?' I said I'd never heard of it so he played a couple of bars. Now it's quite a low song, the lowest note is getting down to the boots for me, but I la-la'ad it through and I managed to hit that bottom note. 'You hit the bottom note, what's the top end of your range like?'

'How high do you want me to go?' So he played another little tune and I sang high.

'You've got a great range, I'll give you a try out.'

So I got the job and about a month later we were doing my first ever 'live' broadcast at the Royal Festival Hall for Radio 2 and I was petrified. Syd had given me a full 90-minute cassette of songs and told me to learn as many as I could and I'd learnt the lot within ten days. That's how keen I was. One song I'd found difficult, 'Elmer's Tune', so I thought I'd leave that one and that was the very song he wanted to do on this 'live' broadcast. It was a vocal group number and I only had a handful of lines to sing so we rehearsed it and I got everything right and then we come to the broadcast. One of the lines in the song went

'What makes a lady of 80 go out on the loose, Why does a gander meander in search of a goose.' Live on air I came out with 'What makes a lady of 80 go out on the beat, Why does a gander meander in search of his feet'!

Syd Lawrence is pretty famous for his death-ray look if you get something wrong and he gave me one of his looks and I just looked back at him very humbly like I'm very sorry Syd, don't sack me, and he just collapsed with laughter! The audience knew I'd messed up because they knew the song backwards, but they also appreciated I was able to carry on.

When Syd left the band and went into semi-retirement he'd given me the ropes, so to speak, to front the show and Brian Pendleton became the MD. I was the front man for two years but it was the same songs, the same music, and I left because I felt I couldn't go any further with the band. I'd learnt all the songs he'd wanted me to learn and I thought what else can I do with this job? I had to move on but I wanted to keep working within a big band format, so with Freddy Staff I formed my own big band and we got *A Swing Affair* off the ground and continued touring.

VIC LEWIS

1919–

Themes 'Jazzmen Blues', 'Blue Champagne', 'Music for Moderns', 'Concepts', 'Play on Blues'

No other British bandleader changed their style quite as often as Vic Lewis, from Dixieland to big band jazz, and his theme music changed accordingly. With the formation of the Vic Lewis–Jack Parnell Jazzmen in the '40s the two leaders co-wrote 'Jazzmen Blues'. The advent of his big band in 1946 with their blue suits produced 'Blue Champagne' and the 20-piece line-up in 1950 was aptly introduced by his own composition 'Music for Moderns'. Another of his originals, 'Concepts', should have provided his audiences with some conception of what they were about to hear in 1953, and he made yet another change in 1958 with his 'Play On Blues'.

Vic Lewis played guitar with George Shearing and Carlo Krahmer in London in the mid-1930s before visiting New York where he recorded with Bobby Hackett and other American jazzmen. He greatly admired Boyd Raeburn, but a decade later it would be Stan Kenton's turn to capture the musical imagination of the pint-sized bandleader who was forever seeking new musical pastures. During the war, as a member of the Bomber Command Sextet led by Buddy Featherstonhaugh, he tired of only ever playing in the rhythm section and got Don McCaffer to teach him to play the trombone!

Often described as the British Stan Kenton, Vic Lewis formed a close friendship with the American bandleader he admired so much and has played a large part in keeping his music alive since Kenton died in 1979.

171

VIC LEWIS

Before the war in my very first band, I had three blind people including a girl. George Shearing was on piano, Alf Hickman on bass, there were only six or eight of us and we would play Slough every weekend. The band I had in 1947 had Ruth Harrison on trombone and then Kathy Stobart, so no one can ever say I was anti-women players!

During the war Jack Parnell and I were both with Buddy Featherstonhaugh and we didn't like the music we were playing. I was very different to Jack because I'd started with Bobby Hackett in America and I was what they call Chicago music. Jack was more of a modernist. I asked Wally Ridley, who ran EMI, why I couldn't make a record as Buddy was doing all this recording. 'You can have a record date,' said Wally. So Jack, who was with me, said, 'Well if he can have a date why can't I have a date?' So everything was fixed.

Two or three days beforehand I had said to Jack, 'What are you going to do?'

'Do about what?'

'Who have you got playing for you?'

'Oh, I'd forgotten all about it.'

'It's the day after tomorrow. I tell you what, why don't we do the session together? You play drums for me and we'll call it the Vic Lewis/Jack Parnell Jazzmen and then we can do four sides instead of two sides.' That was how the band came about.

We recorded 'Sugar' and 'Is You Is or Is You Ain't My Baby' and we had the biggest selling 78 there'd been in God knows how many years. There were about 400,000 copies sold. Then we went on the stage through Jack's uncle, Val Parnell, who owned all the Moss Empires, and when the war was over we went on tour. Our agent said he'd been talking things over with Val and they'd decided two names were a bit too heavy for a band. I didn't know what the names had to do with it as long as the people liked the music! I knew what he was getting at because I think Jack's mother had been getting at Val. So I suggested we ask the band what they thought, and as luck would have it they all decided to stay with me. So it became the Vic Lewis Jazzmen and Jack left and went with Ted Heath. In 1946 we toured Sweden, Denmark, Ireland and we were playing what I call Chicago/Dixieland music. Eventually Dick Katz, who was a wonderful piano player, left and the guy who replaced him was Ken Thorne. Ken was a great writer and he asked if he could map out a few things for the band. I'd written a series of études, so Ken suggested we put one in each week on this series of broadcasts we had: 'Étude in Green', 'Étude in Blue' and so on. They were different from what we had been doing and very modernistic, and that was the beginning of my moving towards Boyd Raeburn's music and eventually towards Stan Kenton's.

We formed the band in 1946 at the Exeter Hotel in Bournemouth. The manager kept coming up to me and saying, 'Can you play "We'll Gather Lilacs" because during the lunch period we want you to play quiet music.' We kept on getting remarks about keeping the music down but we had two fellows who came in every night saying, 'You've got a great band here, if you ever want to leave we've got a ballroom up at Boscombe and you can come there.' Eventually I lost my temper with the manager of the Exeter and told him he'd hired the wrong band and it would be better if we left. So we went up to Boscombe and had six marvellous weeks playing what we liked.

When that summer season finished we went back to town and I augmented to three trumpets, three trombones and five saxes, and we rehearsed for two to three months every day bar Sundays and nobody got paid at all. It was a great band and everybody wanted to be in it – Charlie Granville, Jimmy Skidmore, Ronnie Chamberlain. We had uniforms made but we couldn't afford to pay anyone until we went out, but we wanted to go out and be perfect, which we were. We were all in royal blue with silver grey slacks and when Kathy Stobart came into the band we had a skirt made for her. She was with me off and on for years; wonderful player. It was basically very modernistic and we called it the 'Music of Tomorrow by the Band of Today'.

Parlophone said we could make some sides for them so we started recording some Kenton because at that time no Stan Kenton records were issued in Britain. We got the arrangements sent over and did 'Artistry in Percussion', 'Back to Sorrento', and through that my association with Stan started. We made four records for Parlophone and I told them I wanted an echo, I didn't want the dry sound they got at Abbey Road. But we couldn't experiment because in those days the wax had to be heated downstairs and brought upstairs where the fellow with the magnifying glass looked to see if the grooves were all right; the red light went on, and if you played one wrong note, that wax was finished. Then I had the idea of running the leads from the mikes into the toilet downstairs where there were white tiled walls, have a mike there that picked up the sound, and fed it back to the board. It worked! It gave 'The Man I Love', which became a huge record over here with a Gordon Langhorn trombone solo on it, this huge echo. And when I went to America and took the record for Stan to hear he said, 'How did you get that sound? That's what I've been trying to get.' So I told him how we did it!

The BBC gave us some broadcasts and I was called by the head man and he said, 'If you play any more of that music, you're coming off the air.' 'I'll tell you what I'll come off the air anyway.' Then I realised what I'd done, I'd kicked my own shins!

Pat Dixon did two programmes with us called *Listen My Children* and *Third Programmes Involve Fractions* for the Third Programme. I had the 60-piece George Mitchell Choir, Ken Thorne was doing all the writing, and we played this modernistic music and nobody knew what we were trying to do, but Pat was marvellous telling us to go ahead and do it. The *New Musical Express* had the headline 'Vic Lewis to appear on the Third Programme'.

Then I get called in by the other BBC man – I wish I could think of his name – who said he would give us one more broadcast but said he expected us to bend a bit regarding the content. So we did this broadcast and afterwards he said, 'I gave you one more chance and now you're banned from the air. Fancy doing a tune of Glenn Miller's like 'Adios' and mucking it around.'

'That's as much as you know about music, that *was* Glenn Miller's arrangement!'

So we got taken off the air for playing an original Glenn Miller which we'd only included because we were making an effort to be more commercial!

Now we were doing one-night stands all over the country and people tried to dance to us. We played all the big ballrooms and the City Hall in Newcastle on a Sunday where they were allowed to do concerts. We packed out two houses, that's 5,000 people, and our share was £160 and we had to have a bus to get there! We then started to play ten- and twelve-minute pieces that Ken was scoring. We did 'Porphyria's Lover', and I remember playing at the Capitol in Cardiff where the manager was a real tyrant who, if you said anything, he'd be at the side of the stage. You weren't allowed to talk, wear make up, nothing on a Sunday. You could wear uniform but that was it.

We had a big following and the place was packed and there was one of these jokers up in the balcony. All of a sudden I heard a raspberry and a voice shouting, 'What the hell do you think you're playing down there?' So I looked up at the balcony, which I knew I shouldn't do, it was like committing suicide, and said, 'I'm awfully sorry sir, I can hear you, I can't see you, but I can smell you,' and the next thing I know the manager's at the side of the stage waving me off. I just put up two fingers and got on with the concert. Afterwards he said, 'That's the last time you'll appear here.'

'I don't care two hoots whether it's the first time or the last time, you're the loser. There's a packed house out there and it's like that every time we come here.'

I'd now increased my band to five trumpets, five trombones, five saxophones, five rhythm with bongos, and we weren't going to play any dances, only concerts. We did Hammersmith Palais on eight Monday nights and there was a queue from one o'clock lunchtime to get in! We had 8,000 people come in every Monday night, nobody could dance, they just stood in front of the stand. We weren't going to play dance music and managers like Sam Ramsden in Derby said they wouldn't have us in the ballroom. There was open hostility to what we were doing. We were trying to do something original. It's British music and we were trying to do what Stan Kenton had done in America and all they were trying to do was knock us. That went on until my mother lent me £1,600 to pay off the debts and we didn't have another date in the book and that was it. Finish. 1950. That band lasted six months to the day.

After that band had finished I got on to our agent Harold Davidson and suggested we went back on the boards with a different line-up. We went to the Wood Green Empire, Shepherd's Bush Empire, and did a tribute to Stan Kenton but modified it. I then decided to go back on the road in 1951 and during that year and 1952 we toured the American bases in Germany. We started doing tours with American stars such as Frankie Laine, Johnny Ray, Nat King Cole, Mel Tormé and that took over. I actually played trombone with Stan Kenton at the Alhambra in Paris! Bob Fitzpatrick was taken ill and we were waiting backstage with Artie Shaw who had come to see the Kenton Orchestra. Stan said, 'I don't know what we're going to do because Fitz isn't here.' Then he turned to me. 'You play trombone don't you?'

'Well, yes and no! But I know all your stuff anyway.'

At least I thought I did. There I am with Kent Larson and Carl

Fontana and the first thing they do is 'Concerto to End All Concertos'. I looked at this part and thought, 'Oh my God,' and the fellas said to me, 'What you don't know, don't play.' It wasn't as bad as I thought it was!

I later recorded with my own 20-piece band when I played a blues and you can tell how badly I play, but that used to bring the house down as people couldn't believe I played trombone because I used to play piano and guitar. I had an old trombone which I didn't like to take on the stand, and when I went to play a solo I'd go to the trombone section and say, 'Can I borrow your trombone, I've got my own mouthpiece?' and they would hide their trombones and say, 'No you can't,' because I used to blow so hard that I'd cut my lip and there would be blood all over the mouthpiece. And the fellas would say, 'I'm not going to let you have my trombone and get blood all over it. Go out and buy your own!' Don Lang was my main trombone player with Johnny Keating, Tony Russell and Ken Goldie, all good players, so I had a very good trombone section.

On the whole I wouldn't say I was a disciplinarian but when Johnny Shakespeare was in the band on trumpet, his wife would go around telling all the other wives who had been going out with who, and she nearly wrecked the band. I remember saying to Johnny, 'I want to speak to your wife' and he said, 'What about?' because he was a sweetheart. 'She's been spreading gossip around about what the fellows do. What they do, I don't care, as long as they don't bring ill-repute to the band, but I don't want somebody else coming in and telling them what to do because it will wreck the band.'

The other problem I had was when I found out the guys were smoking pot. After about 1948 I decided I wouldn't go on the bus any more because I felt the guys would have no respect if you're there among them because they can't talk about you. So I decided to go by car and I remember one time saying that I'd see them halfway there at a transport café. When the bus pulled up I opened the door and I could smell pot, and that was one time when I really blew my stack. 'If I'd been a policeman stopping this bus you would have all gone inside and you wouldn't have had a bad name, I would have had a bad name. People would say the Vic Lewis Band are on pot. Do as you like when you're not part of the band. If you want to go round the corner and light up, that's your business, if you get caught that's your business, but when you're in the band bus I don't want anybody smoking in here.' I also said I didn't want anyone making sleeping bags out of our suits that were all hand tailored. I would come on the bus and see them sleeping all night in these beautiful jackets and trousers to save money on their digs, and I was paying them digs money!

RONNIE CHAMBERLAIN *Alto saxophone 1946–56*

I was a founder member of the Vic Lewis–Jack Parnell Jazzmen. Jack's uncle, Val Parnell, wanted it to be Jack Parnell's Band, and as it was a semi co-operative band we thought we didn't want that as Vic had done most of the donkey work, so we more or less voted Jack out. We didn't part bad friends or anything but that was how it happened.

Vic went on for a while with his small band and we won a few *Melody Maker* polls. It was a semi-Dixieland type band. Then he decided he wanted to form a big band and said he wanted me to play lead alto. Well at that time I didn't read very well because I was a jazz player. I could read but not sight read. Vic said he'd try to find a lead alto but it was difficult because everybody was in the forces, so it finished up with me having to learn the parts. Ken Thorne was with us at the beginning and he taught me a lot.

It was just a series of one-night stands for not very much money, and looking for digs and sitting in the bus with no heating. They had one heater in those days and that was at the front, and of course the bandleader sat by that, and his wife, and we sat at the back with newspapers round our legs trying to keep warm!

We made quite a lot of recordings with that band over a period of about ten years. Vic changed his band an awful lot. I played him a record of Stan Kenton and he flipped and wanted to form a band that sounded like Stan Kenton. It was reasonably successful but the standard of musicianship wasn't all that high because to get that many good players in a band of that size isn't easy.

I had this phone call in 1955 from Ted Heath telling me that Roy Willox was leaving the band and going with Geraldo and he'd like me to join the band. I said I'd love to join the band but I'd just signed a contract with Harold Davidson who was Vic's agent. We were doing a tour with Johnny Ray in South Africa and I was sort of deputy bandleader at the time. Johnny Ray tended to bring all his musical problems to me and he more or less stipulated that I should be in the band, so I signed the contract. I told Ted when the contract was up and he said, 'Okay mate,' and put the phone down on me. So I thought my big chance had gone but about a month before my contract was up he phoned me again and I said I'd love to join his band.

BOB EFFORD *Tenor saxophone 1950*

When I joined Vic it was like a copy-cat Kenton band, which is the only way I can describe it. Not a dance band, it was a big concert-type thing like Kenton had. We did theatres mostly and sometimes we did very well, sometimes it was embarrassing. I think I remember playing some place in Brixton or Clapham or somewhere like that and you could hardly see any heads at all when the curtain opened! Out of London some of the attendances were pretty good. It was a concert performance so people that came should have known what they were in for, but I'm not too sure that they always did because it was very far-out music, it was really out there and incredibly loud.

That band didn't last and then it became a regular dance band, but I didn't stay much longer after that. It was a noble experiment that didn't work too well. People weren't ready for that.

PETE WARNER *Tenor saxophone 1950–51*

They were on a sort of Herman, Kenton kick at the time and my audition piece was 'Early Autumn' and Vic said, 'Can you play like Stan Getz?' There was the written Getz solo and I was paralysed with fear but I got through it. Soon afterwards Ronnie Scott joined the band, which was a wonderful opportunity for me to learn a lot of stuff from Ronnie: how to play and whether I was doing things wrong or right, and what you could do and what you couldn't do, chords, section work; great, wonderful experience.

We were on the road and stopped at one of those transport cafés on the A5 and Ronnie says he's going to stuff this cushion up his back and go into this café like Quasimodo, so he goes up to the counter and the guy who comes out to serve him is a real hunchback! Everybody fell about but it was terrible really. That's Ronnie for you. I remember when we were in Leeds he went up to a policeman to ask directions with a 'joint' in his hand. I was horrified but the policeman never said anything!

We did a lot of overseas tours and it was a really great time for me as I'd never been abroad before. Vic was a nice man and the money was a lot better than with Teddy Foster! It was a good band.

JOHNNY KEATING *Trombone 1950–52*

In 1950 I joined Vic Lewis as arranger and trombonist and I have to say that my happiest time as a professional trombonist was my two-year stint on lead trombone with Vic. He was my favourite to work for, and he obviously liked my style of playing. He could have paid me a little more of course!

I recorded three trombone features while I was with him: Pete Rugolo's 'Theme for Trombone', Bill Russo's 'Solitaire' and a Woody Herman classic 'Everywhere' originally performed by Bill Harris.

VIC ASH *Tenor saxophone/clarinet 1953–56*

That was my first big band and Vic was a marvellous little character, still is, and his love is Stan Kenton, but during the period I was with him he was going through a phase of doing all different bands like Billy May and Glenn Miller. It was hardly ever Stan Kenton's music apart from maybe 'Intermission Riff', a couple of things like that. I suppose it was a commercial thing because he wasn't drawing in the crowds with the Stan Kenton music.

He was a marvellous guy to work for. We were the first British band to play Birdland in New York in about 1955 or '56 when we did a tour of American army and air force bases. That was a specially put together band when he put more well known jazz guys in the line-up. Ronnie Ross was there, Jimmy Deuchar, both unfortunately gone now. Birdland was a very nerve-racking experience because as you can imagine dozens of American musicians came to see us. We had Zoot Sims and Buddy Rich out front and we all had our solos to play, and the band acquitted itself very well. When we were over there Vic had this inspiration and he said to Jimmy Deuchar about two days before the event, 'Write me a tune and we'll call it "Britons in Birdland",' and the genius of Jimmy Deuchar really came out because he wrote this very fast, very intricate thing on the coach and copied out all the parts in pitch. That was the genius of Jimmy Deuchar and we played it at Birdland. Vic was knocked out with it.

JOE LOSS

1909–1990

Theme 'In The Mood'

Joe Loss became Britain's youngest bandleader when he formed his first band in 1930 and became its longest-serving leader when he died in 1990, having fronted a highly successful line-up for 60 years. He booked Vera Lynn for her very first broadcast, for which she got paid thirty shillings and his records have sold in their millions around the world. In the 1960s he had chart entries with 'Wheels Cha Cha', 'The Maigret Theme' and 'March of the Mods'.

Joe Loss and His Orchestra were first and foremost a dance band but they were an entertaining dance band, and the main reason for their success was Joe Loss always knew what the public wanted and gave it to them.

His nine-year residency at the Astoria, Charing Cross Road, in the '30s saw his first signature tune, 'Let's Dance at the Make Believe Ballroom', establish him as London's most popular dance band. When he heard Glenn Miller's recording of 'In The Mood' and played it on the air, the reaction was such that he soon adopted it as the band's theme and would often end up having to play it several times in one evening. The band was a firm favourite with the royal family and played for many private dances at Buckingham Palace and Windsor Castle over the years. It also became the first British band to visit China, and in 1973 made the first of what was to become an annual event, the World Cruise on the *QE2*.

HARRY GOLD *Tenor saxophone 1920s*

I met Joe Loss when he and I were students. I saw an advert in the local paper which read: 'Saxophone player wanted, willing to rehearse', signed J. Loss. So I wrote and he answered, asking me to go to his place for a rehearsal. I arrived and there was a drummer, Joe on violin, and a girl playing piano but she could only play on the black notes. So it was G flat mostly! Joe had a piano copy in front of her and he had to transpose from C to D flat or whatever and I, being on an E flat alto, had a double transposition if you see what I mean! I was transposing like mad.

The drummer was Ginger Conn and he was very well known in Archer Street in those days and he was a friend of Joe's and was there presumably to audition us. He was out in the street while we were playing and he came in and said, 'Joe, it sounds like a real band.' The saxophone made it a real band!

I stayed with Joe a couple of months and we did little gigs for half a crown a night. In fact we played at the opening in the East End of a famous salt beef supper place; I've forgotten the name. Half a crown and a salt beef supper! Eventually I said, 'Joe, I'm enjoying it but I have to leave.' 'Why?' 'I'm not learning to read, I'm just learning to transpose!' I did some arrangements for Joe much later on and when he was at the Astoria I used to go and visit him. It was Joe who got me the job with my band at the Hammersmith Palais.

WOOLF PHILLIPS *Trombone 1936*

I joined Joe Loss at the Astoria, Charing Cross Road. They were all past masters in the art of cockney rhyming slang, up the apples and so forth, and I knew they were saying things about me but I could never understand what they were saying, but gradually I learned and I could talk to them!

I liked Joe Loss immensely – a very nice man. Harry Latham was in the band and a chap called Joe Cordell was the trombone player. It was a seven-day-a-week job at the Astoria and we played all the time for dancing. I enjoyed it. I did some arrangements which we recorded and I did some jazz things for him, but we never recorded them.

ROSE BRENNAN *Vocalist 1951–66*

I'd been a dance band singer since I was 11 and Joe's band used to come to Ireland every year after the war. He was one of the first bands to come; Kenton came, Oscar Rabin came, and I remember going to see them all as all I ever wanted to be was a singer with a band.

In those days the singer was invariably blonde, but if there were two there'd be a blonde one and a dark one so they wouldn't fight with each other! They were always slender and they sometimes had the reputation of being the bandleader's perk. You didn't have to sing all that well as long as you looked good. I fell into none of those categories so when I said I was going to be a singer with a dance band on the BBC, everybody said this fat girl from Ireland must be mad!

Danny Miller, who'd been in Joe's sax section from the very early days and was his right-hand man cum fixer cum troubleshooter, came to a ballroom where I was working. He went back and told Joe he'd heard me singing and Joe asked me to go and see him. I came over to London with my aunt, I think I was 17. Very young, convent educated, a virgin and having been shielded by my father who always came and took me home from the gigs. We had a long chat with Joe who was a very shrewd man. I think that was his greatest talent, his shrewdness, and he realised that I was too young. Everybody realised I was too young except me. I remember going with my aunt and sitting at the Hammersmith Palais and Lou Preager was there, and of course that made me even more determined I was going to sing with a dance band on the BBC. The whole atmosphere of the Hammersmith Palais, this glamorous place with the lights, the big band, the revolving stage, the whole thing.

Anyhow I went back to Ireland and was singing with a band. Then in 1951 Joe had a singer called Elizabeth Batey who married Harry Bence and she fell and broke her jaw. She was the absolute opposite to me because she was a bubbly little blonde who sang the 'point' numbers. There was always a point number singer who sang the cute songs. But Joe needed a singer very quickly and Danny reminded him about me because this was three years later. Joe rang the ballroom in Dublin where I was working and spoke to the bandleader first, which again was Joe; one does things the right way, the boss must come first. He asked me if I could still sing, which was a stupid question, and asked me if I could be in a solicitor's office in Dublin the next day, which was a Sunday, with my parents, because I was under age. That was typical of Joe because everything was always done very correctly. He offered me two weeks there and then, to come over to Manchester to the Hippodrome.

I flew over to Manchester on the Monday morning and got off the plane and that was when I knew my life had changed drastically because there were photographers and newspaper reporters. In those days the big bands were the thing like the groups now, like the Spice Girls; I was a Spice Girl! We went along to rehearsal and Joe told me I was singing two songs with Howard Jones, the wonderful Welsh singer. 'September Song' was in the hit parade, which I did, but I also had to sing a duet with Howard Jones, 'How Could You Believe Me When I Said I Love You When You Know I've Been a Liar All My Life', which I had to learn and Joe expected me to do it. I went out on stage that night at six o'clock and I did it and that was the beginning. Two weeks later he offered me a contract and I stayed with him fifteen and a half years.

I had to pay for all my dresses and most of my money went on clothes. Mildred, Joe's wife, took me to this dress designer but she didn't tell me I would have to pay for it! It cost me a bloody fortune, three or four weeks' wages. I had no agent, I had no manager, and never did an audition in my life so I had no idea how it functioned. I didn't come from a theatrical family. I was fixed up with an accountant; again it was his accountant so it cost me an arm and a leg but he reined me in when I started to make more money. The only thing both Joe Loss and Roy Fox asked of me was that I look elegant, and I always did. They both insisted that when you went on stage and appeared before your public you had to look elegant. The only thing that Joe allowed to be dishevelled was his hair! And that was a prop because if you think of Joe and the pushing back of the hair, that was Joe. But the rest of him was immaculate.

And another thing, neither Joe nor Roy would allow you to come down on the dance floor. You were not allowed to dance or mix with anybody. While you were up on stage they were paying to see you; the minute you came down you were one of them, so why pay to come and see you? That was indicative of both of those men, the gentlemen of the business, and isn't it strange that neither of them picked a glamorous bird to sing with the band! I never had glamour but I had presence and you remember the person not for what they look like but for the effect. I still have what was instilled into me from a very early age; I never apologised when I walked out on stage because I knew I would give them what they came for. And I learned that from Joe and Roy Fox. I won the *New Musical Express* Dance Band Singer of the Year Award in 1954, and the following year 'Whistling Gypsy' was named the *Melody Maker* Top Female Record.

Ross McManus, bless his heart, is probably one of my closest friends. He's one of the most creative people I've ever known. Extremely intelligent, and he's also a very generous and, like most intelligent, generous people, can be a swine to get on with at times but lovable, and Ross and I understood each other very well. As for Larry Gretton, I don't think Larry gives a damn about anything. The sky could fall and Larry would still stand at the microphone and go through it. He's been singing one song for thirty-odd years and he still doesn't know the entire lyric! He just sails through life and we got on fine. The band were very protective of me in a funny kind of way.

Although later on Joe became synonymous with Hammersmith Palais, he was really the king of the north, the king of Scotland and the king of Ireland, whereas in London it was Heath, Parnell, Dankworth with all the slick jazz. Joe was a dance band, they weren't. He and Victor Sylvester and probably Oscar Rabin and Lou Preager were, because they played for dancing. Ted Heath, Dankworth and Delaney didn't play for dancers, they tolerated dancers. So really that fact was recognised by the canny northerners. Joe played for them whereas we all know a lot of musicians have a habit of playing for themselves! Joe had tremendous respect for his audience, that's why he lasted so long. His motto was you never short-changed your audience, never. I had great respect for him because I knew I wouldn't be sitting there if they weren't dancing around.

I remember going to a place called Maryport and the town closed down when the coach arrived. They were all standing outside the shops waving to us. Joe Loss was in town! It was like the Beatles coming. At Trentham Gardens they would wait for the coach to see whether we had any tickets, like touts. In the Isle of Man the landladies had to bring forward high tea because if people were going to the Villa Marina they would have to queue up for two hours before they could get in. It's incredible looking back now how much I took it for granted. I wasn't aware at all of what was happening.

Sitting on the stand we would pick out certain things, like one night we would watch ears and ears are fascinating. It sounds awful, but if you watch people's ears as they dance by, the shapes and sizes! And another night it would be noses and feet, and, of course, for the fellas it would be boobs! I used to sometimes pick out birds and say, 'You'd fancy her'.

It was a deliberate policy of mine not to have a boyfriend in the band, not that they would ever have fancied me! I'd seen so much unhappiness with that kind of thing because when you're on the road you're almost married to somebody, and contrary to what people thought, there wasn't that much promiscuity. Most of the fellows in our band were married, they had mortgages, they had cars, they had kids, and I found them really quite boring because they talked about things normal people talk about. They'd get out on stage and blow a jazz solo and come off and be worried about the roof leaking! So basically it was all extremely normal. When I hear now about people having nervous breakdowns, I laugh, they don't know what it was like. We didn't travel in air-conditioned coaches and aeroplanes. The coach call was outside Broadcasting House in Portland Place, just around the corner. So if we were going to Manchester we'd take off on a Monday, ten o'clock on the coach.

I had one of those big basket skips and my entire life was in that! My most precious possession was a travelling iron as in those days the frocks had yards and yards of tulle underneath and all the diamante and they had to be crushed into this skip because I had to have at least seven dresses with me and shoes to match, if we were doing a week somewhere. We'd get on the coach and there was a greasy spoon about 35 or 40 miles away and we'd stop for a coffee about eleven-thirty. There was no motorway and we'd get to Manchester if we were lucky by five, maybe six. We stayed, not at a big hotel, but a comfortable one so you had a bath and something to eat and then you went off and did the gig. You came back that night, no wild parties because everyone was knackered, into bed and on the coach the next morning. We always used to say whoever planned the itinerary was the greatest sadist ever, because we could be Manchester one day and down in Devon the next. We could be on the road for three weeks like that with no let-up at all and we'd rush back on Sunday to do a Sunday broadcast, then it was straight out on the road again. It was hard, very hard, but when you love what you're doing it doesn't matter does it?

At the beginning of the 'sixties I realised that I was beginning to get disillusioned and I thought perhaps I'd stayed too long with Joe, but I was never very ambitious. I'd had a couple of very good offers and Max Dreyfus of Chappell's said I should leave England and go to America because England only wanted the 'girl next door' and I would really come into my own in the States. But I didn't, and I suppose it was lack of ambition.

One of the things that precipitated my leaving the band was on one of our broadcasts we had as guests two young ladies who shall be nameless. One you couldn't hear at all, and she was making a fortune. Then the other one came in after she'd done the broadcast and said, 'Wasn't I wonderful? Have you heard my latest record? You really must hear it, you'll die to play it.' And I thought 'I'm in the wrong business.' I'm not blaming her but that's the way you have to be, and that made me realise this is the confidence you must have and I didn't have it. All I ever wanted to do was sing.

When I got married I realised that choices had to be made because John was a detective in the police force and we were just saying goodbye and hello to each other, and he was quite a handsome man and I thought, 'What did I marry him for if I'm going to leave him lying around?' I had a very good life. I had some very nice friends and I bought some property but it was different then. That was my job, it was my career. Nobody has a career any more. Fifteen and a half years and I could have stayed even longer. When I left I gave Joe six months' notice and he wouldn't believe I was going.

ROSS McMANUS *Vocalist 1954–68*

I was playing jazz trumpet in a great big swinging band in Nottingham Astoria, Miles Davis and Clifford Brown were my idols. I did a few vocals but I wasn't the vocalist with the band, and then one evening one of the older men in the band said to me, 'You're going with Joe Loss.'

'How's that?'

'On the balcony is Danny Miller and he fixes Joe's singers and musicians.'

Nottingham was one of the few places you could get a late-night supper in those days so Danny took me to supper afterwards and he talked about singing with the band and so on, all of which was beyond me. I just wanted to be a jazz trumpet player.

A few months later I got a call to go to the Isle of Man for an audition. The bandleader said he would have to give me the sack. So I told him I had to go because my wife had just had a baby and we were fed up with cardboard shoes and 'coon-skin coats! I went off, did the audition, and thought Joe looked absolutely splendid in his monogrammed silk shirts and cigar. It was another world to me because I was just a jazz club rat!

I got back to the ballroom and the owner said, 'I believe you've had the sack because you went for an audition?'

'Yes.'

'Well I pay the piper and on this occasion I'm calling the tune: you've got your job back.'

A few months later Joe came back to me and asked if I could join the band. He wanted me just as a vocalist and I hadn't foreseen that because I looked very peculiar. I was eight and a half stone with these bent rimless glasses and this huge voice that came out of this tiny little body. The glasses were always hanging off my nose and people used to do impressions of me later on, laughing about how peculiar I looked, but I was a good singer!

Having been in a band the week before that did all Gerry Mulligan arrangements, suddenly I found myself singing 'You Make My Heart Go Ticka Ticka Tock' and clapping my hands. I thought, 'My God I can't sing that, everybody will laugh at me!' This was no way for a grown man to make a living. Anyway Danny Miller, God rest his soul, took me under his wing and said, 'You'll have to get some nice suits and don't carry your music around in a brown parcel, get a briefcase.' He sort of groomed me and got me to do things I would never have dreamt of doing, comedy and things like that. From being a peculiar-looking little person, slowly I found myself, in hand-stitched suits and getting a lot of attention from the ladies and going to expensive restaurants. They groomed me into something totally different and I became a total ne'er-do-well. Before I'd practised every day on my trumpet, wanting to be a jazz musician, now suddenly it was wine, women and song! And I have to blame them for putting me on the slippery path to alcoholism and nymphomania if you can have that!

I suddenly found myself in a totally different world entertaining people and Joe's attitude was the most important people were the people you sang to. They paid your wages and you had to treat them nicely. It's true the fans were actually friends when you think how

Dizzy Gillespie and Miles Davis would turn their backs on people and most jazzmen I knew wouldn't talk to the 'punters', the idiots who knew nothing about jazz. Suddenly I was being nice to the public and I stayed 15 years with Joe like that. I learned a lot which I then took into cabaret when I left. It was a remarkable experience and totally changed my life. I became a totally different person.

Joe was marvellous really, he had great empathy with the public. He knew what they liked because he liked it. I don't mean to denigrate him when I say he was not musically sophisticated. If he didn't like a chord at the end of a song he would say, 'Change that.' Because sometimes the arrangers would put a great big oobley chord on the end and he would change it because if he didn't like it the people wouldn't like it either. So he always went on his own taste, and of course it was a great formula for success because we always did things to please the public.

He was very strict in his way of working, he didn't like you drinking, he didn't like you chasing women or giving the management any grief. Joe's philosophy was, you were making your living playing all sorts of music, whatever people wanted. I remember one of the tenor saxophone players saying to Joe, 'Do you want me to play it exactly like the record? I don't mind playing it that way but . . .' Joe stopped him at the word 'but'.

'What are you talking about? You don't mind, you're not here not to mind you're here to play it.' And that was his philosophy. He was very strict but a good man. I think he thought of himself as a father figure to all of us.

When I joined the band Rose was there. Larry Gretton came in a few months later and Larry was a great big red-faced fellow who looked like a farmer. He won't mind my saying that and we became terrific friends; we never had a cross word. We were perfect foils because I was small and he was big; he was very jolly and I could be a bit neurotic and miserable at times but we did work well together.

The reason I left the band was that Joe said he couldn't afford to pay me any more. He had a new accountant and he said he couldn't give me as much for the last year of my contract but he would offer me less to stay. I had to go and tell Joe I'd decided on a solo career and I didn't think it was right after 15 years to take a cut in wages. I've never said this in public before, but we actually cried that day. Joe said, 'You've been like a son to me,' and he gave me a big hug and we both cried a bit.

SAM WATMOUGH *Trombone 1965–*

I was about to pack the business in having got to 27 and played with most of the bands and never made any money. I'd settled back in Liverpool playing at a ballroom when drummer Red Carter said to me, what is a trombone player like you doing playing in a band like this? I told him the only two bands I would be interested in would be Ted Heath or Joe Loss. Two weeks later he came to me and said that Joe Loss wanted a trombone player.

I typed a letter to Joe, got a reply two days later to go for an audition, and I started the following Tuesday at EMI, which was 7 May 1965. I've never been anywhere else! We were doing television shows every Saturday and toured all over the country. There'd be a regular broadcast every week, a regular recording once a month, a session and a half of Luxembourg. We travelled on a coach which for those days was probably a very fine coach with a heater that would heat the bottom half of the body while the top half froze. It had 'Joe Loss' on the outside and the horn blew 'In The Mood'!

KEN MACKINTOSH

1919–

Theme 'The Very Thought of You'

Ken Mackintosh was born in the West Riding of Yorkshire where his father was a violinist with his own band. He learnt to play the saxophone at the age of 16 and was soon playing in local line-ups and gaining a considerable reputation. His musical career was cut short at the age of 20 when he was called up and sent overseas, finding himself at the evacuation of Dunkirk.

After the war he thought he would try his luck in London and joined Johnny Claes and His Clay Pigeons at the Princes Restaurant in Piccadilly, but the Yorkshire lad was soon homesick for the dales. About to head for home, he got a call from George Elrick and the next twelve months were spent on tour with the Elrick Band playing theatres and one-nighters. A spell with Oscar Rabin followed, but in 1947 Ken Mackintosh found himself back in the West End with Frank Weir's All Star Band, resident at the Lansdowne Restaurant in Berkeley Square. With George Shearing and Ralph Sharon on two pianos, the lad from Yorkshire, soon to be fronting his own band, was playing alongside the top musicians of the day.

KEN MACKINTOSH

While I was with Oscar's band I was a very keen and dedicated sax player and when we spent two or three weeks in a ballroom in Norwich called the Samson and Hercules, every morning I'd be down in this ballroom practising. I was the only one there and the chap who owned the place, Alec Taylor, would come around and listen. He sort of took a liking to me and he would invite me out on his boat on the Norfolk Broads. He was a very wealthy man.

One day he phoned me in London and said, 'Can you come and see me, I want to talk to you.' I went along to meet him and he told me he'd bought a ballroom in Nottingham and wanted me to put the band in. He'd got a chap in there called Billy Merrin, a famous old bandleader, Billy Merrin and His Commanders, and he wanted to make a change. 'I want you to lead the band for me.'

'I haven't got a band Alec and I'm just beginning to do well in London.'

'Well can't you form a band?' He wasn't a musician, you know.

'It's not that easy, and in any case I'm doing so well in London. No Alec,' I said. 'I'm not going to go to Nottingham, get a bunch of boys, and then you decide you don't like us after a fortnight and that will be it, no, no. I've got no contract, nothing.'

'I tell you what I'll do, I'll give you £160 a week for the whole band and I'll draw up a contract now in this pub in Bond Street.' You know the pub, it's next to the Aeolian Hall; we all used to go there.' So he brought a bit of paper out of his pocket, wrote a contract out and put a stamp on it to commence on Easter Monday, 1948.

I go back to Frank Weir's band that night and say to the boys in the band room, 'I've got a job with my own bloomin' band.'

'What do you mean?' they say.

'I've got a job in Nottingham and I haven't got a band.'

Jack Seymour said, 'I'll come with you, I don't like this West End bit, I'll come to Nottingham with you.' Bobby Kevin says, 'I'll come too, we'll form a band here.' So we all sat in the band room over the next few days and I rigged up a band. Jack Seymour knew a chap who was just coming out of the army called Bobby Pratt. He said 'I know just the trumpet player, he's fantastic and he's coming out of the Signals at Kettering. We'll get him, he'll come. And I know an arranger, a pal of mine; he's great – Alan Roper.'

So we get Roper over from Manchester and we booked Bobby Pratt. We had five brass and a vocalist called Roy Edwards, who became quite famous. We all went to Nottingham on Easter Monday with this band and it was a sensation, it just clicked. Syd Lawrence, who was a pal of mine, did some arrangements for us, Roland Shaw did some for me, Alan Roper, Jack Seymour; I scrounged, begged and borrowed and got a library together. We packed the ballroom out there for three years. Alec Taylor made a lot of money and couldn't do enough for me.

Then came that terribly hot summer and the business was right down as everybody was going out swimming and so on and Alec and I had words. 'Look Alec, I didn't want to lead the band in the first place, I'll go back to London and play the sax.'

'All right, finish in three months' time.'

In the meantime Mecca sent for me, and wanted me to take the band to Scotland. The Sunday morning before I went to Glasgow, Alec Taylor told me he had a chance of buying Wimbledon Palais with Oscar Rabin but he would only buy it if I would promise to go and play for him down there.

'No, no Alec, no way because if I'm going to lead the band I'd prefer to do it for a big organisation like Mecca, then if they get fed up with me in one spot I can go to another spot.' We used to broadcast in those days, by the way, from the Midland region in Birmingham.

'You know that if you ever get in the London area, Jim Davidson of the BBC has promised he will look after you,' says Alec.

Jim Davidson liked me and he liked the music and I'll never forget him putting me on a broadcast from Nottingham. There were two bands and Ted Heath was the other half playing from Torquay and I got messages from London saying how well I'd done. So maybe Alec Taylor had a point.

Anyway we went to Glasgow and were a hit there but I'd decided Alec Taylor was right and when the manager of the ballroom said, 'Go down to the tailor and get new uniforms,' I had to tell him we weren't staying! I came to London and opened at Wimbledon Palais in 1950. Once again we were a big hit and we stayed there three years.

Being out front of the band came naturally to me and never presented me with any problems. There was never any shyness; even on that first night at Nottingham I was quite at home. I remember that. It never worried me, that side of it. I always got on well with my musicians. I suppose I used to be a bit tough in those days but we always had laughs and they always respected me and some of the boys were with me 20 years; they stayed with me a long time. They were with me at Wimbledon and went on the road from there, one-nighters, Blackpool, Isle of Man. We're still carrying on playing now, a couple of gigs a week, but the popularity of the big bands is not the same. I hated to have changes with the boys who had been with me for ages. I had one boy come to me and say, 'Ken, I love working with your band, it's fantastic' and the next week he came and gave me notice.

'Hang on a minute, do you remember what you said last Friday?'

'Well Eric Winstone has offered me a job at Butlin's and it's a bit more money.' Things like that used to disappoint me.

We went to Bournemouth once for a concert and I said to my road manager, Vincent, he was an Irish lad, 'If these chaps are late don't wait for them, go.' We'd done a broadcast at two o'clock and we had something like a five o'clock rehearsal in Bournemouth and were on the coach. No motorways in those days. So we get to Bournemouth and there are four or five men missing. 'Hang on a minute Vincent, you've left the drummer behind. If you're going to leave people behind leave the third trumpet, not the drummer!' We went on and did the show without the drummer. I told the boys to stamp their feet!

I had the same coach for seven years with the same driver, little Jack, and we used to pick up in Baker Street. A lot of famous names came out of my band, Bert Courtley, Nigel Carter – Nigel came to me from a building site, very raw but I knew he was a virtuoso, and within 12 months he had that trumpet really going great – Don Lang, Bobby Kevin, Jack Seymour, Ken Jones, Les Wigfield, Pete Warner, Peter Hughes, Dave Sharman and Clive Sharrock, who's in South Africa now; he was with me 20 years.

When we were topping the bill at the Newcastle Empire I kept telling the boys who would go to the pub, 'You know what happens on these shows, the previous act goes off, up goes the curtain and, "Now we have Ken Mackintosh and His Band." They don't wait, so don't be late.' Come Saturday night the curtain flew up and the boys kept creeping on. I'll never forget that. I think I fired half of them. 'I've been telling you lot not to go in that boozer opposite.' They were pretty good lads. If you have a band of teetotallers, you don't have a band do you? I just expect the boys to use their loaf. If you want to have a drink, go and have a drink, it's not a temperance society you work for, but I don't want anybody incapable. You've got to play, you've got a job to do. I didn't have much trouble but there were a couple of incidents. I had one chap who bent down behind his stand and was sick and it all trickled down the stage!

Our first big hit was 'The Creep' and that happened because Don Lang came to me one night at Wimbledon Palais and said, 'The kids don't ask for a dance now they're asking them to come along and do a creep.' I said, 'You're kidding, hey that's a good title for a song,' and never thought any more about it. We were in HMV Records one day with Wally Ridley and we were sorting out a title for Don to sing and Wally asked what we were going to do on the other side. I said, 'I haven't given it a thought Wally,' and Don Lang said, 'Why don't you do that number that we spoke about at the Palais the other night. Do you remember, I said the kids were doing the creep now and you thought it was a good idea for a title?' Wally Ridley said, 'What did you call that?'

'It's a number called "The Creep".'

'It sounds all right to me, do it, Tuesday.'

This was on the Friday and we had to record it two o'clock Tuesday afternoon!

I walked out of Abbey Road that day with Don Lang and I said, 'You've put me in it, I haven't even got an idea for this damn number 'The Creep'. You'd better come down to the Palais in the morning and I'll get a writer in to do the arrangement and I'll think of a few ideas during the night and we'll get something going.' So I phoned Brian Fahey as he lived in Mitcham and said, 'Brian, are you available in the morning, I've got to do a number for the recording next Tuesday and I haven't even got a clue what it is!' We got down to the Palais and at the time 'Hot Toddy' was the big thing so I thought we'd start with the baritone because that sound had clicked. I plonked something out on the piano and Brian wrote it down. I sang a little riff on top of that.

'Got it down Brian?'

'Yeah.'

'Let's make a middle eight, so-and-so.'

'Right I've got enough now,' says Brian. 'Leave it to me. Ready for rehearsal Monday morning at the Palais.'

This is the funny part of it, I remember saying to Don Lang, 'Don't tell the boys that we've done it because if you tell the boys they'll kill it.' English people are like that you know, they'll kill anything of their own. The Americans aren't like that. Bert Courtley was in the band at the time and when we rehearsed this tune, he said, 'Who did that?'

'Oh it's from an American television show.'

'Ooh it's great, let's play it again.' So we played it again and all the boys thought it was marvellous asking, 'Whose show is it from?'

'Oh, Ray Anthony or somebody.', I made it all up!

I remember coming out the Palais that Saturday morning when we'd written this thing and I'd said to the boys if we get it published and anything happens to it, we'll split it three ways. We didn't think anything of it, just a little riff tune. We recorded it and the *Daily Mirror* got hold of it, did a big spread on it, and it took off. Do you know 17 bands recorded 'The Creep' including Stan Kenton. Jack Parnell did it, I think Ted Heath did it, Jerry Gray did it. They all did this blooming thing so it made a certain amount of money. Not a fortune, there were no fortunes in those days when you think of the money these pop boys make. I still get cheques for a couple of hundred quid. And Brian must get the same and Don got the same. It was my wife's name on the song copy, Burton, Andy Burton. Don had the idea, I did most of the writing, and Brian did the arrangement.

After that we did a number called 'Raunchy' which had been done in the States and Wally Ridley wanted me to do this thing with me on the sax and an electrified rhythm section. Phil Seamen played the drums and I remember Bert Weedon was on the session because they kept kidding each other. Phil kept calling him 12-bar Bert! That took off and went to number seven in the charts. 'The Creep' had got to something like number six.

I was doing one record a month you know, and was thinking of ideas and then getting arrangers to jot them down. Another idea I had, which I put to Wally Ridley one day: 'The Americans are full of doing their own streets. 'Memphis Street Blues', 'South Rampart Street Parade'. I'm going to do some tunes on stadiums.' I did 'Wembley Stadium' and 'Hampden Park' and they all had a lot of plays on the radio but they weren't hits. I would think I must have made a couple of hundred records with the band and I've made LPs on the sax. They were not terrific sellers but I did well with them.

I was never happy when I'd done a recording, I never liked it. In fact for years I used to give what we called the white labels, the test records, away. Then one day I thought I'd buy all the records we'd made so I phoned HMV and said to Wally's secretary 'Blanche, can I have copies of all my records?' 'Oh', she said, 'we delete them after 12 months.' So I never had a single record. But if I hear those recordings now I think that band was something else, although we never used to rate it.

I never went abroad with the band although I would have loved to have done that, but I never had a hit over there. You see Ted Heath was on Capitol records and he sold in the States. I had nothing selling in America so there was no point in taking me out there. In 1963 I opened at the Empire, Leicester Square. They'd spent a million pounds on turning it into a ciné/variety theatre with a ballroom downstairs. We were there for seven years doing eight sessions a week, six nights and two afternoons. People like Nigel Carter, Jimmy Hastings and Jimmy Staples were in the band then. From there I went to Hammersmith Palais and that was another seven-year engagement! In fact I swapped with Joe Loss because he came out of Hammersmith Palais and I took his place while he went to the Leicester Square Empire, but he only stayed for about six months. We'd done regular OBs from the Empire and when we went to Hammersmith we were doing *Come Dancing* and the Miss World contest for television.

I've had my band since 1948 and today I run a twelve-piece, three trumpets, one trombone, one tenor, me on alto, an electric rhythm section and two vocalists. We do all the popular medleys. It's not the big band as we knew it but I had to move with the times. Every evening we get asked, 'What about that 'Creep' number?' and I think, 'Not that again!'

A little disappointment in life is the fact I devoted so much time to the sax, playing and teaching my own boy Andrew. He's a terrific player, and I often wish I had dedicated more time to learning to play the piano. I would like to have been a good pianist and have become a fantastic arranger like Gordon Jenkins, Nelson Riddle, Rob McConnell or our own boys, Peter Knight, Wally Stott, Laurie Johnson. I'd've loved to have been one of those, running a band. I missed out not being able to write. I can write, but not as fluently as those boys can. I wish now that I'd done that. That is one disappointment in my life.

PETE MOORE *Piano 1950–53*

Ken had heard some of the writing I'd done for Teddy Foster and he was looking for someone to write charts for the band. At that time Jack Seymour was doing most of his writing and had written a hell of a good book, he and Alan Roper between them. Ken wanted someone to back them up so invited me to join the band.

Wimbledon Palais on a Saturday night became a combat zone. All the gangs used to come up from Elephant and Castle and various other places in south London and quite often there would be a terrible punch-up. Ken would stand there conducting and saying, 'Don't stop playing for Christ's sake, don't stop playing!' There'd be chairs flying and there was a bouncer there, a great big guy called Ernie Woodman, and he'd have two or three of these fellas by the scruff of the neck. He'd be pushing them out the door and someone would go bang over his head with a bottle and he'd just shake it and turn round and go wham. It was like a John Wayne film! It didn't happen every Saturday night but when it did it was like John Wayne in *Dodge City*. We daren't stop playing, it was a bit like the *Titanic*!

The Rabins, who had the lease on Wimbledon Palais, found it wasn't possible to employ a band for five nights a week and make money so they were looking desperately for a way of making it pay with other kinds of things going on. One night a week they'd have wrestling, they'd have Old Time Dancing, and another night they'd have Square Dancing. Square Dancing is the most boring bloody music you'll ever come across. We'd play the first number and Ken would say, 'Keep it going chaps' and he'd be off to the pub! He'd come back ten minutes before finishing time. 'Very good fellas, that's it!' Then we'd all go home so for the three hours we were playing this boring music and Ken would be in the pub!

Jack Seymour had one of the first effective amplified basses. The trouble was, with Jack's set-up every once in a while Kenny Bardell would be singing a heartfelt ballad and all of a sudden this amplifier would pick up the local taxi service. 'Here Charlie, nip down to Trafalgar Square'! Ken would say, 'Switch that bloody thing off!' But this used to happen at least once a night.

I would ride my motor cycle over to Wimbledon Palais from where I lived in Romford. One night I fell arse over head off this motorcycle and I had my dress shoes in a bag tied on to the back. Well I just picked the motorcycle up and went zooming off to Wimbledon Palais and when I got there I found my dress shoes were way back at London Bridge or somewhere where I'd taken the tumble! What am I going to do now wearing these bloody great boots with mud all over them? There was nothing I could do as I had no spare shoes so I just pulled my dress trousers over the top of the Wellington boots and went on the stand. Ken was playing the alto sax out front and, as he turned, his eyes slowly go down until he sees my boots. I got a terrible roasting about that but he was a good guy, Ken.

He was a fine sax player and a very good, considerate guvnor. He's the guy that said to me, 'I like what you're doing, I like the arrangements you're writing, and I want you to write things regularly for me so why don't you go to one of the colleges and learn how to write for strings and so on?' He was the guy who encouraged me to go in that direction, which was a hell of a good steer. It was an area of music and orchestration I knew nothing about and I needed to get started as soon as possible. So I wound up with a fairly full life because I was playing for Ken, writing for Ken, and also working for a music publisher during the day, writing arrangements for various people.

TONY FISHER *Trumpet 1956–59*

That was my first job on being demobbed from the air force after my National Service. That was the high time for the bands and we worked a lot. We were doing six one-nighters and Sunday concerts, and of course we did the Villa Marina on the Isle of Man.

Ken is like a legend in his own lunchtime as they say! He is a very good player and I must say that he's one of the best lead alto players I ever heard in my life. I used to call him posh Yorkshire because being a bandleader he would go on these gigs and do all the talking and make it as 'English' as he could, but he's through and through Yorkshire. He's from Cleckheaton you know, and it used to show horrendously at times! One time we did a gig at the Dorchester and someone handed him some jewellery they'd found on the floor and he said, 'Oh we have a beautiful pair of gilt earrings which have been handed up to me.' And everyone looked at each other and he said 'Oh no, of course we're at the Dorchester, they must be gold mustn't they?' That was classic Ken.

We had a band manager called Vincent. Vincent was a double-strength Irishman and he and Ken used to sit together at the front of the bus and often the whole bus would go quiet because we'd be listening to the conversation that was going on at the front, and sometimes it was absolutely hysterical. Ken was thinking about buying a car and he had a newspaper with advertisements for cars and Vincent is saying, 'That's just the thing for you Ken, a Ford Zodiac and it says £5,000 o.n.o. Only one owner.' And there was Ken nodding in agreement! It was like Laurel and Hardy at the front of that bus.

I was very young when I joined the band and I played the way I thought it was right to play, but he wanted it to be a more vibrant sort of sound and he would say to me, 'Make it sing, kid, make it sing.' He was fantastic to work for and the band was always of a good standard. Ken didn't have much time for inefficiency. And something I appreciate even more nowadays, he always had an eye for putting on a show for the people, instead of 15 fellas just sitting there playing instruments. For instance, we would do Sunday concerts and he had one or two guys in the band who were very good at doing things like impersonations. Johnny Harris, who is now big stuff in America, was on second trumpet and doing some very good arrangements. On the first Sunday concert we did, Ken announced Johnny and I thought he was going to play a trumpet solo but he went down the front and did about 15 minutes of these fantastic impressions of people like Robert Mitchum, and he did them great! I couldn't believe it. It was a good entertaining band, which a lot of the bands weren't in those days.

NIGEL CARTER *Trumpet 1964–65*

I joined Ken on second trumpet at the Empire, Leicester Square, which was a Mecca ballroom, and there would be seven or eight hundred in there most nights. The weekends were quieter. Ken was very good for me because he forced me to play things like 'Concerto for Trumpet' and things like that which I would never have attempted. My brother Roy was in the band as well, on second tenor.

I don't drink now but I did then and I don't know whether the comedy was the result of too much beer, but it escalated out of all proportion and I'm not sure whether Ken liked it or just put up with it. As a result of all these frolics on the stand he suggested I do this 'Post-Horn Gallop' for him. 'Hey kid, we'll get you a new post-horn from Boosey and Hawkes, we'll hire a stage horse and you can come down the front and play the "Post-Horn Gallop" and on cue we'll get the stage horse and the punters will think it's a great joke.' Come the night of the wheeze, I got down the front and I was very fat in those days, a hell of a belly, out here from over-indulging, and I started to play this thing and Ken brought on the stage horse. Now in the front of this stage horse there was this big bouncer and in the back of it this little Pakistani guy and he was a little matchstick guy, very weedy. Ken thought this was wonderful, but of course it all went wrong because he said, 'Get on it kid, ride it, ride it' I get on the horse and I'm about 13 or 14 stone and I landed on this Pakistani guy and the whole thing went down among the music stands. The post-horn got buried underneath all this rubble and I couldn't play for laughing anyway! We all picked ourselves up and of course the brand-new post-horn is bent in the middle in a V shape. Ken's at the other end of the stage and the red's coming down from his forehead and he can get very angry. It was like a silent volcano! 'Don't worry Ken, I'll straighten the thing' But of course they never straighten in the same place and it looked like a level crossing!

We'd do anything that would attract attention to the band and give the idea of show biz. There was another trumpet player, Colin Dobson, and he used to put on these enormous pair of ladies' drawers and go down the front with this accordion. It was Ken's accordion and one night Colin was fooling around and he got hold of the strap bit where the buttons are and hung it over the side of the bandstand and of course the clip came off, the bellows came out, it broke in two and all the keys got kicked around the ballroom! Colin also played the sousaphone wearing this regalia and used to dance with the punters as well. Ken would go along with this with a 'not quite sure whether it was going to be good for the punters or not but give the musicians their head and hopefully fling enough at the fan and some of it's bound to stick!'

There were quite a few casualties later on with drink. The profession is littered with them, especially trumpet players and classical players too – very famous players, and it's no secret they've had problems. The very finest have even committed suicide, Bobby Pratt for one. Freddy Clayton joined Alcoholics Anonymous, that was well known. One or two players in Mackintosh's band had this problem, and of course there was an awful lot of drinking going on everywhere, in the studios, and that was the heyday of studio work.

Ken's was a very good band and by broadcasting standards as good a band as I've heard play. I've got tapes of it now and it stands up great.

Old Clive Sharrock used to play 'Getting Sentimental Over You' and Ken played the occasional waltz. He was quite something on the alto. He was in the Freddy Gardner league, he had a very special tone, and I always used to think it sounded like a very bright soprano cornet, a silvery beautiful tone, effortlessly played. I think most musicians will tell you he was a giant of a player. I never heard him play in a section but as a soloist in the Empire he was quite stunning.

I never went on the road with Ken, he was always in the Empire when I was with him. There were always plenty of girls around the stand. There was one famous lady who would come around the back to the band room and display her breasts for us at the drop of a hat! She was famous. Then there was the lady in white who used to come dressed in a big hat, gloves, shoes and everything and would sit there casting some kind of spell on the band. Every Wednesday afternoon she was there, this lady in white. I think she was a mystic of some sort.

Ken could be quite angry. He would tell you if he didn't like your playing. He would say you were rotten. I remember once we had such a terrific argument on the stand, it developed into about a quarter of an hour battle of words. He would get the rhythm section to go on playing a waltz while we had this battle! And of course we never spoke to each other for quite a while after that. My brother would go in and collect my wages for me. It went on for months.

Ken had every just cause to sack one or two players, myself included I guess, for being just that little bit on the edge, but I never remember him sacking anyone. I think he was a rare breed Ken Mackintosh, a person of great stature and really a very good bandleader. He had that presence about him and he certainly knew how to train a band and how to get a band to play well.

OSCAR RABIN
HARRY DAVIS

1899-1958 1901-1996

Theme 'Dancing Time'

Oscar Rabin never fronted the band that bore his name, leaving that to the more personable and charismatic Harry Davis. Known in the business as the Gold Dust Twins, they formed a powerful partnership with Rabin supplying the business know-how and Davis the show business glamour.

Oscar Rabinowitz arrived in Britain at the age of four, the son of a Latvian cobbler. He won a scholarship to the Guildhall School of Music, formed his first dance band when he was still in his teens, and shortened his name to Rabin. He met guitarist and vocalist Harry Davis in 1924 and together they formed a small co-operative band. By 1930 the band had increased in size and a two-year residency at Wimbledon Palais put them firmly on the London map resulting in a five-year run at one of the capital's premier ballrooms, the Astoria, Charing Cross Road. This was followed by another five-year stint at Hammersmith Palais. An astute businessman, Rabin built up a highly successful agency often tying people to five-year contracts on the grounds that if he made their name, it wasn't for someone else to reap the benefit. Oscar Rabin had no time for musicians who wanted to do their own thing. He knew his customers wanted strict tempo dance music, and if the musicians didn't like it they could go.

When Harry Davis emigrated to America in 1951, David Ede took over as front man and the band landed the residency at Mecca's most coveted ballroom, the Lyceum in the Strand, where their seven-year contract had 18 months to run when Oscar Rabin died.

BERYL DAVIS *Vocalist 1932–47*

My first job with the Rabin-Davis Band, when I was eight years old, was a lovely wedding gig in the West End. 'It Happened in Monterey', sing one chorus, dance two, and I was paid two shillings which was a fortune for me! The band seemed to do every wedding and barmitzvah in London at that time. Daddy was brilliant at the party stuff. I made the grade on that occasion and became 'Little Beryl'! My tap dancing was paramount to me in those days, so everything was sing one, dance two. I worked many nights until midnight, stumbling to school next morning with smudged make-up all over me, and I was a dreadful student at St Martin-in-the-Fields School in Trafalgar Square.

Oscar and Harry found a home at the Astoria Ballroom, Charing Cross Road where Joe Loss was the relief band. I was the regular vocalist and loved every minute. From there we went to the famous Hammersmith Palais where I learnt to rollerskate on the enormous floor during rehearsals, much to everybody's annoyance! We did the first remote TV show from there with my dad compèring the whole thing as usual. Our biggest audience participation number, 'The Big Apple', was enormously popular and quite a sight. Billy Nichols was a smash as a scat singer and pretty brunette Diane sang the ballads. I did the novelty up-tempo tunes though I do remember singing 'Moon of Manakoora' with Eddie Palmer on the Novachord.

That Novachord was featured heavily at the time, and heavy was the operative word. It seemed to take the whole band to get it on and off the stage when we went on tour. We seemed to have a great talent for going to towns that had been pinpointed on the map by the Luftwaffe. Coventry, Manchester, Liverpool, Weston-super-Mare, where the BBC sent the bands for safety. I never remember any fear during those crazy times. It was just a way of life. The air-raids didn't seem to stop the performances at all. The alert would sound around seven and we'd start the theme song 'Dancing Time'. One night a big disaster during a gorgeous Freddy Gardner sax solo on 'Stardust', a direct hit! Daddy screaming 'Beryl, Beryl' in complete darkness and everyone scrambling to get out the stage door. The balcony had split in half and a lady was giving birth to her baby in the audience! We all seemed to be intact on a truck ready to leave when a scream went up 'The Novachord!', still on the now-defunct stage! Everybody back in to lift it out and shove it on the truck where we all hung on to it back to the hotel. Why we didn't drive outside that town I shall never understand. As we all ran in to the lobby and looked at each other we fell about laughing; we were pitch black from head to toe!

We worked in London all through the Blitz, running home from door to door dodging bombs and shrapnel all the way and never going to a bomb shelter! The most we did was to sit on the stairs outside our flat at 30 Stourcliffe Close, Marble Arch, along with one of our agents at that time, Lew Grade of the Collins and Grade Agency.

That band was my great learning experience. God knows it's hard working for your dad but I seemed to handle it quite well in my own way. I received incredible training from him and many great laughs from my Uncle Oscar. I loved his humour and the big family, Auntie Leah, Bernard, David, Marlene; they became my family too.

Those were great days. My last show was a special guest spot just before I sailed to America in January 1947, at a big venue in Bristol. It was a very tough moment for me as I was due to sing 'You Made Me Love You' with my dad but broke down emotionally and was a total mess! Still can't sing that song without a problem. What a wonderful start the Rabin–Davis Band gave me. Yes, I was extremely lucky to be a part of it and I'm still swinging!

HARRY GOLD *Tenor saxophone 1939–42*

Oscar Rabin sent a message saying he needed a second alto player in his band and would I be interested? I told him I wasn't playing alto any more but I could quite easily transpose the parts on tenor as I could transpose anything.

Oscar was at Hammersmith Palais so I was in town, I was at home. Okay it's hard work but it's not really hard work when you're blowing. I enjoy whatever I do when I'm blowing. All my life I've been a blower, a musician, I know nothing else. Then the war broke out and the government decided there would be no entertainment. They were frightened of people gathering together in case of mass bombing. As you know it started with the phoney war, I think they called it, and there was no work. What were we going to do?

I heard they were lining up at Hammersmith Town Hall to do labouring so I joined the queue and went to be a labourer. You had to get money somehow and I don't mind work, I couldn't care less as long as I get paid! Standing in line I was watching a real labourer trundling a one-wheel wheelbarrow with a load of sandbags on it. He was a hefty man, nine feet tall and ten feet wide, the British workman, look at him! I got the job along with Oscar Rabin's son Bernard. He was only 16 but he was a big fella and looked much older. My first job was to carry sandbags on my shoulder and it was like two rows of ants, one lot of guys going one way with the sandbags and another line coming back to pick them up.

Thinking of this guy I'd seen trundling the barrow, I thought, 'I'm going to show them'; I was pretty strong and still am. So I'm rushing along when a fellow coming the other way to pick up his bag shouted, 'What the f– you think you're doing?' It suddenly hit me they got a union as well! So I started slowing down. Then I got moved up to a wheelbarrow and now I'm going to show that fellow with three bags on it. Oscar's son was with me so I told him to put the bags on the barrow, come on keep going. I went to lift the thing and it wouldn't move so I take one bag off and it still wouldn't move. I eventually got down to three and I could lift that! You learn by experience!

I did labouring until the Palais reopened in about a month when the government decided it was a false alarm. There were two bands, Oscar was the main band and we did three until five in the afternoons, tea dances. Evening was eight to eleven or twelve. Beryl Davis was the vocalist with Diane, who married Bernard and became Oscar's daughter-in-law.

Oscar was a lovely fellow, he was really kind. In fact it was through him that I started the Pieces of Eight. At one time I did all of his arrangements because publishers used to pay for them to be done in those days. Being a broadcasting band he would need special arrangements and he didn't want publishers' arrangers, he wanted his own arranger. So I did all right out of that. We did one broadcast a week and you couldn't keep on playing the same numbers so it was good.

Oscar was a very shy man, very humorous in the band room where he could tell funny stories, but once he got out in public he was lost completely. He played fiddle quite well and occasionally in a waltz he might come out and do that. Harry Davis was the guitar player and he dressed well, looked well and could speak well, so he was the front man. Oscar also played bass sax, usually two in a bar, boom boom, boom boom. He had to do something and as arrangements got more modern he couldn't play the fiddle. One day I said, 'Look Oscar, I hope you don't mind me saying this but you're not in tune with the bass player. This might sound very hard and very rude of me but pretend to play it and I'll take the reed off.' And he went along with it! I had a bass sax but I didn't play it in that band.

We used to stay in the Palais as once the bombs started falling we couldn't go home. My wife stayed as well and they made bunks for us in a little room. Later on when I went there with my own band that room was a dressing-room and it had just a thin wooden roof, so we could have been destroyed but we didn't know that then! When the bombing started, Oscar was very, very nervous, terrified, and so we left the Palais and went on tour playing dances, and then we went into variety. One day I said to him, 'Oscar, it would be a good idea if you had a band within a band as you still want to do some jazz and it will help the show. Make it a Dixieland band, I'll do the arrangements and I'll pick the guys I think will be suitable.' I thought, 'I don't want this to be Oscar Rabin's band, I want it to be my band.' So I said I wanted to use my name and he said, 'Sure, no problem.'

We were in Glasgow at that time, staying with my wife's sister and her husband, and I told them I wanted a name, something like the Five Pennies. We sat up most of the night thinking of names and my brother-in-law as a joke said, 'Pieces of Eight, ha, ha, ha.' I said, 'That's it!' That was absolutely right so I went back the following morning to Oscar and said, 'It's going to be called Harry Gold and His Pieces of Eight' 'Fine, fine,' said Oscar, and that was the start of the Pieces of Eight.

He really was a lovely man. The tough man was Harry Davis and he took on the personality of a bandleader, but Oscar was a lovely man and he'd joke with the lads and everything.

WALLY STOTT *Alto saxophone 1941–43*

I'd been with Bram Martin's band for the whole summer on the North

Pier in Blackpool and Oscar Rabin's band came to the theatre for the week and I went there and asked for an audition. They had four saxophones: Harry Gold on lead alto, really a tenor player, Harry Conn was second alto, and the tenors were Benny Keane and George Roberts who had been with Ken Johnson, the band that was half decimated at the Café de Paris when a German bomb came in through the roof. I did this audition on first alto, got the job, and two weeks later I joined the band at Weston-super-Mare.

In those days the BBC would send a band every week to a studio or church hall in Weston-super-Mare and you did a broadcast every day as the Band of the Week. We were on tour playing the Moss Empires and occasionally we'd go to Green's Playhouse in Glasgow which was a huge ballroom. It could take thousands of dancers and we would go there for six weeks and then we would set off on tour again and occasionally go to Weston-super-Mare.

Oscar Rabin was a little man who didn't have the personality to be a bandleader and he knew that, so he had a partnership with Harry Davis, Beryl Davis's father, who was a very handsome-looking man. He dressed immaculately, could speak, could announce things, and could keep his head and count the band in. So it was called Oscar Rabin and His Band with Harry Davis. I think Harry Davis's instrument was the guitar, but I never heard him play it. Oscar sat in the band and he played a bass sax doubling on the string bass parts. He would do that for a bit then he would have a rest and a look around and count the seats, see how many people in the audience and think what the receipts would be, then he'd play a bit more.

Beryl Davis was a wonderful singer. She was an amazing young lady because when she was in her early teens, maybe 15 years old, she was singing with the Hot Club of France in Paris. Stephane Grappelli was a family friend. I was 17 and a half when I joined the band but I think she might have been slightly younger than me. Of course, she didn't look like a child.

Eddie Palmer, the pianist, would do a feature, and this was the thing that made the Rabin Band a little different. He had a Novachord which was a kind of synthesiser which they rented from Boosey and Hawkes. It was full of valves and things and was more like a synthesiser than an organ but it was always going wrong and breaking down. They didn't play it in the band but it would have its own numbers with the rhythm section. They would say, 'Now at the Novachord we have Eddie

Palmer.' The drummer was Bobby Richards who was the first drummer I heard that played like Buddy Rich and did a drum feature. It was a lot of fun being in that band.

KEN MACKINTOSH *Alto saxophone 1945–47*

I was with George Elrick and he decided to disband – he must have lost money or something – and I was walking along Oxford Street in Manchester with some of the boys and we bumped into Harry Davis and Oscar Rabin. We started to talk and Harry Davis asked who I was working with. I told him George Elrick but he was finishing so he said, 'We're looking for a sax player to take Wally Stott's place, would you like to join our band?' I said I wouldn't mind at all so I joined on lead sax as Wally Stott had gone to Geraldo.

One of the best features of the Rabin Band in those days was its sax section, which came to light when we did a programme called *Reeds and Rhythm* which I'd suggested to Oscar. He thought it was a good idea and took it to the BBC. It was all fast technical sax playing in those days and we made quite an impact with that recording, and people still talk to me about it today.

At the end of the war we went to Paris to play at the Marigny Theatre in the Champs Elysée while the Glenn Miller Band was at the Olympia, so we saw a lot of them. We would go to their rehearsals and they came to ours.

I toured all over with Oscar. We did Ireland, we did Scotland, everywhere in the British Isles, and during that time Frank Weir was forming an all star band and he phoned me and asked me to join.

MARJORIE DAW *Vocalist 1949–54*

In those days Oscar would look at the boys' nails before they went on stage. You had to be perfectly clean, you couldn't go on stage looking rough. The discipline was incredible although the boys hated all that! The singers with the band when I joined were Marion Davies, who later married Ken Goldie, and Denis Hale. Then a Scots girl joined, Patti Forbes, and then Marion Williams. There were always two girls and one fellow.

Harry and Oscar were both very nice to me. I'd come over from South Africa and knew nothing about being with musicians and I learnt more in my first three weeks with that band than I'd learnt in my whole life! But nobody used any bad language or anything like that in front of the singers.

We were touring and there were always girls at the back of the bus who the musicians had picked up in the ballroom and they would be dropped off at the next town or somewhere! Some of those girls, the boys married. As Kenny [Clare] always said, the drummers never got a girl because they were so busy packing up the drums, so he had to find a singer!

Kenny joined the band six months after I did. He'd just finished his National Service so he was 20 when he joined and he chased me for two years because I was older than him! Nobody knew we were going out together until we decided to get married.

The band was at the Lyceum and Oscar said we had to get married on our day off, which was a Monday, and we could have Tuesday and Wednesday off but he wanted us back at work on the Thursday! On the Sunday, Oscar made this announcement that we were getting married the next day. There was this fellow who always sat up in the balcony with dark glasses on, looking at the girls. And we used to say, 'Which one is he looking at tonight?' Anyway that night when I got to the stage door, carrying a large glass bowl that Patti Forbes had given to me, this fellow came up to me and he said, 'You can't marry Kenny Clare, I'm madly in love with you, you can't.' There wasn't a soul behind me at the stage door and I said, 'If you don't leave me alone I'll hit you on the head with this bowl,' and he disappeared and I don't know who it was to this day. The next day in church I was so worried he was going to turn up and shout something!

I eventually decided to leave the band as I got fed up with it being every afternoon and evening except Mondays, and even then we'd sometimes go and do another gig somewhere. When you joined a band in those days you had to sign a five-year contract, but when I told Oscar I wanted to leave he let me go. Soon after that Kenny had a telegram from Ted Heath asking if he could join the band as Jack Parnell was leaving. Ken went to Oscar and asked if he could leave and Oscar said, 'You've still got some of your contract to go but if you pay me £100 you can leave.' We didn't have £100 so Ken turned Ted down.

Many years later, when we were at one of Ted's parties, because Ken worked with him on and off, he asked Ken why he turned down his offer and when Ken told him it was because he didn't have £100 to pay Oscar, Ted said, 'I would have paid the £100 for you'!

PETE WARNER *Tenor saxophone 1951–53*

Arthur Greenslade left Vic Lewis to move to Oscar Rabin and recommended me, and Rabin was a much bigger name at that time. David Ede was fronting the band, good clarinet player and of course a few years later he went to Blackpool with the band after Oscar had died and went out on a yacht which overturned and he drowned.

We were resident at the Lyceum in the Strand. Six afternoons, six evenings, a one-night stand on the day off, a broadcast on the Friday morning, you never stopped work and the embouchure was like cast iron! We could dress well, eat well and live well, and that's what everybody wants really. Bernie Sharpe and I had a flat in Lancaster Gate and we would practise yoga in order to keep going. We'd be running up the stairs at the end of the night when the rest of the guys would be dragging themselves up!

Sunday was Jazz Day and we got to play jazz all day and all night. There'd be a line down the middle of the Lyceum with the black folk on one side and the white folk on the other side and then you'd just wait for things to start happening and it always did. There would always be some sort of trouble, fighting and so on, but it was still a very enjoyable night. We would have Benzedrine strip and Green Chartreuse, which was about 98 per cent proof, to keep us going! Oh yes, we were very 'alert' but it was all legal; if you were going to get raving there was the legal way to do it.

On listening to the recordings made by the Rabin band, it was a beautifully balanced band, the arrangements were beautiful, the singers were great and Oscar never troubled us at all. He was a lovely man, a real gent.

GARRY BROWN *Trombone 1952*

I went back to the north of England in 1952 and I'd only been back a few weeks when I got an urgent phone call that Charlie Messenger had been taken ill and I had to come straight down to town and go into the Lyceum in Charlie's place.

I used to do Oscar's broadcasts and when I got to the Lyceum I knocked on Oscar's door and he tweaked my ear, he always did that to everyone! 'Thanks a lot Garry for coming down, I see you've got the uniform and it fits okay.' Charlie and I were about the same size so that was all right but what I didn't know was that Charlie had German measles! Nobody had told me that and I was wearing his uniform!

I did odds and ends for Oscar but I was never a member of the band for longer than a few weeks, but I would do a lot of his broadcasts on bass trombone because there was really only Jimmy Coombs and I who were actually playing B Flat and F instruments.

I remember getting off the coach at Baker Street at six in the morning after travelling all night and going straight to the Playhouse Theatre and starting the rehearsal at nine for a broadcast with Oscar, who was sat back in the stalls. He'd stopped touring then and the band was resident at the Lyceum. In the coffee break he came up to me, tweaked my ear and said, 'You look tired Garry. Why don't you stop all this touring and join my band at the Lyceum. You can come in there and be home every night. You know son, I toured for years . . . in a Rolls-Royce!' That was Oscar.

HARRY ROY

1899–1971

Theme 'Bugle Call Rag'

Harry Roy made his West End debut as vocalist and soprano saxophonist in his brother's band at the Café de Paris in 1924. Sid Roy and His Lyricals were the toast of the town, but Sid was never in any doubt that it was Harry who had the best potential as a bandleader and showman. Six years later Sid Roy took a back seat in order to encourage Harry to start his own band, which he did in 1930 with a quartet at the Bat Club where they were known as the Bat Club Boys. In August of that year, RKO opened their Leicester Square Theatre with a spectacular stage show featuring Harry Roy fronting a 13-piece line-up called the RKOlians. The band included such future stars as Joe Daniels, Nat Temple and Sid Millward, with Ivor Moreton and Dave Kaye on two pianos.

First and foremost Harry Roy was a showman, greatly influenced by such performers as Ted Lewis and Cab Calloway, whose scat singing he adopted. From the RKO Theatre he went to the Café Anglais where his twice-weekly broadcasts brought in some 2,000 fan letters a week. But when the band was booked to appear at the Mayfair Hotel in 1933, sceptics from Tin Pan Alley to Archer Street predicted disaster. No way would the upper crust of London society accept this scat singing, clarinet tooting, rowdy showman. How wrong they were. It wasn't long before Harry Roy had the Mayfair clientele in the palm of his hand.

213

NAT TEMPLE *Clarinet 1931–40*

Harry and I came in contact with each other because he lived in the next road to me in Stamford Hill where the whole of the Temple family were practising at the same time, much to the annoyance of the neighbours. Harry passed by, liked what he heard, and gave me an audition.

He had become the bandleader at the RKO Theatre in Leicester Square where I soon got the bullet. And the reason I got the bullet was my face was covered in pimples, I was only 15, and they didn't think that would look very nice, but eventually they took their chance, the pimples went away, and I stayed with Harry for nine years!

From the moment we started at 12.30 p.m. it was a mixture of films and a show with the band doing their own show and backing the other artists. Naunton Wayne was one, Jack Hulbert, Claude Hulbert, Florence Desmond, and other stars of that era and it went on until midnight. We just stayed there the whole day. The boys used to play cards between their various appearances and once they overdid it. The idea was we came up in a pit that rose as we were playing, which was a sensational innovation. This particular time the pit did rise but there was no band, they were playing cards. It just rose up with nothing on it and then went down again! Harry would have been playing cards too and probably losing his lot! He was a bit of a gambler.

I think that engagement lasted for six months and then we went to a little restaurant in Northumberland Avenue and from there to the London Pavilion, which was non-stop variety and you could sit there all day from 12 to 12 and see the thing umpteen times.

It was BBC producer Pat Dixon who got Harry the audition for the London Pavilion. He did a lot for Ted Heath, he did the *Goon Show*, *Take It From Here*, *Hancock*; he fought his way through all the opposition to push a show. He had tremendous courage and would put his job on the line. I remember being in the office when he was told to take me off the Braden shows because they had a 'house' band. I was there when Pat said, 'No, don't tell me how to run my show, Nat stays.' Bang, the phone went down! Not many people would do that. I've never forgotten him, he was a great guy.

As a player, Harry was terrible. He was way out of touch with what had happened to the clarinet and the style of playing. He belonged to the Ted Lewis school which was play a high note and hold on to it for three hours and growl and laugh and all that sort of thing. He also told musical lies because if he was asked by a fan if he'd played this or that and how wonderful he was, he wouldn't come clean and say it wasn't him. He once confessed to me, 'Nat, I've had to tell people that it wasn't me playing the clarinet introduction on "Rhapsody in Blue", but I think that's the only time he confessed to not doing something and it was going on all the time.

I played first alto and clarinet on recordings and broadcasts. Harry seldom played on broadcasts; in fact I don't think he ever did. That was always me on the band as it was. He would sing a lot and he certainly had an individual style! It was based on that old razzmatazz style of growl. But there were many other aspects to Harry's character, apart from musicianship. There was his showmanship, business ability, and all those things that help one be successful, and he was terribly popular. I've seen the fire brigade called out to keep the crowds back. He was really something. I've never reached that stage!

I never knew anybody who hated Harry or even disliked him, and I suppose that is rare when you think of leaders like Goodman or Shaw, you will find people who thought they were not as nice as they should have been. His playing was an absolute joke but they appreciated the showmanship. The crowd at the Café Anglais would gather around when he was holding this high note one-handed while the other hand was at the back of his neck! That was showmanship.

You certainly appreciated he was your paymaster and he was a famous band; we did umpteen command performances. He married a very sweet girl, Princess Pearl of Sarawak, but he was a little unfaithful here and there and that led to trouble and they broke up.

Jack Collier was on bass, Joe Daniels on drums; later Ray Ellington took his place, great drummer and a good singer. Harry Hayes came in very occasionally on baritone. On recordings Ivor Moreton and Dave Kaye with Joe Daniels were called the Tiger Ragamuffins, and one night at the Mayfair Ivor Moreton and Dave Kaye handed in their notice because they'd arranged to set up their own little band, and of course Harry was broken-hearted and thought the end of the world had come. He never spoke to them again, he thought that was a terrible blow because to him Ivor was the keystone of the whole band. I was half pleased because although they were good they didn't have the sort of musicianship that I idolised. Stanley Black was a good friend of mine and I brought him into the band and Harry accepted him almost out of despair. But it was a big step up musically because Stanley came in with his writing ability and his brilliant playing and that improved the band no end.

The Mayfair was very posh indeed. We played *sotto voce* because in those days people insisted on that so they could carry on talking while they were dancing past the band without having to raise their voices. That was essential: you must play quietly. The clientele were the aristocracy, you didn't take much notice whether they were dukes or earls, they were just there with their funny evening dress. The jackets were always wrong or the sleeves didn't come down right. They had no idea how to dress, it wasn't a Savile Row exhibition. But they were charming people and they had a code of behaviour which was admirable, at least outwardly. We played from nine until two with no interval, but the band would split so a few of us would go off for a break at a time. Harry would very often be off chatting. Most bandleaders would be asked to go over to a table for a drink of champagne, that was quite normal. Some overdid it and would go straight to a table and the band would take no notice and play on, but that wasn't approved of.

When we went to South America we were probably the highest-paid band in the world at that time, and that was a fabulous trip. There were aeroplanes flying overhead as we sailed in: 'Welcome Harry Roy'. We took 17 days to get there and landed in Buenos Aires, but we weren't a success in spite of all the ballyhoo. There was something missing. We didn't draw the crowds and I don't think they liked us very much, but that is my personal opinion.

The opening night in Buenos Aries was disastrous. We'd finished the stage show and the idea was for the curtains to swing down but they didn't. Nobody had thought to work that one out and in that particular theatre the curtains moved about an inch at a time and as the applause had died away and we were still on the stage, it felt like a week until the curtain dropped!

We were out there for four months. The contract said they could employ us for x number of hours a week for the same salary, so that meant if they put us in one place for half an hour and we were due to play four hours, they could send us anywhere and the time only counted when we were playing, not for the journey to get there. There were a tremendous number of rows over that. Going to Peru for just half an hour and things like that! We went everywhere by car and I remember driving across the Andes, very dangerous I thought. You'd look down thousands of feet and there was no barrier to stop you going over. I think Harry knew, deep down, that it wasn't the success he'd hoped for, but he must have been getting a lot of money which made him happy. Of course when we came back, according to the publicity, it had been a big success!

When war broke out everything shut down, but it was the so-called phoney war and when it all started to get back to normal we went into the Café Anglais. It was crowded as nobody stayed at home; they went out dancing, and if there was a very heavy air-raid, they'd stay underground in some of the places. Quaglino's used to have a very good underground shelter. The Café de Paris was the same; we did tea dances at the Café de Paris and evenings at the Café Anglais. They were the same company.

The band went on working as most bands did, but they had to lose key personnel because of the call-ups so there were always people coming in and going out. I joined the Grenadier Guards as solo clarinet, but in those days once you'd done your duties and played in this, that and the other you could do what you pleased, so I could rejoin the band on a sort of ad hoc basis. When I went overseas with the Grenadier Guards I had to leave Harry. His band started to go down in popularity but that was inevitable. I think Joe Loss was about the only band that really survived and probably improved his status.

HARRY HAYES *Baritone saxophone 1934*

Harry Roy had been driving me mad to join his band and I used to say to him, 'Harry I love you but I couldn't possibly stand that music you play!' Then I got this phone call from him saying 'Listen to this, you know I'm at the Mayfair Hotel and I'm going to do six months at the London Palladium in the Crazy Gang Show. Now the money will be fantastic, does that interest you?'

'Mmm, okay I'll come, what will I play?'

'Play what you like.'

'Well let's see, you've got four saxophones so I'll play the baritone.'

I hired a baritone and it was the funniest six months I've ever had! Bud Flanagan's dressing-room was on the same level as the band's and on Wednesdays and Saturdays, matinée days, his dressing-room was like a betting shop! Bud used to walk across the stage from the side, wave to the crowd and turn round to us and say 'It won' or 'It lost'. While we were there Bud was told by a jockey he knew, to back the Aga Khan's horse in the Derby, Mahmoud at 33 to 1. The whole Palladium backed it and it was a matinée day, a Wednesday, and he walked across the stage and said, 'It f–ing won!' The whole Palladium went mad because everybody had backed it! The party went on all day and night. What a marvellous tip, 33 to 1!

STANLEY BLACK *Piano 1936–38, 1941–42*

I joined Harry Roy on 10 January 1936, to the disgust of everyone in the profession. Stanley Black going with the 'cowboy band', as it was called, because they were fooling around all the time and music was secondary. It was the show, the comedy that was all important.

The night I joined Harry Roy at the Mayfair Hotel we played for about ten minutes when the head waiter came and whispered something to Joe Crossman who was sort of the deputy leader. Bill Curry, the vocalist in the band, waved us to a standstill, came on to the bandstand, switched on the microphone and made an announcement I shall never forget: 'Ladies and gentlemen, there will be no more dance music tonight, the King is slowly passing away.' We packed up and we all walked down to the palace and saw the notice put up when he died later that night. So my first date with Harry Roy consisted of about ten minutes.

Harry was a big confidence trick really. He had a brother named Sid who started the Harry Roy dynasty as it were. Sid was known to all and sundry as the bastard because he was the one that argued about money and asked why you hadn't had your dinner suit pressed and things like that, while Harry walked around with a halo round his head! Harry was a great showman but as a musician he had a sort of gropy kind of technique, rather like a bad suit: it fitted where it touched! He was a Ted Lewis kind of player. He would forgive you anything you may have missed musically as long as you sat there and smiled. That was the thing, you had to smile all the time. And that was it, you could do the most maniacal things, it didn't matter. If the audience laughed you keep it in and you do it every night! He always said we should memorise every note we were going to play on the show and he insisted on it. There were no music stands on stage and everybody had to memorise everything. He was a showman in that sense. You walked onto the stage with a little bit of manuscript paper, the bit you hadn't memorised yet, and a soda water siphon. Halfway through if you got a squirt of soda that was fine and towards the end of the show when the fun really started we picked up the siphons and the battle began. The rhythm against the saxes and the brass and everybody and everything getting wet!

One August we had a farewell concert because we were all going on holiday. It was in Manchester and the stage was swimming with water creeping down towards the footlights. The act finished that night, with the band still playing, nothing stopped that, but with two stagehands in front of the audience sweeping the water back up stage! All those mad band ideas emanated from Harry.

He was a stickler for that sort of discipline. It was a vaudeville discipline rather than a musical one. I was at the Mayfair with both Harry Roy and Ambrose and they were very different. With Harry everything hung out, it was more fun once you realised you weren't playing for any *Melody Maker* contest. Miraculously we still managed to produce quite a good sound when we were playing seriously but soon the fooling would start whereas with Ambrose it was all meticulous – no messing around.

My big memory of Harry Roy was going to South America with the band. That's when I acquired my taste for Latin American music. I used to walk around with a notebook making sketches, listening and really taking it all in. I took it very seriously because I became known eventually as something of an authority – horrible word – on Latin American music.

I joined him again after being invalided out of the forces when I got a cable saying, 'Going out on tour can you join me?' signed Harry Roy. Although people didn't like working for Harry because they were worried about their reputations, so many places had folded and there was so little doing that Harry could virtually pick and choose.

We were playing the number one Moss Empires and it was a little frightening in places like Leeds and Manchester. You'd play the first house while it was still light but the moment darkness began to fall the air-raid sirens went. It was a case of dodging between the stage and the shelter. There would be an announcement along the lines that things were hotting up and for the safety of everyone would you follow the attendants into the shelter. Then the all clear would sound and we would all troop back. It played havoc with the length of the show!

EDNA KAY *Vocalist 1941*

Harry was very gentlemanly towards me because people had forewarned me that he could be a bit of a naughty boy. But he was very good because he knew that Stanley Black was my steady boyfriend. One day after a rehearsal Harry said, 'Come on, come and have a bite to eat.' I think his brother was there too but excused himself and we went to the Ambassadors which was a very smart club, known as Les A. We had lunch there and I don't know whether he was trying to impress me but he said, 'You realise that Stanley Black could never take you to a place like this?' I didn't answer and he went on, 'Not that I'm saying anything against him but he'll never be able to take you to anywhere like this.' I had to bite my tongue because it was so funny!

Harry's claim to fame was having been married to Princess Pearl of Sarawak, so he was obviously trying to impress and I don't know why because I wasn't giving him a 'come on' at all, and I don't think he was with me, it was just a Harry thing, trying to impress. He had lots of girlfriends.

One would do concerts at air bases during the war and very often the commander of the base would present me with a present of parachute silk. And I would also try to scrounge coupons from all the family so I could have dresses made.

WOOLF PHILLIPS *Arranger/ trombone 1940s*

In 1942–43 I get a letter from Harry Roy's office with a song copy of 'Brazil'. Could you do an arrangement of this etc. I hadn't seen Harry Roy since I played cricket with him eight years earlier and from then on I did a lot of arrangements for him. I got on very well with Harry and I liked him immensely. He was the corniest thing in the world as a player and he wrote all those compositions which were dreadful so I used to make them into good numbers. '9 o'clock Bounce' etc.: I did so many of them.

When I came home on leave I would play trombone with him when he played at a night club called the Milroy. My brother Sid played at Le Suivi; everybody played at Le Suivi and he was there for a couple of years. He was a corporal before he took his commission as an intelligence officer. I remember one time I was on leave with him and we were playing with Leslie 'Jiver' Hutchinson on trumpet, Yorkie de Sousa playing piano, Max Abrahams on drums, I was playing trombone and it was great. Sid was in the RAF and I was in the army but we were in evening dress. This particular night the place was packed and all the big shots were there. Robert Newton, the actor, was lying drunk on the stand. We'd just started and we saw a man who was obviously a Marshal of the Royal Air force. It was Air Chief Marshal Sir William Sholto Douglas and he was dancing and I thought, 'Oh, what's going to happen now?' As he came dancing past he said, 'Hello Sid, everything fine?' 'Yes sir, thank you very much,' and I thought why doesn't he say 'Shoot him'! Sid is standing there in an ordinary suit and he's in the air force; you can't do this. So Sholto Douglas was also a Sid Phillips fan! Can you imagine that?

LITA ROZA *Vocalist 1942–43*

I saw an ad in the *Liverpool Echo* for a girl singer in Southport in a night club cum restaurant and I asked my mum if she would take me to the audition; I was just coming up to 16 at the time. I remember singing 'Moonlight Becomes You', and I got the job and was paid five pounds a week. I kept that job for about 16 weeks, I remember that clearly because I saved up sixteen pounds out of the money I earned to come to London to see what I could do. My mother said I could go, but only for two weeks, and if I hadn't got a singing job by then I had to go home.

I took what they like to call a studio flat in Mornington Crescent. Oh it was dreadful, and I lived on beans on toast and did the rounds of the music publishers every day to find out if they had any news of anyone wanting a singer, and it was always 'no'. Then I went into the Norris Music Publishing company and there was this man sitting playing the piano and he said, 'Can I help you?'

'Yes, I want to be a singer.'

'Can you sing?'

'Well I think so.'

I can't remember what it was I sang for him but at the end he said, 'I'll take you to the Star Sounds Studios and we'll make a record.' They weren't called Demo Discs in those days so I thought, 'My God I'm making a record!' I had no idea what the intention behind this was. We did it and when I heard my voice coming back through the speakers I couldn't believe it was me. You don't sound on record the way you think you sound in your head.

Anyway, he was quite impressed and said he was going to send it off to Harry. 'Harry who?' I asked. 'Harry Roy.' I thought, 'My God, Harry Roy' because he was the big news in those days. This man's name was Sid Green and he told me Harry was looking for a girl singer to replace Rennie Lester. He had two girl singers, one was Rennie Lester and the other was Marjorie Kingsley. 'I'll send this up to Harry as he's at the Coventry Hippodrome this week and if you come in at the end of the week I'll let you know what he says.' A couple of days later I heard that Harry wanted me to go up to Coventry so he could have a look at me. But I had to tell Sid Green I didn't have the money for the fare so he said, 'That's all right, I'll pay your fare.'

Harry liked me and I got the job. I took Rennie Lester's place and Rennie eventually became Suzi Miller. I worked with the band for almost a year. I remember I had my 17th birthday when I was with him. I think I started on about twelve pounds a week, but I had to pay for my digs.

Harry was terrific because he was such a personality. I think at the time he was having an affair with Marjorie Kingsley because she was the sultry songstress and I was the personality girl and I had to sing all the up tempo numbers. Marjorie was very sophisticated and married to an American and I was sort of in awe of her because I thought she was the very essence of sophistication. How wonderful to be like that!

We were mostly doing weeks in variety as Harry was a big variety draw and he would take the whole of the second half. He had a gimmick where he used to invite people up to lead the band. They would be doing numbers like 'Hang Out the Washing on the Siegfried Line', then Marjorie would come on and add a little sophistication and I would come on and sing a Betty Hutton number and then Harry would invite people to come and lead the band who were all ready to make an absolute mess of it, however they were conducted, and it was a great success.

When I joined Harry I had two evening dresses from my work at Southport and then Marjorie sold me one of her dresses and I felt I'd arrived as I was in a glamorous gown. I stayed for almost a year and then in 1943 the band was going out to Egypt to entertain the troops, and of course I was only 17 and couldn't leave the country. Bandleaders had subsidiary bands and Harry had one working at the Regal Ballroom, Marble Arch, so he said I could go and work with his band there until they got back. Now here's a strange thing: about three years ago when I was at the Barbican with the Heath Band an elderly man came up to me and he said, 'You won't remember me but I was the bass player at the Regal Ballroom, Marble Arch, when you and Frankie Abelson were singing with the band.' There was a boy singer with the band and I only knew him as Frankie Abelson but of course that was Frankie Vaughan, and Frankie has never mentioned that.

I stayed at the Regal for a while and then I discovered they wanted a girl singer at the Embassy Club in Bond Street. So I went to see Art Thompson, did an audition, and got that job, so I had two jobs going.

When my contract was up at the Regal Ballroom I got another job from eight until eleven at the Albany Club in Savile Row with Mickey Wood's Trio. Then I would go to the Embassy Club and finish at three thirty in the morning. I was now living in a luxury flat in Luxborough Court and was quite rich! My mother was quite shy about it all but my father loved it as I think really I was doing what he had always secretly wanted to do, to be an entertainer.

Marjorie Kingsley rang me one day and asked me to lunch as she wanted me to meet a Flight Lieutenant in the RCAF, very handsome, and evidently he'd seen a photograph of me with the band and asked Marjorie to arrange a meeting. Three days later he proposed and I accepted. I thought this was great, getting married in secret and surprising everybody, but you couldn't in those days because you had to be 21 and I was only 18. I had to take him up and introduce him to my mother and that was the first lie I ever told her as I said I'd known him for a year. I couldn't have been in love with him – let's face it, after three days that's impossible – it was just the romance of it all. So I married him at Marylebone Registry Office and eventually we went to America.

FREDDY STAFF *Trumpet 1953–54*

I was on the halls with Harry for almost a year. The 'Met', Edgware Road, and all the different places, and Butlin's at Filey for the summer season. My audition was in the office in Lower Regent Street and after I'd played for him he said, 'That's fine, the only trouble is do you have to wear glasses because I've got eight of the band with glasses already!'

The funny part about working with Harry was we had to wear make-up on stage. It used to be embarrassing getting the all-night bus home with the make-up on my shirt collar. In those days you were a 'Nancy boy' with make-up, but we didn't have time to take it off!

Harry was a lovely guy and he was great with kids, marvellous. At Filey if he couldn't bring comics on the beach he'd buy annuals and books. He'd come loaded with stuff. I don't know whether he had any children of his own, I don't think he did. His second wife Sonia was there at Filey.

After leaving Harry I joined Woolfy Phillips at the Pigalle because Woolfy had all the sessions in those days.

LEW STONE

1898-1969

Theme 'Oh Susannah'

Lew Stone was a natural musician. As a child he took piano lessons but, being a keen footballer and cricketer, never had time to practise. Twenty minutes' concentration at the keyboard before an exam was sufficient to ensure success.

Drummer Bill Harty got him his first job playing in a club for ten shillings a night after it had been raided and the original pianist was too scared to play there any more. But Lew Stone's first band of note was the Savoy Havana Band directed by Bert Ralton. It was for them that he did his first arrangements, and it was as an arranger that he was to find fame before, somewhat reluctantly, becoming a bandleader.

Lew Stone had already acquired a formidable reputation as chief arranger for Ambrose when he joined Roy Fox at the Monseigneur Restaurant on piano and began writing most of the band's scores. When Roy Fox was taken ill Lew Stone took over, and in 1932 led the restaurant's resident band under his own name. Later he was to be much in demand as musical director for West End musicals such as *On Your Toes* (1936), *Under Your Hat* (1938) and *Annie Get Your Gun* (1947). He also composed and conducted the music for 42 films.

JOYCE STONE

After we were married I would copy the orchestrations and I took over the fan mail for one week and there were something like 90 letters. Lew's sister Sally had been doing them and I told her she could have the whole lot back as I couldn't bear it. Dirty little bits of paper from what I imagine were poor little girls who were drudges in big houses, and Lew would say, 'Answer those first as it makes their day. The ones on printed notepaper, don't bother about them. Remember the ones that are hard up,' and I did but I got fed up within a week.

We used to go to the Leicester Square cinema quite often and Lew would pop into wherever he was playing and pick up his post and it came in a small sack. We would wait for the end of one film and before we would go in to see the next film, we'd sort the letters out while we were waiting, over a cup of coffee.

When he took over from Roy Fox at the Monseigneur, Roy had been taken ill and had gone to Switzerland because he had a touch of TB. Lew was on piano and they wanted him to lead the band. That was when he first started doing regular broadcasts, and I've got a cutting from the *Melody Maker* saying 'Lew Stone Band takes over at the Monseigneur and becomes famous overnight'.

So Lew abandoned the piano to Monia Liter and after that he was the conductor, although he didn't want to be. He wanted to make music but he didn't want to be a bandleader because he was a very retiring person. He wasn't a showman and he couldn't sell himself. People came to hear Lew because they liked his music. Leaders like Jack Hylton could show off, but Lew was much too retiring to want to stand up in public.

They broadcast every Tuesday night from ten thirty until five to twelve. And they would put notes on all the tables saying that the band would be broadcasting as they did some comedy numbers and people would have wondered what the hell was going on. Some people who were great fans would go in deliberately on a Tuesday night to listen rather than dance. When Lew started broadcasting he got Joe Crossman to do the announcing but one day he decided he would announce. I think it happened twice and it was on the second occasion he said something like, 'Good evening all and those of you who haven't paid your licences.' The BBC said, 'Never again'!

In those days you weren't allowed to play any music from an

American show until it arrived in England. The publishers were very, very strict about that and Teddy Holmes of Chappells told Joe Crossman, Lew's lead sax player, to tell him that he was coming in that night and not to play certain numbers as the show hadn't arrived over here. Well Joe Crossman completely forgot until he saw Teddy Holmes coming down the last three steps into the Monseigneur. It took Lew exactly four bars to turn what they were playing into 'Don't Tell a Soul'. That's a true story!

Al Bowlly sang with the band all through the Monseigneur days and then he left the band to go to America with Ray Noble. People think that Al came back from America to have an operation on his throat, but he came back because he was homesick. He missed London. Lew always used Al with the band when he could as he always preferred him to anyone else.

Lew liked to do his own arrangements and that is what made him so unique as many bands would use the printed copies and Lew wouldn't. His choice of signature tune, 'Oh Susannah', had something to do with the rhythm of a horse because he was a very good rider. He was in the Cavalry Brigade during the First World War although the war finished before he was old enough to go abroad. The way he played 'Oh Susannah' was to lift it on the off beat so you really felt the movement of a horse.

The Café de Paris at that time was run and owned by a man called Poulsen who was Danish and was known to the profession as the Danish Pig! He could be very tough and was an awful snob as you can imagine. He loved all the society people going in there and the Kents and the Mountbattens would come in as a foursome on average once a week. They always had to play softly in the Café de Paris so the trumpet was nearly always muted and as you know to play any instrument with a mute in all the time is very tiring. Lew had a small band there, four saxes, one trumpet and rhythm but Ambrose, who I think followed Lew in, took his full band and it was awful. We gave a dinner party there one night and we just couldn't speak to each other because the band was too loud. Ambrose would never play with a small band. His Octet went on tour but not with him.

Later during the war, when the bombing started, Poulsen got killed in an air-raid. He was a bit of an idiot because the Café de Paris is below ground with a rather gracious staircase going down with a balcony and he sandbagged all of that but did nothing at the back which was the Rialto Cinema. The bomb came through the cinema and landed at the band's feet. There was a double balcony with a stairs coming down each side and the band were between the two staircases. 'Snakehips' Johnson, the bandleader, was killed outright and the bass player, Tommy Bromley, was blown right through to the band room at the back and had both his legs broken.

After the Café de Paris Lew did two shows with the Hulberts, and then when the war started we opened in a show called *Orchids and Onions* with Carroll Gibbon's wife at the St James's which no longer exists. It was at that time that Lew did the theatre, then walked up to the El Morocco which was just off Bond Street, and then home to our flat in Berkeley Square about four in the morning. El Morocco was a typical night club where you had to become a member and had to order your bottle 24 hours before you went in and then you put your name on it. Because I didn't like drink I think I had my one bottle of gin probably longer than anyone! I had to have an escort because although Lew was on the bandstand I couldn't have sat at a table by myself, it wasn't that kind of place.

Lew was at the Dorchester Hotel right through the Blitz, playing to all the VIPs, people like Portal, Lord Halifax, the Duchess of Argyll, who were living there. Lady Diana Cooper used to come in but everyone was very tired. You've got to remember everyone was doing something all day long, voluntary work or otherwise. When the band finished at night we were jolly glad to get down into the basement and sleep if we were lucky. We were given two camp beds in the guest air-raid shelter and they fed us up in the courier's room with the private secretaries, ladies' maids, people like that. The band weren't allowed to eat with us, they had to eat in a separate room and where they might have a dried egg omelette, which was pretty foul; we would be given the legs of chicken because the guests wouldn't eat the legs, only the breast! The follow-on was an orange sort of ice-cream which was so hard you couldn't get your spoon into it so it never got touched and was sent back. That same bit of orange ice-cream would come up night after night and was nicknamed Orange Pneumonia! We'd stay all night until the all clear went and then we'd go home. The band played all through the air-raids; they never stopped under any circumstances; bombs or no bombs, they went on playing. One night there was a stick of seven bombs that came down and Lew got the band to play 'The Anvil Chorus' so quickly that a bomb came down between each beat of the tune! It stopped any panic because everybody was laughing!

At the request of the government we left the Dorchester and went on tour. On medical grounds Lew could have stayed but he got itchy feet. So when we were asked to go and play at Bomber Command and all the little tin-pot theatres, we did. It was the hardest job ever because you played a different camp every night. You stayed in digs or a hostel and you did two shows a night. If the concert place was small they'd ask you to do three shows if the musicians were willing, and they were only earning ten pounds a week, but they would do it. Very exhausting. In November 1944 Lew was playing in Coventry just after that major blitz and he said, 'I can't go on, I'm exhausted; ring up the agent and cancel everything.'

He was playing to the Americans down in Southampton for the last four months of the war when his singer was 14-year-old little Helen Mack, but when he went to the Embassy Club we had to dispense with Helen because you couldn't take a 14-year-old child into a club and keep her awake and singing until four in the morning. She wouldn't have been allowed in anyway.

Lew had West End tempo, as did Ambrose, Roy Fox, Carroll Gibbons and Harry Roy to a degree. You didn't play fast and you didn't play slow, you played somewhere in between. I was talking to Tiny Winters not long before he died and I said, 'Tiny, I could wake up in the night and I could start that tempo immediately.' 'Joyce, so could I, let's do it now.' And we did! The society people didn't dance slowly, nor quick steps; they bunny hugged, cheek to cheek, and they'd sort of loll around in almost total darkness. I was at Quaglino's one night with Lew as guests and we were dancing and the band got slower and slower and the lights got darker and darker and more and more smooching went on, and the manager sent for the head waiter and said, 'For heaven's sake man, tell the band to play something quick!' Lew would never have allowed that. As soon as people started to flag and smooch he would 'up' the tempo.

STANLEY BLACK *Piano 1931–33*

Lew Stone's was a wonderful band, I thought it was the best. I joined him at the Monseigneur which was a restaurant, but it had a different kind of aura, a different kind of clientele, fairly youngish, more of the

'Hello Henrys'. It was a thrill to work in that band and I did a lot of writing for Lew.

Of course he was a fine arranger himself, but his second claim to fame was he was the clumsiest so-and-so that ever walked the earth! He was marvellous! If we were doing a broadcast from the studios, we'd pile into taxis, get there and get set up as quickly as possible. On the air at 10.30p.m. until midnight. Those were the days when they'd have a dance band session every evening with a different band each night. Lew would still be in his dress wear but without the jacket and there were flaps and things flying all over the place. When the band was playing he would turn around and fly towards the control room and take two music stands with him on his braces!

Lew was a good musician and he was given the job of MD of a show, and one night as he was going off after the show had ended, there was a huge hole in the middle of the stage where they used to put the piano so that it dropped down and reappeared again, and Lew fell down the hole. He was suddenly missing and no one could find him until someone heard him groaning under the stage. He was so incredibly clumsy. He'd turn around and bang his head on the mike!

NAT GONELLA *Trumpet 1932–35*

I was with Roy Fox at the Monseigneur in 1931 when he was taken ill; he had a bit of trouble chest-wise and he had to go to Switzerland to recuperate and he did this a couple of times. While he was away Lew Stone took over the band and made a big success of it because he featured different members of the band who could sing or could put a number over. I think practically every member of the band sang a number that Lew had picked out for them. He studied the musicians and their characters all the time. He was a very studious sort of man.

I was one of the lucky ones to do 'Georgia', which became very popular. The recording manager at Columbia told Lew Stone that if he recorded any more numbers like that they'd go skint, and of course it became one of the biggest hits they had for that particular period!

The Prince of Wales would come in, look over his girl's shoulder and wink at me. He liked my 'Georgia', and when we did it on a stage show he actually came around and told me he liked it. He was a whale of a man really because he liked women and he would dance around there and it was a lovely club. You always had to use the back entrance at the Monseigneur because you were just staff really. It was a very posh place, down in the basement in Jermyn Street, very near Piccadilly Circus.

When Roy Fox returned, Lew Stone kept the band and, being an American, I don't suppose Roy Fox could say too much having been away. He was such a debonair, strait-laced man and looked fabulous from the back and everybody loved him. He always wore tails, immaculate, better dressed than a woman! But the management of the Monseigneur were then more in favour of Lew Stone because he played more novelty numbers, although we still had to play pretty softly.

The trombone player who sat on my right was Jewish, as was Lew Stone of course, and when Lew sat at the piano and turned sideways this trombone player would say, 'Look at that conk.' That was always a big laugh! Musicians are the lowest form of humanity aren't they?

We were getting seven pounds a week and that was a lot of money. We started lateish, playing from ten until two in the morning, and before that we would be playing in a stage show somewhere in London like the Holborn Empire or Finsbury Park Empire. I don't remember any of the musicians drinking in those days at the Monseigneur Club. In fact you weren't allowed to drink as there was no bar for the musicians. It was different in ballrooms where you got time off and would go out to the pub and have a few drinks. At the Monseigneur we'd have no break between ten and two, but if the band was playing a waltz or a tango then someone would be on violin so you weren't playing.

I remember the first dance band I played in at the Plaza Ballroom in Belfast; we played from eight until two in the morning – one band. I was playing trumpet in the brass section, then I was featured on clarinet with the saxophones, and then I was on second violin in the tangos and waltzes. One night I went off the stage and said in the dressing-room, 'I never get a rest, I'm doing everything' and I smashed my violin on the table and it broke into a hundred pieces! It had cost me 39s 6d! So I never played it again. I played drums as well but I wasn't too good on the double-handed thing!

Sitting on the stand at the Monseigneur, I'd see the people looking at me; I was handsome and blond in those days. They'd look at me with a little bit of a grin and then they'd see Al Bowlly and they'd take their eyes off me and it was Al Bowlly from then on. He was dark and swarthy and really handsome. Al was a very jovial sort of fellow and very popular. I gave him some marriage guidance when we were at the Monseigneur! We'd go to a night club and play a bit of jazz after work and then on to Lyons Corner House in Coventry Street where you could get coffee, breakfast, anything you liked, all night.

One night Al came in. I knew him very well and he said, 'Who's this woman coming in the door?'

'That's the hostess with the mostest.'

'She's all right, she's nice.'

So when she sat down I went over to her and before I could say anything she said, 'Who's that fellow you're with?'

'That's Al Bowlly, do you want to meet him?'

'Yes.'

So I introduced them and within a week they were married, and within another week they had left each other! That was my marriage guidance!

KENNY BAKER *Trumpet 1940*

I came down to London in 1940 with tuppence in my pocket and I always remember my mother and father saying, 'There's no money here so if you go, keep the money for your train fare back so if you don't get a job and want to come home, you'll have your train fare.' So I always kept a couple of quid or whatever it was.

I was getting very low on loot when I got a job out of the blue at Streatham Locarno: five pounds a week and the pianist was dear Norman Stenfalt; that's when I first met him. I started on the Monday, played the Tuesday, and on Wednesday went down the 'Street', Archer Street, where all the boys used to go looking for work. Somebody came up to me and said, 'Hey, Lew Stone's looking for a trumpet player for a show in the West End. Why don't you go and get an audition?' I went to see Lew and he gave me an audition and said he'd give me two weeks starting on Monday. So I started at Streatham Locarno on the Monday and handed my notice in on the Thursday saying, 'I'm sorry but I've got a good job in the West End, I'm leaving Saturday.' They were furious!

Now I'm up to eight guineas a week; from nothing I'm suddenly making a lot of money, so I got myself a flat. Come the end of the fortnight, I'm standing at the stage door quaking in my shoes because nobody has said anything. I said to the stage doorkeeper, 'I don't know whether I've got the job or not.' And at that moment Lew came by, said goodnight to the stage doorkeeper and went. 'What do I do now, he didn't tell me?' and the chap said, 'I'd just turn up on Monday.' I did and I never did know whether I'd got the job! I did the run of the show and then joined Sid Millward who went on tour with a pukka big eight-brass swing band.

TOMMY WHITTLE *Tenor saxophone 1943–44*

When I joined Lew Stone he was playing variety theatres, a week at a time. A couple were in London and then we went around the country. We used to do the last forty minutes of the show and it was a very good band. The lead alto, Jimmy Easton, used to go out front and do a comedy number with the singer, Helen Mack, who was very young.

We used to open the show with his signature tune 'Oh Susannah' which we would play on clarinets, so my saxophone was on its stand in front of me. One night the curtain went up, caught hold of the crook of my sax, and took it way up. I saw this little silver blob disappearing, it was frightening! They had to bring the curtain down of course, so it was a real misfire for a start! But at least it came down safely and it didn't fall down.

I was only 17 and I really loved it in that band, I thought I'd arrived! When I turned 18 I was called up and had my medical in Glasgow while we were at Green's Playhouse. I had a little problem with my shoulder so I was graded 3 which meant I was supposed to do munitions work, but Lew Stone managed to get me an ENSA card. That was good for me because I was able to stay playing as a musician and I didn't have to do the munitions work and I didn't go in the army either. Lew was marvellous, he was so thoughtful and kind and a very good musician.

AND MANY, MANY
MORE . . .

EDNA KAY *Vocalist, Carroll Gibbons and The Savoy Orpheans 1945–47*

My brother would pick me up and watch over me like a hawk, particularly at the Savoy where all the officers would be staying and the American boys too. You would see all these highly respectable girls meeting up with them and going upstairs. The Americans were a bonus because they could get nylons and things!

Carroll Gibbons was quite a devout Catholic when it suited him and he also drank quite a bit. I used to kid him about that, saying you can't possibly get very drunk the night before and be with whoever and then go along to confession the next morning! He was quite a ladies' man, and for the society ladies it was very glamorous for them, but he was absolutely charming.

We were rehearsing for a broadcast one afternoon at the Savoy and the orchestra, Carroll and myself were running through a number when the Maître d' came over and Carroll stopped us and he said something to him and then we carried on. I was sitting on a table, swinging my legs and singing, and the door opened and a group of gentlemen came in and waited there as we carried on. I was oblivious as I was thinking about where to come in and so on, and then they walked across the room and went out. As they left the room Carroll stopped, and you know how musicians when they finish play discords and things, so it was all a bit like that. Carroll looked up and said, 'Thanks fellas, that was Winston Churchill and Anthony Eden,' The Maître d' had come in to tell us to carry on and not take any notice and I was so busy I hadn't looked up!

ROY WILLOX *Alto saxophone, Henry Hall 1946–47*

They wanted to inject a bit of younger blood in the band. When I went in I was 16 and the nearest to me was Ted Alexander the drummer and he was 32, double my age! So I was really the kid and very lonely in a way because I couldn't go to the pub and have a drink. That's where I learnt to become solitary.

I'd been there about eight months when I heard that the other lads were getting more than me so I went in to get my money and said, 'Guvnor, do you think it's about time I had a rise?'

'No, I don't think so, why?'

I never asked again!

PETER HUGHES *Saxophone, Henry Hall 1948*

We were told not to call him Henry or Mr Hall, but Guvnor; he liked the respectful informality of that. When we were on stage for the show *Something in the Air*, our pianist Bert Marland would end with The Lancashire Concerto, a pseudo-classical version of 'I'm a Lassie from Lancashire'. One night he was off ill and the Guvnor informed us he would play the piano. We were relieved to hear he wasn't going to attempt the concerto but would play a selection of popular tunes instead. During rehearsal Alan Hodgkiss, the guitarist, asked what chords the Guvnor was using as he changed from one tune to another. 'Chords?' queried the Guv. 'Don't worry about the chords, just strum!'

KENNY BAKER *Trumpet, London's West End 1940s*

Jack Harris was an American bandleader who came over, I think before the war and played at a club called the El Morocco. It was like any of the West End society gig bands. He picked up some of the good musicians and just played music for the dancers. He'd got a way with the public; they liked him, but I think he was a bit of a gangster. He was a sharp dresser, always looked good. He was a good front man but a bad violinist. I don't think he ever played it!

I did a society gig with him once and there was a drummer, a very nice gentleman called Johnny Rowlands. We were sitting in the rest room in between the sets and there was champagne and all sorts of food and Harris came in and said, 'You doing all right fellas, everybody okay?' and he looked over and saw that Johnny hadn't got a drink. 'What's the matter, you're not drinking?'

'No, I never drink on the job.'

'Have a drink, you can't play any worse.'

That was Jack Harris for you!

I first worked with George Shearing at Hatchett's in Piccadilly. That wasn't my regular job either but the band was run by a guy called Chappie D'Amato and I think the job belonged to Dave Wilkins, the trumpet player with the 'Snakehips' Johnson Band. I remember going in there one night and putting my case in what I thought was an empty dressing-room. I'd come in early and was going next door to have a drink, and before I put the light on in this black room, a voice said, 'Hello.' I put on the light and there was George Shearing sitting in the corner reading a Braille book! Happy memories.

PRIMROSE *Vocalist, London's West End 1930s and '40s*

When I sang with Sidney Lipton at Grosvenor House the Sultan of Jahore used to be a regular. His wife was Romanian or something and they had a permanent suite in Grosvenor House and he sent me this beautiful perfume.

When I worked Sunday nights at Lansdowne House with Tim Clayton, I was very naïve, and the young Duke of Kent would come in with Princess Marina and one night they asked me to sing 'I'll See You Again'. Afterwards they sent up a ten-pound note and I said to the waiter, 'I can't take that, no, no, take it back.' The band were going to kill me and Ted Heath, who sat behind me, said, 'What do you think you're doing Prim?' Of course I didn't know. I'd know now, but I didn't know then!

HARRY HAYES *Alto sax, London's West End 1930s and '40s*

I had a band at Churchill's Club in Bond Street which was the band George Shearing was playing in immediately before he went to America. The female vocalist was my wife, Primrose, and she sat in the bow of the piano immediately next to George. She wore a silver fox bolero around her shoulders which she took off and placed on the corner of the piano when she stood up to sing. One night, while she was singing, the bolero slipped onto the piano keyboard. George was terrified of cats and as his hands encountered the fur he leapt to his feet, hands waving wildly, and shouted, 'Cat, cat!' Everybody in the band stopped playing except the bass player and the drummer and the dancers were completely startled. It took quite a while before George could be persuaded it was a fur belonging to Primrose!

He had a marvellous sense of humour, everything was a joke. If Primrose sang a wrong word, he would wave his fingers; he knew the words of every song and all the vocalists were terrified of going wrong because George used to wave his hand!

At the Café de Paris, the Prince of Wales, a great lover of women, used to come in with Lady Furness five times a week and they would shut the door after he came in so nobody else could get in. He was a very nice chap. 'I say, old boy, will you play so-and-so?' He was quite good at that!

I was in the English/American line-up at the Savoy, Fred Elizalde and His Band, and there were three very famous American musicians including Adrian Rollini, who was a god in those days. He was getting seventy-five pounds a week, that's about four grand now I should think! I was getting eighteen and as we also did sessions, I must have been earning about twenty a week, and a thousand a year man in those days was a prince! I sat in front of Adrian Rollini for about 18 months and if I hadn't learnt to play sitting in front of that I would have been a right idiot. When I left there in 1934 I went to Ciro's Club with Sidney Kyte.

DON LUSHER *Trombone, Joe Daniels, Lou Preager, Maurice Winnick 1940s*

Joe Daniels and His Hot Shots were looking for a trombone player and were holding auditions. I arrived at this place in Lisle Street and I couldn't think why there were so many friendly ladies. They came up and spoke to me and I thought, 'Gosh, this is a very friendly place.' Of course years later I realised that they were prostitutes! I went upstairs, did the audition, and Joe said, 'You can start,' and that was wonderful.

I went with Joe and after a month that folded and then I was out of work for a long time until I got a telegram: 'Come to Hammersmith Palais, audition with Lou Preager', and I nearly died because that was big stuff to me. I got on a train, did the audition, and broadcast with the band that same night, and I remember what really turned me on was the eleven pounds a week. Incredible! My Dad didn't get five a week until he was managing a hardware store during the war, so that was big money to me.

Lou was a strict bandleader. It was a good band and guest bands came to Hammersmith Palais including Ted Heath and Billy Ternent, who we thought of as a rinky-tink band, but it was excellent and would you believe he used to tune the band on the stand before every session. Right round the band!

Going with Maurice Winnick was a cultural shock. I'd never been in a big club before, and what a difference in atmosphere. Many of the guys didn't talk to me, not a word. There were big timers in this band, doing sessions, much older and more established than myself. I was there a month before I got the sack and there must have been four or five of those guys who never, ever said a word to me. One gentleman asked Jock Bain, 'Who's the trombone man?'

'Don Lusher.'

'Where's he from?'

'Lou Preager.'

'My God, a palais band player'!

SYD LAWRENCE *Trumpet, Sidney Lipton 1952*

Sidney Lipton was a gentleman. He would play some nice violin solos with Billy McGuffie accompanying him at the piano early on when people were dining. Occasionally you'd get some rich guy come up and ask for 'McNamara's Band' or something like that and we'd all play it in unison for him and he'd drop a ten-pound note to Sidney and that's like dropping a hundred pounds today! Instead of having the money we'd have cigarettes and we'd finish up with three packets of Players each!

GARRY BROWN *Trombone, George Evans 1948–49*

George was a musical perfectionist and his library was beautifully copied by his wife, Jane. She wasn't a musician, she was an artist, and it was incredible how she looked at it like a pattern or design. They were incredible arrangements to play.

George was the top arranger with Geraldo and then when he started his band with ten saxophones he became very ill and came back with eight brass and six saxophones. The best residency in the country was the Oxford Galleries in Newcastle, and after touring 17 months we got this residency and I resigned at the first rehearsal! We'd wanted a residency but as soon as we got one I couldn't stand it. You would finish a dance at midnight and George would call a rehearsal!

That was a band that was half semi-professional and half professional which was very difficult, and there wasn't a lot of money. The professionals got seven pounds for three gigs so we used to call it Sevens with Evans! The semi-pros got six. But there were some great players in the band like Gracie Cole and Bill Geldard. I remember one night, half-way between Grimsby and the next gig in Wolverhampton, they'd left Gracie's trumpet behind and we had to go back for it. We get to Wolverhampton but we're late so we have to go straight on the stand. It was the Civic Hall and it was mid-winter. The only two who had digs were Gracie and Bill. Some of the guys used to sleep in the coach because we weren't getting much money. We came off the stand at one o'clock, it's snowing, and we have no digs. The regular sleepers in the coach had all the blankets and so on but the rest of us didn't have much to keep warm. It must have got to about two o'clock and Brian Gary and I decided we were going to freeze to death if we didn't get out of that coach. We went round to the police station, they didn't want to know; went to the fire station – they didn't want to know; went to the railway station, but they weren't open until five so we couldn't get in there. Then we saw a telephone kiosk and we went in there and Brian was tall so he could reach up to the light bulb and warm his hands, but I couldn't and he lifted me up! We found an all-night snack bar, an oasis! We went in and had a cup of tea, but after about 20 minutes the guy behind the counter says, 'All out.' There were about six of us in there, four drop-outs and us two!

'The law says I've got to close for 30 minutes.' So we're out front of this snack bar with the four tramps waiting for him to open up again!

BARRY ROBINSON *Alto saxophone,*
George Evans 1953

When I left school I was having lessons with George Evans's brother Les, and he took me up on the train to Newcastle and I played for the afternoon tea dance as an audition and I got the job. I was 16 and I got paid thirteen pounds a week which I thought was fantastic!

On one side of the stage there were four alto players who all doubled baritone sax and clarinet with the lead alto on soprano. Then the other side of the stand there was the proper baritone player, three tenors, and the end guy played bass sax. George had these wonderful tea dance arrangements where he'd score one chorus of a tune and if you used the same fingering it automatically transposed the parts so you could play the same part on alto, baritone or clarinet. It was a very simple and effective way of doing arrangements for tea dances.

FREDDY STAFF *Trumpet, George Evans 1949–50*

They had this three-week payment system worked out so if there was seven jobs in one week, you didn't get seven lots of money. Somehow it worked out that you lost out! But it was a good training ground because we were all very young and inexperienced. Gracie Cole came in after about six months and at first the reaction was strange. She was courting Bill Geldard which made it easier for her in the band.

We were at the Hammersmith Palais for about 12 weeks and I heard that George was going to the Oxford Galleries, Newcastle, and being a Londoner and I'd just got married no way was I going to go, and that's when I left. I took a job on the *Queen Mary* with Geraldo's Navy with Stan Tracey on piano who couldn't play a waltz! I don't think he can now! I still don't understand his piano playing!

BILL GELDARD *Trombone, George Evans 1949–51*

I was still in the air force at the time and George got me weekend leave to go and play. In April 1950 we went to Grimsby for six weeks and while we were there Bernie Sharpe, the lead trumpet, left. Fred Staff was the 'bumper' so he extended what he was doing but the trumpets never settled after that. There always seemed to be a hole in the trumpet section and nothing was happening.

While we were in Grimsby Ivy Benson's band arrived for a week at the Palace Theatre. George knew Ivy well and they decided to get the two bands together and get the press in, and they got a whole page in the *New Musical Express*.

We took our library along to the Palace Theatre, which I suppose was a bit of a liberty, and we sat down with the girls interspersed between us. Gracie Cole, Sylvia England and Dorothy Burgess were up with the trumpets and these girls could play. They had our library and they played it. Suddenly some of the trumpet parts that had been missing were coming through loud and clear.

A little while after this George got together with the brass section to sort out what they were going to do about the trumpets, so I said, 'Gracie Cole played well when she was here, why don't you ask her?' George was a friend of Ivy's and he didn't like the idea of stealing her first trumpet, so I was given the job of approaching Gracie and asking if she'd like to join the band. That was the way it happened, and for Gracie it was a terrible drop in salary but I think she thought it was worth the sacrifice. After she joined another weak link left and then the trumpets became a good team. I think it worried them now and again that a girl could play this well, but Gracie and Fred split the leads between them.

Gracie joined the band in the August and we got married the following February in Glasgow.

GRACIE COLE *Trumpet, George Evans 1950–51, Squadronaires 1951*

It was a lovely experience with George Evans, I enjoyed it tremendously. He was very good to me and he used the system of marking the trumpet parts so that you either had 1, 2 or 3 written on the arrangements. The idea was to get a good overall sound so that if you split leads the sound would be ongoing, and he did that for a while.

It wasn't always easy in the Evans Band and hadn't been since my days in Grimethorpe Colliery Band – male prejudice! Looking back, one can understand it was a man's world, but having Bill in the band made a difference.

We suddenly got a phone call from Tommy McQuater asking us to meet him at a pub to discuss the possibility of Bill and I joining the Squadronaires. That was the thrill of my life playing trumpet next to Tommy; he was wonderful. The sad part that broke my heart was when he eventually had to leave the Squads. Twinkle, his wife, thought he should have a rest from the touring after all those years on the road, and so he left and joined the Skyrockets at the Palladium.

Bill had been asked to join Ted Heath, who had already suggested to me that I might form a girl's band, and that's what I did. Later, when Bill was with John Dankworth, John wrote 'Cole Storage' for me, and that became my signature tune.

DUNCAN CAMPBELL *Trumpet, Tommy Sampson 1947*

We rehearsed solidly in Scotland for six months and then Tommy reckoned we were good enough and he wrote to the BBC and they came to hear us and gave the band a broadcast in London.

We got this old, left-hand-drive, big American truck and one of the guys in the band was a joiner and he made beds in this truck and we were off to London! We came right down to the Paris Cinema and parked for a week round the corner by the Captain's Cabin! Yellow lines hadn't been invented! We'd have a wash in the Paris Cinema and they allowed us to rehearse there and we'd go up to Lyons Corner House for breakfast. That was our only decent meal all day!

Tommy lost £10,000 on that band, which would be like a million pounds today. It was his dad's money. It lost money all down the line because we played dances and they'd come up and ask for a waltz and we didn't like playing waltzes or tangos, we just played jazz. We did a week at Redcar and some nights there were so few people in that we went out and played in the middle of the floor!

HENRY McKENZIE *Clarinet, Tommy Sampson 1947–49*

I was one of the first to join and the last to leave. It was all one-night stands and once he hired a cattle truck! Things weren't quite organised in the Sampson Band and I think we were playing in Hull and we had to get to Bolton. It was a Bank Holiday Monday and the only way we could get there was by cattle truck. When we arrived in Bolton the people were all queuing up as they dropped us off at the front of house and all these chaps were getting out of this cattle truck making animal noises! I was a bit embarrassed and stayed in the truck until it went around the back.

We played ballrooms but they couldn't dance to us. If they asked for a waltz Tommy would play a Stan Kenton number, but even our waltz arrangements you couldn't waltz to! I think even Ted Heath began to get a bit worried because the band started to get very popular with the musicians. We were resident at the Eldorado in Leith, and all the touring bands like Oscar Rabin and Joe Loss would come as the main attraction, but it was a disaster for them because the Sampson Band was so much better.

Tommy was easy going, probably too easy going. He could be led by people in the band. Having been a prisoner of war he wasn't too bothered about discipline, he just wanted to have a good time with the band.

ROSEMARY SQUIRES *Vocalist, Tommy Sampson 1948*

I joined Tommy in Germany because he'd been let down by his singer who had backed out at the last minute. I had to go out there on my own, get on a train, and nobody told me it was going to separate so all my luggage went off to Hanover and I got off at Hamburg. I was left with just my toothbrush and face flannel! Tommy didn't look too kindly on me for that when I got there.

I had no idea what I was going to sing and he flung about a dozen songs at me that I didn't know very well and I had to learn. A dress was loaned to me by a very portly lady who ran the hostel. If you can imagine this thin little thing with pins all round, praying at the side of the stage! I was a quivering mass of nerves and it was quite horrendous, but I got through it somehow.

They were a rebel band, nobody had an evening dress suit and nobody was going to buy one. Tommy was immaculate of course in evening dress, and we had the Merry Macs with us who were very well groomed. On the first night all the heads of the armed forces came to hear us and afterwards a memo was sent to Tommy saying if the band didn't get proper band jackets or suits they would be shipped back home immediately. So the next day, round they go to a black market dealer and all they can find is a kind of hessian material which is very stiff, in a choice of two colours, black or a sort of chocolate, but that was all they could get and it was paid for with cigarettes and drink! They got these band jackets made up very quickly and when the commanding officer saw these from out front he said, 'Ah, that looks better.' Everything was fine while the band were standing up, but when they sat down, these jackets didn't give, they stayed rigid. The fellas were really annoyed and couldn't see the funny side of it!

But what a band that was! It was billed as Tommy Sampson and His Powerhouse Band. Tommy was a very good trumpet player and nearly all the arrangements were done by Edwin Holland. The band's signature tune was 'Comin' Thru the Rye' and Tommy would do a lot of Stan Kenton stuff. It was far too progressive for the dancing public and Tommy wouldn't commercialise; in fact the band wouldn't, they weren't going to play any rubbish or square stuff! Nobody could dance to it, they would all stand around watching and listening.

KEN MACKINTOSH *Alto saxophone, Frank Weir 1947*

When Frank Weir formed his All Star Band he had Aubrey Franks on tenor, Bill Lewington second alto, Alan Franks played trumpet, Bobby Kevin was on drums, Jack Seymour on bass, but the feature of the band were two fantastic pianists, one being George Shearing and the other Ralph Sharon. They were both playing in the band when we opened at the Lansdowne Restaurant in Berkeley Square, and to see the customers watching these two pianists play, George especially, they would stop the show. Ralph went on to become Tony Bennett's MD, and of course George went to America. I remember going to his farewell party.

Frank Weir was a very good alto player, good clarinet player as well, and a bit of a playboy. An elegant type of man, good-looking, he was a real West End boy, he had flashy cars and all that.

DON INNES *Piano, Billy Ternent 1956–58*

Billy was a brilliant guy but his temper got the better of him sometimes. He was a disciplinarian, but don't forget it must be difficult to run an outfit without discipline.

You had to play everything exactly as it was written, although once in a while there would be a jazz solo marked, but apart from that everything had to be exact and very precise. They were very cleverly written, and when I began to arrange for him I did a few arrangements in that tickety-tock style. The brass section with tight mutes going tickety, tickety, tickety. He had a sound and he was very popular.

DON SANFORD *Guitar, Billy Ternent 1969–77*

He was always very accurate and knew exactly what he wanted. He could tell even a large orchestra exactly who played what, and if it was the fiddle section he'd point to the fiddle player who'd dropped a wrong note. He was a good shouter, a big Geordie shouter, but you took everything he said with a pinch of salt and underneath he was a good soul.

FREDDY STAFF *Trumpet, Billy Ternent 1974–75*

When I was doing a broadcast series with Billy Ternent and we were on the radio twice a week, he would write wrong notes in on purpose to show off to the producer how he could pick them out. Billy would spot these semiquavers.

'Duncan, you played a G natural.'

'That's what's written here Billy.'

'It should be a G sharp, change it.' Of course the producer's very impressed. One day on a 'take' I nudge Ronnie Hunt. 'I'm going to play three wrong notes on this take, Ron.' Good 'uns they were on the inside parts, and Billy didn't even spot it! How horrible we could be!

Ronnie Hunt was lead trumpet, the triple-tonguing expert! I was the sweet lead and Duncan Campbell was the hooligan jazzer. We were the trumpet section. Don Lusher and Harry Roche were the trombones, and one day when Don was off and Dorsey's 'Marie' was in the broadcast, Harry didn't want to play it so he slipped off the side of the stand on purpose and said he'd damaged his trombone. So Ted Barker played it and played it great. From that day on I had Rochie under control because he could be pretty horrible. He was a hard man in the Heath days and could be pretty horrible to people. He was anti-semitic and he used to be very sarcastic and say to me, 'Here's the Jew boy.' 'I'm not Jewish Harry.' But once he'd done that I'd got him and he used to get the trumpet in the back of his neck and, 'Is "Marie" in the programme today?' Punishment! Religions are evil you know!

GEORGE CHISHOLM
Trombone

Ambrose 1937–39
Squadronaires 1939–50
BBC Showband 1950–55
Goon Show
Black & White Minstrel Show

There are some great players around today but there are also some very pretentious players who think there is no such thing as a wrong note any more. They fly up and down their instruments picking any note they like, and if you complain they tell you to move with the times. I remember the days when if a saxophone squeaked he'd apologise to the other four in the section and change his reed very quickly. Now it sounds like a fire in a pet shop.

There ought to be another word for that kind of music; they shouldn't use the word 'jazz' to describe what they're doing. I like to think I communicate with an audience which is what a lot of avant-garde, free-form guys don't do. You must let an audience in, you must say hello and explain this is such-and-such. Because if some musicians can't understand what these guys are playing, what chance has the audience got? None!

George Chisholm, 1987

INDEX

248